W9-BWJ-292

DISCARDED
Fordham University Librarie

PARAPSYCHOLOGY:
SOURCES OF INFORMATION

Compiled under the auspices of the
American Society for Psychical Research

by

RHEA A. WHITE

Director of Information, A.S.P.R., and
Assistant Reference Librarian, East Meadow Public Library

and

LAURA A. DALE

Editor, Journal and Proceedings, A.S.P.R.

The Scarecrow Press, Inc.
Metuchen, N. J.   1973

BF
1001
A1 W15
cop.2

Fordham University
LIBRARY
AT
LINCOLN CENTER
New York, N. Y.

Library of Congress Cataloging in Publication Data

White, Rhea A
    Parapsychology: sources of information.

    1. Psychical research--Bibliography. I. Dale,
Laura A., joint author. II. American Society for
Psychical Research (Founded 1906) III. Title.
[DNLM: 1. Parapsychology--Abstracts. Z6878.P8
W587p 1973]
Z6878.P8W47   016.1338   73-4853
ISBN 0-8108-0617-7

Copyright 1973 by Rhea A. White
and Laura A. Dale

to

IRVING ADELMAN

who has the answers to most questions,
and for those he does not,
knows where to find them

TABLE OF CONTENTS

ACKNOWLEDGMENTS

The authors wish to express their appreciation to the following members of the staff of the East Meadow (Long Island) Public Library who considerably lightened the burden of compiling this book: Irving Adelman, head of the Reference Department, who served as consultant and general problem-solver at every stage; Thomas E. Dutelle, director, who permits R.A.W. a highly idiosyncratic schedule, without which this project could not have been undertaken; Selma Quigley for heroically typing the book review citations; Iris Quigley for checking her mother's work; and Caroline Rocek who, beyond the call of duty, obtained needed volumes from all over the country with speed, dispatch, and a smile.

We are especially grateful to Jean Angstadt Spagnolo, who devoted many hours to checking, rechecking, and proofreading the manuscript. Thanks also go to Dorothy H. Pope for supplying material and checking several items, and to R.A. McConnell for providing information not otherwise available.

FOREWORD

Parapsychology: Sources of Information is a book that had to be written. The small band of active research workers in the pioneering branch of science called parapsychology or psychical research has become increasingly aware that the long struggle to gain wide public attention is ending. We find ourselves today increasingly concerned with the problems that arise from this success.

The demands to be met come in many forms. A high school student has chosen extrasensory perception (ESP) as the topic for a term paper and he writes in desperation for the information he needs. A college student wants to know what graduate schools offer higher degrees in parapsychology. A graduate student who has discovered that serious scientific work is being done in this area would like to know about the active research centers and whether there are career opportunities in the field. Serious-minded persons desiring to become reliably informed about parapsychology want advice regarding the best investment of their limited reading time. Without help anyone seeking such information may flounder in the morass of sensational journalism that surrounds this field without knowing that safe paths to knowledge are available.

This book answers to these needs and many more besides. It is not offered as cover-to-cover reading for either the academic scholar or the involved adult, but rather as the key to unlock the right doors for entering the field and advancing through it. Under the circumstances the prospective user of this unique reference work may properly want assurance that the key fits the right locks. Who, he may rightly ask, are the authors and why should they be trusted to give sound advice about information on parapsychology? What are their qualifications for making the many decisions of what to include in a reference work of this kind and for giving evaluative judgments about the selected books as well as other relevant publications and scientific activities in parapsychology?

I cannot think of any other two persons who would
be as well qualified as Rhea White and Laura Dale to
author a book such as this one. They have both been
actively connected with the field for many years, at first
as research workers who established their reputations as
investigators through their publications in the scientific
periodicals, the Journal of Parapsychology and the Journal
of the American Society for Psychical Research. Mrs. Dale
has served as editor of the latter publication and of the
Proceedings of the Society from 1944 to the present, except
for three years (1960-1962) when she was relieved by Miss
White. They were both Charter Members of the Parapsychological Association when it was formed in 1957 (Miss
White was its first Secretary) and remain active in that
professional organization. Both are on the staff of the
American Society for Psychical Research. Mrs. Dale de-
votes full time to editing the Society's scientific publications
and Miss White is Director of Information (part time) with
responsibility for its large and growing library and archives.

So far I have emphasized those respects in which the
authors' careers have followed closely parallel courses.
The reader is also entitled to know important respects in
which their qualifications for this special task of authorship
are complementary.

Miss White attended the Utica College of Syracuse
University for two years and transferred to Pennsylvania
State University for her B. A. (English, 1953). After a
period as a Research Fellow in the Parapsychology Laboratory of Duke University (1954-1958) and subsequent work in
connection with the A. S. P. R. in New York, she studied
library science at Pratt Institute and was awarded the M. L. S.
degree in 1965. Since that time she has served as Assistant
Reference Librarian at the East Meadow Public Library on
Long Island. In 1965 she was chosen by the New York Chapter of the American Documentation Institute (now the American Society for Information Science) as the recipient of the
Hans Peter Luhn Award in recognition of her outstanding
service to library science and the profession.

Mrs. Dale attended private schools in New York
City and the Sorbonne in Paris. She was attracted to the
field of parapsychology in 1941 and her scholarly and scientific contributions to the field appeared frequently in the
A. S. P. R. Journal from 1942 through the 1950s. In 1961

she collaborated with Gardner Murphy on <u>Challenge of Psychical Research</u>. She has, over the years as editor, won the highest esteem and the undying gratitude of her scientific colleagues, especially for her unequaled knowledge of the literature of the field.

Not only did this book call for the collaboration of just these two authors; it also demanded the right publisher. That need was ideally filled when the authors were brought into contact with the Scarecrow Press, a modest contribution that I am proud to have made toward the bringing about of this major labor of devotion and service to parapsychology. My reward will be the ready-made and ideal answers that I will be able to give from now on to the mounting flood of letters I get asking for information about parapsychology. May other active research workers in the field find themselves similarly blessed.

J. G. Pratt

Division of Parapsychology
Department of Psychiatry
School of Medicine
University of Virginia

INTRODUCTION

Parapsychology (the modern and more restrictive term for psychical research) is the field which uses the scientific method to investigate phenomena for which there appear to be no normal (that is, sensory) explanations. Basically this refers to phenomena subsumed under the general term psi, which in its motor aspect is called psychokinesis* and in its more familiar mental aspect, extrasensory perception (comprising telepathy, clairvoyance, and precognition). All these phenomena have been observed under laboratory conditions. In the vastly more complex and intricate world of actual life, some form of psi often seems to be a probable explanation of such human experiences as dreams that come true, waking visions of events occurring at a distance, inexplicable hunches, and similar occurrences. Psi is also a useful concept in explaining much that happens in mediumship. Since parapsychologists have established that psi is a part of living behavior, many have hypothesized that what in the early years of psychical research was thought to be evidence of communication with the dead can better be explained in terms of the combination of some form of psi with the dramatizing propensities of the unconscious minds of the medium and the other persons involved.

It is these building blocks of telepathy, clairvoyance, precognition, and psychokinesis that parapsychology uses to extend the bridge of knowledge into the unknown. But contrary to uninformed popular opinion, parapsychology does not deal with astrology, numerology, Tarot cards, theosophy, witchcraft, or other occult systems or practices--or, if so, only insofar as they empirically demonstrate that at their base some form of psi is operating. Dr. Gardner Murphy, one of this country's most prominent psychologists as well as a parapsychologist of note, has pointed this out:

---

*For definitions of this and other terms, see Part VI, Glossary of Terms.

In these as in all other movements in which one feels something of the near scientific, the would-be scientific, the not-quite scientific, claiming to deal with aspects of human nature less mundane than those with which science is concerned, the question is always whether they offer anything like verifiable facts. It would be ridiculous for me to set myself up as arbiter here, or elsewhere. I can only say that so far as I know, the consistent differentiation between psychical research and these many other fields is that despite many maddening difficulties and much ridicule, the areas noted by the psychical researcher are marked here and there with what appear to be facts, which are at least capable of gradually improved analysis and authentication; while the other fields noted are best known by their repeated assertions, in the absence of those orderly research techniques which might work toward ultimate authentication, corroboration, and repetition of the claims [(with Laura Dale) Challenge of Psychical Research: A Primer of Parapsychology; New York: Harper & Row, 1961; p. 289].

In a recent survey* of the sale of occult books at an American university bookstore, it was found that a huge majority of them dealt with subjects such as astrology, black magic, UFO's, etc., while only 3 per cent were concerned with hard-core parapsychology (i.e., "presumptively scientific or scholarly works about psychic phenomena, or books that to a substantial degree treat scientific or scholarly research in this area..."). It seems to us, however, that at least some of these buyers may have been disappointed in their purchases; that although they wanted sound books on parapsychology, they were unable to select them from the countless others confronting them.

The main purpose of this book, then, is to assist librarians, students, and others interested in psi phenomena to select wisely from this mass of material currently flooding the market, as well as from older material, by providing an annotated list of worthwhile books in English on

---

*R. A. McConnell and T. McConnell, "Occult Books at the University of Pittsburgh." JASPR, 65: 344-53 (July 1971).

parapsychology and related areas of study.* Additionally,
we present sections on parapsychology in encyclopedias, on
organizations, periodicals, and significant events in academic
acceptance of the field, and on terminology for those desiring further sources of information and more background
knowledge about the development and current status of parapsychology as a scientific discipline.

The books included in the annotated list in Part I
represent the thinking of sensible, thoughtful people with a
broad knowledge of the literature of psychical research, or
who had personally experienced or experimented with the
subjects about which they wrote. A book was rarely selected if it did not provide sources for the cases, information, or other statements made in it. And perhaps most
importantly, these titles were chosen because they were
written primarily to explicate the subject, not to exploit it
for financial gain. This is definitely not the case with
many books, especially paperbacks, now appearing in an
effort to take advantage of what has been called "the occult
revolution." Both out-of-print and in-print books are included.

The criteria for selecting a title differed somewhat
according to whether or not it is in print. Generally speaking, the out-of-print books in the list are among the best
of the thousands that have been published over the years.
However, many authors still cited today whose methods or
conclusions might be considered questionable for whatever
reason were not included, nor were the writings of famous
men in other fields who are believed to have had an unduly
credulous view of psychical phenomena.

However, the selection standards were somewhat
more lenient in the case of in-print titles. Since literally
hundreds of books are available for purchase, the novice
is, as we have already mentioned, confronted with a

---

*It should be pointed out that books on the subject are
primarily of value as introductions or overviews. Actually,
the best sources of information are not found in books at
all, but in the papers published in the serious parapsychological periodicals (see the titles listed in the first section
of Part IV). Moreover, most of the worthwhile books on
parapsychology are based to a greater or lesser extent on
material originally appearing in the journal literature.

bewildering task in choosing the best books, or even the
better ones, from among the unreliable ones. Thus it can
be assumed that a book published prior to July 1972 which
is still in print but which is not included in the list, did
not meet minimum standards of reliability.

Finally, it should be pointed out that the selection
of books in a field as diverse and complicated as parapsychology is bound to reflect, to some extent, the biases
of the compilers. In the present case, however, their
biases are complementary, one tending to be speculative,
lenient toward new ideas, and placing function before form;
the other skeptical, hard-nosed, and placing form before
function. It is hoped that their tug-of-war has resulted in
a selection broad enough to include parapsychological topics
of interest to most thoughtful people without misinforming
them or providing them with unfounded information. The
reader must learn to be his own best guide. The most useful suggestion we can offer is to keep in mind that parapsychology does not provide a philosophy of life; for the
most part it is not even a body of definitive, organized
facts. At present, and probably for some time to come,
parapsychology is primarily a growing body of methods for
investigating unexplained observations. It would be well
to keep in mind when reading any book on the subject, including this one, that the "facts" are only as good as the
methods used to ascertain them and the conclusions only as
sound as the mind making the interpretation.

R. A. W. and L. A. D.

The American Society for Psychical Research
December 1972

I. ANNOTATED LIST OF BOOKS

(Guide to the Arrangement of This List)

Every effort was made to provide as much information as possible about each title, keeping both readers and book purchasers in mind. Although some pieces of information included (such as type of library for which a book is suited and its reading level) may seem relevant only to in-print titles, * they were nevertheless provided for each item because some persons might want to obtain the books on the out-of-print market, or in the form of xerocopies, † or because they might be reprinted. Anyone who does not have available the resources of a large public, college, or university library should ask his public library, no matter how small, to borrow a needed title from another library by means of interlibrary loan. As long as accurate information is provided as to the author's name, book title, publisher, and date of publication, most libraries will try to perform this service.

---

*In order to find out whether the books listed below are in print, <u>Books in Print</u> (1972), <u>British Books in Print</u> (1971), <u>Forthcoming Books</u> (1972), and <u>Paperbound Books in Print</u> (Nov. 1972, cumulative edition) were checked. In some instances, in-print information was obtained directly from the publishers.

†As an alternative to obtaining a book from an out-of-print dealer, University Microfilms provides a photocopy (hardcover or soft) of any title for which an original can be located to copy and which is in the public domain. The minimum charge per volume (including paper editions) is $6.00, with an additional charge of five cents for each page over 120. Further information can be obtained from University Microfilms, 300 North Zeeb Road, Ann Arbor, Michigan 48106.

General Arrangement

The books are arranged in numerical order by book
(or item) number and alphabetically by author under 24
broad subject headings. (These headings are listed in the
Table of Contents.) Under each heading there is an introduction to the subject matter of that heading and an overview
of the books included; this is followed by a paragraph which
lists additional books also treating that subject found under
different headings in the bibliography.

Book or Item Number

Each of the 282 titles listed in the bibliography is
entered under its own individual item number (which in the
case of books is referred to as a book number). Whenever
a title is mentioned elsewhere in this compilation, its number, rather than the author, title, or page number, will be
used to identify its location. Item numbers have also been
assigned to the encyclopedias, organizations, and periodicals
described in Parts II through V and will be used to locate
them.

Bibliographic Citation of Books

For each title the following bibliographic information
is given: author(s) and/or editor(s); title; subtitle; trans-
lator, if any; name of person writing the introduction,
preface, or other front matter; place of publication; publisher; date of publication, preferably of in-print edition(s);
number of pages (for at least one edition); series title,
if important; hardcover price; paperback price; original
publisher and date, if the in-print edition is revised or a
reprint; and the symbol OP, if the book is out of print.
In the case of books translated into English, the original
foreign-language title is also given wherever possible.

It should be noted that in listing editions, the in-
print edition (if any) is given first. Some of the titles
were published both in the United States and in Great
Britain. When this is the case, the original edition is
given first, unless it is out of print. If a title is in print
in the United States and was first printed here, no effort
has been made to ascertain if it is also in print in Great
Britain. If a title is out of print but listed in University

Microfilm's <u>Books on Demand</u> as being available in the form
of a xerocopy, it is treated as an in-print edition.

A key to the abbreviations used in the bibliographic
citations is given in Appendix 6.

<u>Book Annotations</u>

The purpose, principal contents, and any special
features of each book are described in an annotation which
follows the bibliographic citation. Occasionally, brief biographical information about the author is also included if it
is helpful in elucidating the contents. Specialized parapsychological terms used in the title or annotations are defined in the glossary (see Part VI). At the end of each
annotation, information is given concerning illustrations,
glossaries, type of bibliographic citation, and indexing.
This information is indicated by means of several terms
used consistently throughout the annotations, as follows:
(a) Illustrations are shown in two ways: "Illustrated" indicates that more than one illustration is included, while
"Frontispiece" is used if it is the only illustration in the
book.* (b) If a book contains a list of definitions, this is
shown by the word "Glossary," preceded by the number of
items included.** (c) Several types of bibliographical citations were used, sometimes two or three in the same title.
The terms indicating them are "Bibliographic footnotes,"
"Bibliographic references incorporated in the text," "Bibliography by chapter at the end of the book," "Bibliography
at the end of chapters," and "Bibliography." When other
specially-titled lists are provided, the title used in the book
is given in quotation marks, e. g., "Suggested readings,"
"Recommended books," etc. In the case of bibliographies
or other lists, either the number of pages or the number
of items is given.† (d) The type of material indexed is
indicated by "Name index," "Subject index," and "Index of

---

*Since illustrative parapsychological material is often
needed, but difficult to locate, an index of books containing illustrations is given in Appendix 2.
**An index of books with glossaries is provided in
Appendix 1, since there is no standard dictionary of parapsychological terms.
†Titles with bibliographies of a hundred or more items
are listed in Appendix 3.

cases. " "Index" alone means that both names and subjects
are included in a single index.

Reading Level Ratings

As an aid in selecting books in the library or to
purchase, the reading level of each title is indicated by an
underlined number from one to three at the end of the annotation.   These ratings indicate the following reading levels:
1 (Non-technical)--introductory work, written for laymen,
suitable for high school students; 2 (Semi-technical)--does not
require prior knowledge of the subject, but contains some
technical information; and 3 (Technical)--primarily of interest
to graduate students, professionals, persons engaged in research, or those well acquainted with the literature of parapsychology.   Book numbers by each category are presented in
Appendix 4.

Type of Library Indicators

As a guide to libraries in purchasing books and to
readers in giving them an idea of what types of library
would be likely to own particular books, an indication of the
type or types of library for which each book is suited is
shown by means of a capital letter or letters which follow
the reading level ratings at the end of each annotation.   The
letters used and the kinds of libraries they stand for are as
follows: H--high school; S--small public library; M--medi-
um-sized public library; L--large public library; C--college
library; U--university library; and A--all libraries.   Book
numbers by categories (except L and U) are listed in
Appendix 5.

In deciding which books should belong in each type
of library, limitations of budget were kept foremost in
mind.   If a title was recommended for a small public
library, it was usually also suggested for libraries with
larger budgets.   In the case of smaller libraries, only the
most basic and representative books were selected, except
for a few titles where it was felt that the library should
have them because of their broad general interest--e. g.,
some of the books on altered states of consciousness, and
Jung's autobiography.

As already mentioned, under each subject heading
there is an introduction which provides an overview of the

aspect of parapsychology being considered and briefly indicates which titles are specially recommended. This is intended to supplement, though not necessarily to mirror, the type of library indicators. For example, reasons are given for purchasing Ullman and Krippner's Dream Studies and Telepathy (66) and Proceedings of an International Conference on Hypnosis, Drugs, Dreams and Psi (18), even though both are indicated only for large public, college, and university libraries.

Book Review Citations

It was considered a useful adjunct to the annotations to give citations to reviews of the books in order to facilitate checking our opinions against those of others as well as to supplement them. Reviews in all the major English-language parapsychological periodicals have been included, and also those in general periodicals such as Time and Nation, in major newspapers, in library and book-trade journals such as Library Journal and Publishers Weekly, and in professional journals from fields such as anthropology, psychology, philosophy, religion, psychiatry, and sociology. Since more of the books listed were reviewed in parapsychological periodicals than in non-parapsychological ones, and since the reviews in the parapsychological journals are generally longer, we decided to cite these reviews separately. Moreover, since the same parapsychological journals are cited so often, we have not used the rather lengthy standard abbreviations for them, but have made up much shorter ones. The titles of both parapsychological and non-parapsychological periodicals, with the abbreviations used for them, are given in Appendix 6.

The citations to reviews in non-parapsychological periodicals are given immediately following the citations to the parapsychological periodical reviews, which come immediately below the annotation for a given book. In citing these periodicals, it was decided to spell out in full any titles consisting of only one word. For titles composed of more than one word, we followed as closely as possible the rules for periodical title abbreviation suggested by Committee Z39 of the American National Standards Institute. *

---

*American National Standards Institute. Standards Committee Z39. NCPTWA Word-abbreviation List. Columbus, Ohio: National Clearinghouse for Periodical Title Word Abbreviations, 1971.

Words such as "the" and "of" are omitted in the abbreviations, but the ampersand is used for "and," e.g.: J. Nerv.
&Ment. Dis. The word-by-word method of alphabetizing is
used and the titles are in alphabetical order by abbreviation
rather than by title spelled out in full. The ampersand is
treated as if it were spelled out. To illustrate, periodicals
beginning with the words "science" or "scientific" are alpha-
betized as follows: Sci. Am.; Sci. &Soc.; Sci. Bks; and Science.

All reviews in parapsychological periodicals were in-
spected by the authors, but no effort was made to check the
citations in non-parapsychological periodicals, except for an
occasional scanning of Choice, Contemporary Psychology,
and Library Journal. For the remainder the information
was obtained from the following indexes: Book Review Digest; Book Review Index; Index to Book Reviews in the
Humanities; Index to Religious Periodical Literature; Mental
Health Book Review Index; Nineteenth Century Reader's Guide;
Reader's Guide to Periodical Literature, v. 1; Philosopher's
Index; and Social Sciences and Humanities Index.

If more than one edition of a title was reviewed, we
listed all available reviews, regardless of edition. Wherever
possible we have given the volume of the periodical followed
by the pages, with the month and the year in parentheses.
However, some newspaper-type periodicals such as Spectator
and the Times Literary Supplement do not use volume numbers. In these cases the pagination is given first, indicated
by "p," followed by the date. Not all indexes gave the inclusive pagination for book reviews, so if only one page number is given in a citation, there is no way of determining
the length of the review; that is, the page number may indicate the first page, or it may indicate that the review was
only one page long. Finally, the bulk of the non-parapsychological periodicals cited were taken from the Mental
Health Book Review Index. This index provides volume
number, inclusive pagination, and year, but does not give
the month or issue number of the periodical cited; in these
cases we also had to omit this information.

Finally, where reviews are cited in periodicals that
have changed titles, whichever title was in use when any
given review appeared is the one used in the book review
citation. For example, A. L. A. Booklist and Booklist are
both cited, referring to different issues of the same periodical.

Following is the Annotated List, by subject (see Table of
Contents).

ALTERED STATES OF CONSCIOUSNESS

Only six of the books listed in this section deal substantially with psi and altered states of consciousness (6, 9, 11, 18, 19, 25), but the others are also cited since there is increasing evidence that psi is more likely to occur in an altered state than in an ordinary state of mind. Thus basic books on altered states are important as background material for the understanding and investigation of optimal conditions for psi occurrence. Some of the titles below deal with classical studies or descriptions of altered states (5, 12, 14, 17, 20, 22), while others describe exciting new methods of approaching the subject (2, 3, 4, 13, 16, 21, 23).

Of the 25 books in this section, the most necessary for a basic collection are Aaronson and Osmond, Biofeed-back, Dingwall, Jones, Laski, Masters and Masters, Naran-jo and Ornstein, the Parapsychology Foundation Proceedings (18), Rappaport, and Tart (23).

Additional books with material on altered states: Myers (169, 170) dealt extensively with unusual forms of consciousness. Two of the Parapsychology Foundation Proceedings (89, 90) have substantial amounts of material on altered states. Two of Crookall's books (116, 212) and Muldoon and Carrington (120) deal with out-of-the-body experiences in various altered states. Ullman and Krippner (66) deal with dreams and psi and Edmunds (158) has a long section on hypnosis and psi. Three titles offer suggestions for psychological conditions favorable to success in psi experiments in altered states (129, 167, 197). The volume put out by the Bucke Memorial Society (32) and The psychic force (87) both contain several papers on altered states.

1 Aaronson, Bernard, and Osmond, Humphry (eds.).
   Psychedelics: The uses and implications of hallucinogenic drugs. Garden City, N.Y.: Doubleday,
   1970. 512p $2. 45 (pap)
   This is a collection of essays by scientists, psychologists, sociologists, and religious leaders on the characteristics of the psychedelic experience; the relation of
psychedelics to anthropology, sociology, religion, and
mysticism; and the therapeutic and other uses of psychedelic

drugs.   Especially valuable is a section on non-drug ana-
logues to the psychedelic state in which other ways of inducing altered states of consciousness are discussed, such
as by meditation and hypnosis.   References to psi phenomena
and psychedelics are scattered through the book.   Analyzed
in Essay and general literature index, 1972.   20-page bibliography; index. 3. M-L-C-U.
      Choice 9:720 (July-Aug. 1972); Contemp. Psychol. 16:
105-06 (Feb. 1971); J. Anal. Psychol. 17:222-23 (July 1972);
TimesLit. Suppl. , p738, June 25, 1971.

2 Assagioli, Roberto.   Psychosynthesis: A manual of
        principles and techniques.   New York: Hobbs Dorman,
        1965. 323p $7. 50;   New York: Viking, 1971. $2. 75
        (pap)
        This is a summary of an important European school
of psychotherapy founded by the author, an Italian psychiatrist, and termed by him "psychosynthesis. " It is a system
of methods aimed at synthesizing the various aspects of personality around the central core of the self.   Some of the
techniques described are for the purpose of activating the
unconscious by means of visualization and meditation, and
the integration of the material thus produced.   These techniques may also be adaptable to methods of activating psi
phenomena.   Assagioli includes parapsychology as a field
of study which is adding significantly to our knowledge of
human nature.   Bibliography at the end of most chapters
(159 items); bibliographic footnotes; bibliographic references
incorporated in the text; index. 3.   L-U.
      IJP 10:98-103 (Win. 1968).
      Contemp. Psychol. 11:268 (May 1966).

3 Barber, T. X.   LSD, marihuana, yoga and hypnosis.
        Chicago: Aldine, 1970. 337p $8. 95
        The author is best known for his controversial views
on the nature of hypnosis.   In this book he presents his
explanation of the effects of hypnosis, yoga, and psychedelic
drugs, and questions the assumptions usually made in regard to them.   His approach differs from that of most
writers on these subjects in that he sees them as being
continuous with other known psychological phenomena and
as a part of social psychology.   His remarks, especially
with regard to hypnotic trance, are by analogy applicable
to mediumistic trance and to other altered states of consciousness with which psi phenomena are said to be associated.   Bibliography at the end of each chapter (49 pages);
name index; subject index. 3.   M-L-C-U.

JASPR 65:488-92 (Oct. 1971).

Aust. J. Psychol. 23:95 (1971); Behav. Res. &Ther. 9:
384 (1971); Br. J. Psychol. 62:429-30 (1971); Choice 8:913
(Sept. 1971); Compr. Psychiat. 12:488-89 (1971); Contemp.
Psychol. 16:597-98 (Sept. 1971); J. Am. Soc. Psychosom. Dent.
18:70 (1971); Ment. Hyg. 55:547 (1971); Psychol. Rec. 21:278
(1971); Psychosomatics 12:140 (1971).

4   Biofeedback and self-control: An Aldine reader on the
    regulation of bodily processes and consciousness.
    (Joe Kamiya and others, eds.)   Introduction by Neal
    E. Miller.   Chicago/New York: Aldine/Atherton,
    1971. 806p $17.50

This is an anthology of 75 previously published
papers on or relating to conscious control of bodily and
other processes usually considered to be autonomous.   It
surveys the literature of the subject up to 1970.   The
burgeoning work in this area is now being covered in volumes issued annually (those for 1971 and 1972 have already
been published by Aldine/Atherton).   Of special interest to
parapsychologists are the sections on relaxation, hypnosis,
meditation, and control of alpha waves.   Although the papers
collected here are not specifically related to psi phenomena,
this book should provide valuable background material for
parapsychologists.   Bibliographic references at the end of
most chapters (1540 items); name index; subject index. 3.
M-L-C-U.

Contemp. Psychol. 17:381-82 (July 1972); Libr. J.
97:1332 (Apr. 1, 1972); Psychol. Rec. 22:278-79 (Spr. 1972).

5 Bucke, Richard Maurice. Cosmic consciousness: A
   study in the evolution of the human mind. New Hyde
   Park, N.Y.: University Books, 1961. 326p $5.95;
   New York: Dutton, 1969. 384p $7.95, $2.95 (pap);
   New York: Citadel, 1970. $3.95 (pap); New York:
   Olympia, 1922. $1.65 (pap) (Orig. publ. by Innes
   in 1901. OP)

This work on mysticism by a medical doctor sets
forth the hypothesis that mankind is evolving into a higher
form of consciousness and illustrates this with biographical
and autobiographical materials from the lives of some
famous and some virtually unknown people.   As a psychological study of the state of illumination or ecstatic consciousness, this book is a classic.   The descriptions and discussions are not simply academic and theoretical, for Bucke
himself once had an experience of cosmic consciousness.
Contains "A note on the author and his book" by Beatrice

Simpson. Frontispiece in some eds. 208-item bibliography.
2. S-M-L-C-U.
     No reviews.

6 Cavanna, Roberto, and Servadio, Emilio. ESP experi-
     ments with LSD 25 and psilocybin: A methodological
     approach. New York: Parapsychology Foundation,
     1964. 123p (Parapsychological Monographs No. 5)
     $2.50 (pap) (Available only from the Foundation)
     This is a report of one of the first attempts to in-
vestigate experimentally the possibility of a relationship between psychedelic drugs and ESP. The authors' backgrounds
--biochemistry (Cavanna) and psychoanalysis (Servadio)--en-
abled them to collaborate in providing an excellent discussion
of the methodological complexities involved in experimenting
with drugs and psi. Having set forth the criteria for research, they applied their methodological principles to four
subjects who were intensively studied. The results of this
pilot experiment are reported together with suggestions for
further research. Illustrated; 44-item bibliography. 3.
C-U.
     JASPR 60:84-88 (Jan. 1966); JP 29:63 (Mar. 1965);
JSPR 43:149-50 (Sept. 1965).

7 Clark, Walter Houston. Chemical ecstasy: Psychedelic
     drugs and religion. New York: Sheed and Ward,
     1969. 179p $5.00
     Based on his own observations and experiments as
well as on those of others, the author presents the hypothesis that psychedelic drugs can lead to authentic religious experiences. In two chapters he provides cases of ecstasy,
non-drug-induced, and compares them with drug-induced
cases. He reviews contemporary investigations of drugs and
religion. There is a discussion of psychedelics in relation
to both law and organized religion. Bibliography at the end
of each chapter (125 items); "Selected references" (21 items);
index. 2. M-L-C-U.
     JASPR 65:233-35 (Apr. 1971).
     America 122:51 (Jan. 17, 1970); Christ. Cent. 87:144
(Feb. 4, 1970); Contemp. Psychol. 15:678 (Nov. 1970); J. Sci.
Stud. Relig. 9:263-65 (Fall 1970); Libr. J. 95:500 (Feb. 1,
1970); PastoralPsychol. 21:63-66 (Sept. 1970); Psychol. Today
3:10 (Apr. 1970).

8 Cohen, Sidney. The beyond within: The LSD story.
     Rev. ed. Foreword by Gardner Murphy. New York:
     Atheneum, 1967. 268p $6.95; London: Secker and

Warburg, 1967, under title Drugs of hallucination
(1st ed.) £.50 (pap) (Orig. publ. by Atheneum in
1964. OP)

Gardner Murphy writes that this book will "profoundly
interest those who have a deep concern with the broadening
of human consciousness. It is a book at a scientific level
which is at the same time a book stretching the imagination
as to what this new world of chemistry may bring us" (p. ix).
By a psychotherapist who has worked extensively with LSD,
the book is primarily about research on the hallucinogens,
especially LSD. Both pros and cons are presented. The
characteristics of the "LSD state" are described, with considerable attention to the negative ones. Bibliography by
chapter at the end of the book (21 items); index. 2. M-L-
C-U.

JASPR 59:338-42 (Oct. 1965).

Am. J. Ment. Def. 70:933-34 (1965/66); Am. J. Psychother. 20:537-38 (1966); Br. J. Psychiat. 112:869 (1966); Contemp. Psychoanal. 2:62-82 (1965/66); Contemp. Psychol. 10:
301-03 (July 1965); Libr. J. 90:258 (Jan. 15, 1965); N. Y.
TimesBookRev., p12, Jan. 3, 1965; NewRepub. 151:15 (Nov.
28, 1964); Observer, p28, Oct. 3, 1965; PsychedelicRev.
no. 5:124-26 (1965); Psychosom. Med. 27:397-98 (1965).

9 Dingwall, Eric J. (ed.). Abnormal hypnotic phenomena:
   A survey of nineteenth-century cases. 4v. London:
   Churchill, 1967. £8.00 set; £2.50 each; New York:
   Barnes and Noble, 1968. $32.50 set; $8.50 each

This is a geographically-arranged survey of psi
phenomena occurring in the mesmeric and hypnotic states.
The areas covered are as follows: v. 1, France; v. 2, Bel-
gium, the Netherlands, Germany, and Scandinavia; v. 3, Russia and Poland, Italy, Spain, Portugal, and Latin America;
v. 4, United States and Great Britain. It was written by
seven experts, the editor being responsible for all or part
of three of the four volumes. The purpose of the book is
to fill the gap in standard histories and textbooks of hypnosis, which rarely include reports of psychic phenomena in
spite of their prevalence. Bibliographies in each volume:
v. 1, 406 items; v. 2, 39 items; v. 3, 40 items; v. 4, 152
items. Name index and subject index in each volume. 2.
L-C-U.

JASPR 64:104-10 (Jan. 1970); JP 32:219-22 (Sept.
1968); JSPR 45:408-13 (Dec. 1970).

Br. J. Med. Psychol. 42:97 (1969); Choice 6:916-17
(Sept. 1969).

10   Ebin, David (ed.).   The drug experience: First-person
     accounts of addicts, writers, scientists, and others.
     New York: Grove, 1965. 385p $1.75 (pap) (Orig.
     publ. by Orion in 1961. Hardcover ed. OP)
         This is an anthology of firsthand descriptions of ex-
     periences with hallucinogenic drugs.   The editor points out
     that "all accounts are autobiographical--subjective efforts to
     describe and to evaluate what the experience was and was
     thought to mean; what men say they saw when their con-
     sciousness was altered and what changes may have been
     made in their mode of thinking and being" (Introduction).
     Some of the material had not been previously published.
     The sections, and number of accounts in each, are: Hemp
     9; Opium 3; Opiates, Addicts, and Cures 7; Peyote 6; Mush-
     rooms 2; and LSD 2.   Each section as well as each autobi-
     ographical account is preceded by an introduction.   Biblio-
     graphic references incorporated in the text. 1. M-L-C-U.
         JASPR 56:199-200 (Oct. 1962).
         Atl. Mon. 209:99 (Jan. 1962); Chic. Sunday Trib. , p2,
     Nov. 12, 1961; Contemp. Psychol. 11:478 (Oct. 1966); Kirkus
     29:961 (Oct. 15, 1961); Libr. J. 86:3967 (Nov. 15, 1961);
     Ment. Hyg. 46:655 (1962); Nation 194:106 (Feb. 3, 1962);
     Psychosomatics 3:332-33 (1962); SanFranc. Chron. , p35, Jan.
     14, 1962.

11   Green, Celia E.   Lucid dreams.   Foreword by H. H.
     Price.   London: published for the Institute of Psycho-
     physical Research by Hamish Hamilton, 1968. 194p
     (Proceedings of the Institute, v. 1) £1. 75
         Lucid dreams are dreams in which the dreamer is
     aware at the time that he is dreaming.   This book is both
     a survey of the literature and a report of original research.
     Many of the cases cited were collected by the Institute of
     Psychophysical Research when the author was its director.
     She describes the experience of lucid dreams, the imagery
     involved, and ways of inducing and controlling them.   She
     also discusses out-of-the-body experiences and ESP in lucid
     dreams, and reports on experimental work on hypnosis and
     lucid dreams.   Bibliographic footnotes; name and title index;
     subject index. 2. M-L-C-U.
         JASPR 64:219-27 (Apr. 1970); JSPR 45:21-25 (Jan.
     1969).
         Listener 80:217 (Aug. 15, 1968); TimesLit. Suppl. ,
     p751, July 18, 1968.

12   James, William.   The varieties of religious experience.
     New York: Modern Library, 1961. 526p $2.95; New

York: Collier, n.d. $1.95;   New York: New American
Library, n.d. $1.25 (pap) (Orig. publ. by Longmans,
Green in 1902. OP)
Based on James' Gifford Lectures, this classic of the
psychology of religion has been included because of the analogies that can be drawn between altered states of consciousness (in this case, mystical consciousness) and certain states
of mind in which psi phenomena occur. This book could
serve as a model for a future parapsychologist wanting to do
for the psi experience what James did for the mystical.
Scattered throughout are references to psychical research,
particularly survival. Bibliographic footnotes; index. 2. A.
IJP 5:347-48 (Sum. 1963); PSPR 17:403-11, Pt.45
(1901-03).
Athenaeum 2:282-83 (July 19, 1902); Bookman[Lond.]
22:170-71 (Aug. 1902); Dial 33:322-23 (Nov. 16, 1902);
HibbertJ. 1:182-87 (Oct. 1902); Independent 54:2251-53 (Sept.
18, 1902); Nation 75:155 (Aug. 21, 1902); Outlook 72:991-95
(Dec. 27, 1902); Science [n. s.] 16:301-05 (Aug. 22, 1902);
SewaneeRev. 10:493-97 (Oct. 1902).

13 Jones, Richard M.   The new psychology of dreaming.
      Foreword by Montague Ullman. New York: Grune
      and Stratton, 1970. 221p $7.95
      The innovation of studying dreams by the Rapid Eye
Movement (REM) technique has resulted in a tremendous
upsurge of research on sleep and dreams. The author has
provided a summary of theories of dream formation and
interpretation, of the wealth of new observations flooding
the literature, and of what all this portends for the future
study of dreams. Of special importance for parapsychology
is the inclusion of a section entitled "Telepathic communication." In it Jones describes current studies of telepathy in
dreams using the REM technique. This book provides an
excellent example of how open-minded researchers in other
disciplines can make productive use of psi observations and
theories to enhance their own studies. 257-item bibliography; index. 3. A.
      No reviews.

14 Laski, Marghanita.   Ecstasy: A study of some secular
      and religious experiences. Westport, Conn.: Green-
      wood, 1968. 544p $18.50 (Orig. publ. by Indiana
      University Press in 1961. OP)
      The author is a novelist whose heroine, in The Vic-
torian chaise-longue, is transported backward in time by
means of an ecstatic experience. Struck by the fact that

readers took this in their stride, she made inquiries to discover how common ecstatic experiences are. The results
of her investigations are here analyzed in detail, including
types of ecstatic experiences (both spontaneous and induced),
their characteristics, and their disposing circumstances or
"triggers." Negative experiences are also described. The
final third of the book is on inspiration, conversion, and the
role of religious faith. Laski is particularly interested in
the relationship between ecstasy and inspiration. Bibliographic footnotes; index. 2. L-C-U.
        JASPR 59:86-88 (Jan. 1965); JSPR 41:323-26 (June
1962).
        Guardian, p7, Nov. 3, 1961; J. Sci. Stud. Relig. 4:106-
08 (Oct. 1964); NewStatesman 62:746 (Nov. 17, 1961); Sat.
Rev. 45:32 (Aug. 4, 1962); Spectator, p717, Nov. 17, 1961;
TimesLit. Suppl., p844, Nov. 24, 1961.

15 Masters, R. E. L., and Houston, Jean. The varieties
        of psychedelic experience. New York: Holt, Rinehart,
        and Winston, 1966. 326p $ 7.95
        This is one of the most thorough treatments of what
the psychedelic experience is like. The entire range of responses is described and amply illustrated with quotations
from actual experiences. The religious aspects are treated
in depth. The role of the "guide" is stressed and a systematic method of selecting and training persons for this role
is presented. Although the authors say they are skeptical
about psi, they have included a section entitled " 'Telepathic'
and other 'ESP' experiences" in which they review the literature and describe some ESP experiments they conducted with
LSD subjects. Bibliographic footnotes by chapter at the end
of the book (72 items). 2. M-L-C-U.
        IJP 10:311-14 (Aut. 1968); JSPR 44:255-57 (Mar. 1968).
        Am. J. Clin. Hypn. 9:220-21 (1966/67); Am. J. Psychiat.
123:902 (1966/67); Am. J. Psychother. 21:311-14 (1967);
America 115:100 (July 23, 1966); BookWeek, p7, July 24,
1966; BookWorld 1:23 (Nov. 12, 1967); Bull. MenningerClin.
30:384 (1966); Christ. Cent. 83:892 (July 13, 1966); Commonweal 85:264 (Oct. 2, 1966); J. Crim. LawCriminol. 58:385-86
(1967); J. Forens. Sci. &Soc. 7:56 (1967); Kirkus 34:356 (Mar.
15, 1966); Libr. J. 91:2857 (June 1, 1966); Listener 77:564
(Apr. 27, 1967); N. Y. TimesBookRev., p1, July 25, 1966;
PsychedelicRev. no. 9:85-90 (1967); Publ. Wkly 192:55 (Aug.
7, 1967); Ration. Liv. 2:31-32 (1967); TimesLit. Suppl., p534,
June 15, 1967; WallSt. J. 47:8 (Jan. 30, 1967).

16 Naranjo, Claudio, and Ornstein, Robert E. On the psy-
    chology of meditation. New York: Viking, 1971.
    248p $8.95
    Part One of this book, entitled "Meditation: Its spirit
and techniques, " is by Naranjo. He synthesizes and classi-
fies the various Eastern and Western meditation techniques
and points out the unity behind each approach. Ornstein
wrote Part Two, entitled "The techniques of meditation and
their implications for modern psychology." He relates meditation techniques, Eastern and Western, to current concepts
and methods in psychology and physiology. Bibliography by
chapter at the end of the book (191 items); "Selected bibliography of introductory reading" (14 items). 3. M-L-C-U.
    Critic 30:81 (Mar. 1972); Libr.J. 96:3145 (Oct. 1,
1971).

17 Pötzl, Otto, and others. Preconscious stimulation in
    dreams, associations, and images: Classical studies
    by Otto Pötzl, Rudolf Allers and Jakob Teler. Trans.
    by Joan Wolff and others. Introduction by Charles
    Fisher. New York: International Universities Press,
    1960. 156p (Psychological issues, Monograph 7)
    $4.50 (pap) (Orig. title in German unknown)
    This is a translation of papers by Pötzl, Allers, and
Teler on the experimental investigation of subliminal perception (or subception) in various states of consciousness, with
an introduction that includes a survey of the literature
(which has since abounded). Although psi phenomena are
not dealt with in this monograph, it is included here because
of the many analogies that can be drawn between subliminal
and extrasensory perception and because it presents seminal
material on altered states of consciousness. 93-item bibliography. 3. L-U.
    No reviews.

18 Proceedings of an international conference on hypnosis,
    drugs, dreams, and psi: Psi and altered states of
    consciousness. (Roberto Cavanna and Montague Ull-
    man, eds.). New York: Parapsychology Foundation,
    1968. 208p $6.00 (Available only from the Founda-
    tion)
    This is a collection of full-length papers by 17 para-
psychologists, psychiatrists, physiologists, and other
specialists. There are six papers on hypnosis and psi,
three on psychedelics and psi, three on dreams and psi,
and a paper each on psi and pharmacology, altered states,
and yoga, respectively. An especially noteworthy contribu-

tion is Raul Hernández-Peón's "A unitary model of hypnosis,
dreams, hallucinations, and ESP." John Beloff provides a
summary. Lively discussions are recorded throughout.
Illustrated; bibliographic references at the end of each paper
(206 items). 3. L-C-U.
     JASPR 64:117-21 (Jan. 1970); JP 33:167-76 (June,
1969); JSPR 45:175-79 (Dec. 1969).

19 Proceedings of two conferences on parapsychology and
    pharmacology. Preface by Eileen J. Garrett. New
    York: Parapsychology Foundation, 1961. 86p $3.00
    (Available only from the Foundation)
    Psychiatrists, biologists, medical doctors, pharma-
cologists, theologians, and parapsychologists met at two
conferences sponsored by the Parapsychology Foundation and
the material presented at each is summarized here. The
first conference, "Parapsychology and psychedelics," was
held in 1959. After an overview of the conference, one- to
three-page abstracts of the 15 papers are presented. Among
them are theoretical and methodological papers dealing with
mediumship, psi, and psychedelics. The second conference,
"Parapsychology and pharmacology," was also held in 1959.
A summary of the conference is given, followed by abstracts of 14 papers dealing with biochemical elements in
mediumship, psychedelics and personality variables, suggestions for research, and methods of investigation. 2. U.
     JASPR 57:49-51 (Jan. 1963).

20 Rapaport, David (ed. and trans.). Organization and
    pathology of thought: Selected sources. New York:
    Columbia University Press, 1951. 786p (Austen
    Riggs Foundation, Monograph No. 1) $16.00
    This collection of source materials on thinking has
been included because psi phenomena cannot be considered
in isolation from problems of consciousness as such. It is
very likely that in this important collection of papers, many of
which appeared in English for the first time in this book,
lie clues to the nature of the psi process and how to induce
it. The selections are arranged under the following broad
headings: Directed thinking, Symbolism, Motivation of
thinking, Fantasy-thinking, and Pathology of thinking. A
number of the papers deal with thinking in various altered
states of consciousness. 787-item bibliography; index. 3.
L-C-U.
     J.Abnorm. Psychol. 47:268-74 (Apr. 1952).

21 Richardson, Alan. Mental imagery. New York: Spring-
   er, 1969. 180p $6.75
   This is a survey, by an Australian psychologist, of
"inner experience" from a post-Titchener and post-behavior-
ism viewpoint. Both facts and hypotheses are presented.
Richardson made an effort to include "as much empirical
material of a behavioural and experimental kind as relates
to the nature of imagery ... and to the part played by
imagery in such other cognitive processes as perception, re-
membering and thinking. In addition, a considerable amount
of space has been devoted to the consideration of methodological issues, especially the difficult but crucial problem of
finding objective neurological, physiological or behavioural
indices that parallel subjective reports of mental imagery..."
(p. xi). This is a good source of background material for
anyone studying the mind. 14-page bibliography; name index;
subject index. 3. M-L-C-U.
   Aust. J. Psychol. 22:212-13 (1970); Br. J. Educ. Psychol.
40:237-38 (1970); Br. J. Psychiat. 116:338 (1970); Br. J. Psychol. 61:281 (1970); Choice 6:1838 (Feb. 1970); Contemp.
Psychol. 15:566-69 (1970); Int. J. Clin. &Exp. Hypn. 18:134-35
(1970); Percept. &Mot. Skills 29:1015 (1969); Percept. Cogn.
Dev. 6:618 (1970); Psychol. Rec. 20:13 (1970).

22 Singer, Jerome L. Daydreaming: An introduction to the
   experimental study of inner experience. New York:
   Peter Smith, 1966. 234p $4.25; New York: Random
   House, 1966. $2.25 (pap)
   This book is about the characteristics of daydreams
and fantasies, their psychology, and their positive contribution to personal adjustment and growth. The author begins
with an account of personal experiences reflected in autobiography and self-experimentation; he then goes on to examine
group data obtained by various methods and outlines the
practical applications of the findings. 11-page bibliography;
index. 2. M-L-C-U.
   JASPR 65:357-58 (July, 1971).
   Choice 3:857 (Nov. 1966); Contemp. Psychol. 12:78
(Feb. 1967); Sci. Books 2:166 (Dec. 1966); Science 153:626
(Aug. 5, 1966).

23 Tart, Charles T. (ed.). Altered states of consciousness:
   A book of readings. New York: Wiley, 1969. 575p
   $10.50; Garden City, N.Y.: Doubleday, 1972. $4.95
   (pap)
   This is an anthology of writings, mainly by psychologists and psychiatrists, on altered states of consciousness.

The papers are arranged under the following headings: general views, hypnagogic states, dream consciousness, meditation, hypnosis, minor psychedelic drugs, major psychedelic
drugs, and the psychophysiology of some altered states of
consciousness.   There are 35 papers in all, illustrating the
variety of altered states, their effects, and some of the
techniques for producing them.   These selections demonstrate
that such states can be investigated scientifically without inhibiting the richness of the experiences for those having
them.   879-item bibliography; author index; subject index.
3.   M-L-C-U.
            JASPR 65:103-10 (Jan 1971); JSPR 45:245-46 (Mar.
1970).
            Am. J. Clin. Hypn.   12:274-75 (1969/70); Br. J. Psychiat.
116:117 (1970); Brain 93:228 (1970); Contemp. Psychol.   15:
184-85 (Mar. 1970); Int. J. Clin. &Exp. Hypn.   18:309-10 (1970);
J. Am. Inst. Hypn.   11:86 (1970); J. Transpers. Psychol.   2:79
(1970); Psychol. Rec.   19:659 (1969).

24   Tart, Charles T.   On being stoned: A psychological
            study of marijuana intoxication.   Introduction by Wal-
            ter N. Pahnke.   Palo Alto, Calif.: Science and Be-
            havior Books, 1971.   333p $7.95
            This book is a report of a federally-financed study
the author made of the effects of marijuana on 150 experienced users, and it offers valuable insights into why people
smoke pot.   Of special interest is a chapter entitled "Os-
tensible paranormal phenomena (ESP)."   Among the psi
phenomena considered are telepathy, precognition, psychokinesis, and out-of-the-body experiences.   Tart concludes
that there is a decided link between the use of marijuana
and the incidence of psi.   The discussion of altered states
of consciousness and methods of inducing them is also of
relevance to psychical research.   121-item bibliography; index.   2.   M-L-C-U.
            JASPR 66:415-18 (Oct. 1972).
            Choice 9:286 (Apr. 1972).

25   Van Over, Raymond.   Unfinished man.   New York:
            World, 1972.   210p $6.95
            This is an up-to-date account of current work in
several fields which have one thing in common: the opening
of subjective pathways to the mind.   The author is concerned
with the phenomena of hypnosis, mediumship, dreams (including precognitive ones), ESP, and psychedelic drugs.   In
each case the mind-expanding aspect of the phenomenon is
emphasized.   More than half the book is devoted to psi

phenomena, and there is an appendix in which several key
ESP experiments are described.   Bibliography by chapter at
the end of the book (202 items); index.   2.   M-L-C-U.
     Libr.J. 97:1817 (May 15, 1972).

ANPSI

There is no really satisfactory book on anpsi, or psi
activity in animals; the best material on the subject can only
be found in the parapsychological journals.   However, there
are a few books which touch on the problem, at least peri-
pherally.   Some of these present observations of unexplained
animal behavior for which psi may account (although these
books do not establish that it does); others deal with investi-
gative problems of biology and psychology, especially in regard to "clever" or "thinking" animals, which are similar
to the problems raised in experimenting with animals alleged
to have psi ability.   The only general book included in this
section is The strange world of animals and pets, which is
useful as a popular introduction to how psi may be expressed
in animals, but not as a guide to established facts.   The
book by Pfungst, especially with Rosenthal's introduction, is
an excellent guide to methodology.

Additional books with material on anpsi: A critique
of "talking horses" is given in Vogt and Hyman (41) and the
Ciba Foundation symposium (88) contains chapters on bird
navigation and homing.   Vasiliev (68) has a chapter stressing
Russian work on anpsi.   The best coverage of anpsi in book
form is provided by Pratt (174).   He has a chapter on homing, a subject on which he has done extended research, and
a long chapter on anpsi in general which includes a description of his work with the dog, Chris.

26 Gaddis, Vincent, and Gaddis, Margaret.   The strange
        world of animals and pets.   New York: Pocket Books,
        1971. 243p $.95 (pap) (Orig. publ. by Cowles in
        1970. Hardcover ed. OP)
        In this book the authors are concerned with the won-
ders of animal behavior and intelligence.   About half of it
is devoted to behavior suggestive of anpsi: animal communication, homing, psi-trailing, precognition, "talking" ani-

mals, animal apparitions, and instances of seeming clairvoyance and telepathy.   Although written in popular style
and compiled largely from accounts in newspapers and magazines, some of the major cases cited come from the literature of psychical research.   Bibliography by chapter at the
end of the book (182 items).   1. A.
    JP 35:73-74 (Mar. 1971).

27 Kindermann, Henny. Lola; or, The thought and speech
    of animals. Trans. by Agnes Blake. With a chapter
    on thinking animals by William Mackenzie. New
    York: Dutton, 1923. 188p OP (Orig. title in German
    unknown)
    This is a book about animal intelligence, particularly
in dogs, but some of the abilities described are suggestive
of psi (e.g., Lola's apparent knowledge of facts not known
to her questioner).   The author summarizes Karl Krall's
work with the Elberfeld "thinking" horses and work with Rolf
of Mannheim and four other dogs.   The bulk of the book is
a record of her own experiments with Lola, an Airedale
terrier, the daughter of the famous Rolf, whom she deliberately trained as a "thinking" animal.   Appended is " 'Thinking'
animals: A critical discussion of developments from 1914
to 1919" by William Mackenzie.   He reviews the work on
"thinking" animals and suggests two hypotheses to account
for the phenomena which seem to involve psi.   15-item bibliography. 2. L-U.
    JSPR 21:122-24 (July, 1923/24).
    N.Y. Trib., p18, Apr. 22, 1923; Spectator 129:881
(Dec. 9, 1922).

28 Maeterlinck, Maurice. The life of the bee. Trans. by
    Alfred Sutro. New York: Dodd, Mead, 1901. 427p
    $4.00 (Orig. publ. in French in 1901 under title
    La vie des abeilles)
    Maeterlinck's imagination was fired by the mysteries
of the social insects.   He wrote three books about them,
the first being the one under review.   (The others are The
life of the ant and The life of the white ant, still available
from Allen and Unwin.)   For 20 years prior to writing this
book Maeterlinck had been, among other things, a beekeeper.
Here he first uses the phrase "the spirit of the hive," by
which he refers to the fact that the thousands of bees in a
hive behave as if they were under the direction of a single
mind which is aware of all aspects of the ongoing life of
the group.   It is this behavior that gave rise to the hypothesis that some form of psi holds the individual members of

a hive together. 4-page bibliography. 2. A.
   Athenaeum 2:633 (Nov. 18, 1911); BostonEve. Trans.,
p6, Dec. 7, 1911; Dial. 53:452 (Dec. 1, 1912); Nation 95:
562 (Dec. 12, 1912); Sat. Rev. [Lond.] 112:618 (Nov. 11, 1911).

29 Marais, Eugene N. The soul of the white ant. With a
      biographical note by his son. Trans. by Winifred
      de Kok. New York: Kraus Reprint, 1969. 184p $9.00
      (Orig. publ. in English by Dodd, Mead in 1937. OP)
      The author, a South African amateur biologist, pre-
ceded Maeterlinck as the propounder of the theory of the or-
ganic unity of the termite colony, although the latter generally receives the credit for this. In this book Marais
describes the termitary and illustrates how the various individuals in it function as one organism. He points out that
the behavior in the termitary is as mysterious as telepathy
in humans and that any explanation must take into account
"a subtle immaterial influence which functions at a distance"
(p. 141). Illustrated; index. 1. M-L-C-U.
   N. Y. Her. Trib. Books, p18, Oct. 31, 1937; N. Y. Times
BookRev., p12, Aug. 1, 1937; Nature 140:suppl. 622 (Oct. 9,
1937); Sat. Rev. 16:21 (Aug. 14, 1937); TimesLit. Suppl.,
p444, June 12, 1937.

30 Pfungst, Oskar. Clever Hans (the horse of Mr. von
      Osten). Introduction by Robert Rosenthal (ed.).
      Prefatory note by James R. Angell. Introduction to
      the first American edition by Carl Stumpf. New
      York: Holt, Rinehart and Winston, 1965. 274p $6.95
      (Orig. publ. in German in 1907 under title Das Pferd
      des Herrn von Osten)
      This classic of psychology, long out of print, is once
more available, augmented by a long introductory survey
with a 39-item bibliography by Robert Rosenthal, who ties
in experiments in animal intelligence with current research
on the influence of the experimenter in psychological research. Although Pfungst established that Hans obtained
many of his answers by means of unconscious sensory cues
unwittingly provided by a questioner who knew the correct
answers, there is a residue of unexplained behavior on the
part of Hans and some of the other famed "thinking" horses
of Elberfeld. Frontispiece; 124-item bibliography. 2. A.
   Contemp. Psychol. 11:362 (July 1966); Dial 51:20
(July 1, 1911); Independent 71:100 (July 13, 1911); J. Philos.,
Psychol. &Sci. Method 8:663 (Nov. 23, 1911); N. Y. TimesBook
Rev. 16:456 (July 23, 1911); Nature 88:173 (Dec. 7, 1911);
Sci. Am. 216:144 (Mar. 1967).

31 Selous, Edmund. Thought-transference (or what?) in
        birds. New York: Richard R. Smith, 1931. 255p OP
        This little-known book by an observer of wildlife, and
especially of birds, is a study of unexplained bird behavior
suggestive of the operation of psi. It is primarily a record
of the author's field notes and observations. He decries the
fact that the psi hypothesis has been proposed in connection
with the human species, but is rarely considered in connection with other forms of life. He concludes that if some
form of psi is the explanation for his observations of birds,
then however inferior in quality the human manifestation of
psi may be, "yet with birds it is incomparably more perfect
in its application to the needs and acts of daily life, [and]
also of very much more frequent occurrence" (p.xi). Index.
2. U.
        JSPR 27:190-91 (Jan. 1932).

ANTHROPOLOGY AND PSI PHENOMENA

        The idea that psi might be more prevalent in primi-
tive than in civilized cultures has often been suggested.
Rose was the first to test the hypothesis empirically. The
Bucke Memorial Society at McGill University was founded to
study mystical states by scientific means. In its collection
some stimulating new ways of conceptualizing and studying
trance and possession are presented, stressing primitive cultures. This volume is outstanding as a multi-disciplinary
and many-faceted approach to the study of trance and possession states.

        Additional books with material on anthropology and
psi phenomena: In The book of dreams and ghosts (232)
Lang views accounts of psi experiences as folklore. Besterman (37) does the same for scrying, as do Vogt and Hyman
(41) for dowsing. One of the four conferences summarized
in a Parapsychology Foundation Proceedings (91) was devoted
to anthropology and parapsychology. Papers on anthropology
and psi are included in the Ciba Foundation symposium (88)
and in Besterman's Collected papers (153). Francis Huxley
has a paper on anthropology and ESP in Smythies' anthology
(93), and many references to anthropology and parapsychology
are cited in the bibliography by Techter (210).

32 Bucke (R. M.) Memorial Society. <u>Trance and posses-</u>
       <u>sion states</u>. (Raymond Prince, ed.). Montreal: The
       Society, 1968. 200p $4.00 (pap) (Available only from
       the R. M. Bucke Memorial Society)
       This volume comprises the papers delivered at the
second annual conference of the R. M. Bucke Memorial Society, McGill University. Part I is on the distribution and
patterns of trance and possession states throughout the world.
Part II: deals with methods of studying such states and tying
them in with ego psychology and other altered states of consciousness. The third part is entitled "Meaning and purpose";
it deals with possession states in various cultures as psychotherapy and on the views about such states held by various
religions. Bibliography at the end of some papers (277
items). <u>3</u>. L-C-U.
       Contemp. Psychol. 14:215-16 (Apr. 1969).

33 Lang, Andrew. <u>Cock lane and common-sense</u>. New
       York: AMS, 1970. 357p $12.00 (Orig. publ. by
       Longmans, Green in 1894. OP)
       This is a collection of 10 essays on various aspects
of psychical research. Many cases are given, with emphasis on experiences in primitive societies. Lang points out
that although cultural or other circumstances "may bring
these experiences more into notice at one moment than at
another ... they are always essentially the same" (p. 32).
He deals with apparitions, poltergeists, hauntings, scrying,
clairvoyance, and table-turning. He proposes that psi phenomena are at the base of all religions. Bibliographic footnotes. 2. M-L-C-U.
       JASPR 65:355-56 (July, 1971).
       Critic 25[n. s. 22]:117-18 (Aug. 25, 1894); Dial 17:126
(Sept. 1, 1894); Nation 59:161 (Aug. 30, 1894); Outlook 50:
596 (Oct. 13, 1894); Spectator 73:45-46 (July 14, 1894).

34 Oesterreich, T. K. <u>Possession: Demoniacal and other,</u>
       <u>among primitive races, in antiquity, the middle ages,</u>
       <u>and modern times</u>. Trans. by D. Ibberson. Intro-
       duction by Anita K. Gregory. New Hyde Park, N. Y.:
       University Books, 1966. 400p $10.00 (Orig. publ.
       in English in 1935 by de Laurence under title <u>Obses-</u>
       <u>sion and possession</u>, OP, and in German in 1921 under
       title <u>Die Besessenheit</u>)
       This book is an immense record of cases of posses-
sion and multiple personality from antiquity to modern times,
including Oriental cases and material from primitive peoples.
In interpreting the cases, Oesterreich dismisses the spiritis-

tic hypothesis, but is unable to account for them in terms
of abnormal psychology and dissociation. In an "Appendix
on parapsychology" he ties in the phenomena of mediumistic
trance with those of possession. Bibliographic footnotes;
index. 3. L-U.
IJP 9:60-61 (Spr. 1967); JSPR 43:432-33 (Dec. 1966).
Booklist 20:82 (Dec. 1923); Nature 111:840 (June 23,
1923); Spectator 130:933 (June 2, 1923); TimesLit.Suppl.,
p366, May 31, 1923.

35 Rose, Ronald. Primitive psychic power: The realities
    underlying the psychical practices and beliefs of Aus-
    tralian aborigines. Foreword by J. B. Rhine. New
    York: New American Library, 1968. 224p $.75 (pap)
    (Orig. publ. by Rand McNally in 1956 under title
    Living magic. Hardcover ed. OP)
This is a popular account of parapsychological investigations carried out by the author (a psychologist employed
by the Australian government) and his wife "to determine the
fact or fancy underlying their magic" (p.11). They interviewed shamans and administered questionnaires concerning
paranormal experiences. Anecdotal accounts of psi as used
by the natives in their daily life and rituals are also included. The Roses were the first to administer ESP and
PK tests to primitive peoples. The PK test results were
not significant, but the author concludes that ESP is more
widespread among Australian aborigines than among whites.
1. M-L-C-U.
JASPR 51:118-23 (July 1957); JSPR 39:193-96 (Mar.
1958).
Booklist 53:137 (Nov. 15, 1956); Psychoanal.Q. 26:
558-60 (1957); SanFranc.Chron., p22, Jan. 13, 1957; Spectator, p709, Nov. 22, 1957.

AUTOMATISMS

As defined by F. W. H. Myers, an automatism ex-
presses "such images as arise, as well as such movements
as are made, without the initiation ... of conscious thought
and will" (169, v. 1, p. xv). He distinguishes between sensory
automatisms (such as crystal-gazing and shell-hearing) and
motor automatisms (such as automatic writing and dowsing).
Automatisms are not always associated with psi, but may

sometimes serve as a vehicle for expressing information obtained by psi. The Barrett-Besterman book on dowsing and Besterman's Crystal-gazing are classics in the field and well worth owning. The two volumes on Patience Worth, the recent one by Litvag and Prince's masterful study, are also valuable.

Additional books with material on automatisms: There are significant sections on automatisms in Barrett (152), Dingwall and Langdon-Davies (156), Holms (162), Knight (164), Myers (169, 170), and Tyrrell (241).

36 Barrett, William F., and Besterman, Theodore. The divining-rod: An experimental and psychological investigation. Foreword by Leslie Shepard. New Hyde Park, N.Y.: University Books, 1968. 336p $7.50 (Orig. publ. by Methuen in 1926. OP)
  This is the best and most complete work there is on the subject of dowsing. It is in three parts. The first is an historical and geological survey. The second deals with experimental studies, past and contemporary, with both amateur and professional dowsers. The final part is a discussion of the mechanisms involved in dowsing and of the various theories that have been offered. There are three appendices, two of which are on dowsing in the United States. Illustrated; 19-page bibliography; index. 2. M-L-C-U.
  JSPR 24:16 (Feb. 1927).
  Abst. FolkloreStud. 7:45 (Sum. 1969); Choice 15:983 (Oct. 1968); Nature 119:310-12 (Feb. 26, 1927).

37 Besterman, Theodore. Crystal-gazing: A study in the history, distribution, theory and practice of scrying. Introduction by Eve Juster. New Hyde Park, N.Y.: University Books, 1965. 183p $5.00 (Orig. publ. by Rider in 1924. OP)
  This is the classic work on crystal-gazing, or scrying. It is aimed not only at the psychical researcher, but the anthropologist and student of folklore as well. The author describes the various types of scrying and then reviews scrying in legend and literature. There are four chapters on scrying in ancient and modern Europe, in Asia, Africa, and America. Two chapters are devoted to a valuable discussion of the psychological mechanisms involved. Besterman relates scrying to various other automatisms and to hauntings, raps, and multiple personality. The concluding chapter is entitled "The rationale of scrying." Bibliographic

footnotes; 12-page bibliography; index. 2. M-L-C-U.
        IJP 8:335-36 (Spr. 1966); JP 29:2̄10 (Sept. 1965);
JSPR 21:358-59 (Dec. 1924).
        Libr. J. 90:2567 (June 1, 1965).

38 Litvag, Irving. Singer in the shadows: The strange story
        of Patience Worth. New York: Macmillan, 1972.
        293p $7.95
        This is the first complete account in book form of
one of the most intriguing cases in the annals of psychical
research. Having studied all the records of the case, the
author has produced a highly readable account of Pearl Curran, a St. Louis housewife who, in 1913, began to receive
material (including poems and complete novels) of a high
literary order through the ouija board from Patience Worth,
who claimed to have been a 17th-century Englishwoman. Although the book is as readable as fiction, the facts have
been meticulously researched and documented, and no aspect
of the case, pro or con, has been omitted. "Bibliographic
notes" by chapter at the end of the book (267 items); index.
1. A.
        JASPR 67:102-05 (Jan. 1973); JP 36:73-77 (Mar. 1972).
        Libr. J. 97:2850 (Sept. 15, 1972); Publ. Wkly 201:44
(July 10, 1972).

39 Mühl, Anita M. Automatic writing: An approach to the
        unconscious. Introduction by William A. White.
        Foreword by Eileen J. Garrett. New York: Garrett/
        Helix, 1964. 186p $4.50 (Orig. publ. by Steinkopff
        in 1930. OP)
        Part One of this book deals with ways to develop auto-
matic writing and other automatisms such as automatic drawing and speaking. The author, a psychiatrist, discusses
various forms of dissociation and the development and ex-
pression of secondary personalities. She considers the role
of automatisms in personality growth and also the dangers in
their use. Examples are given of how she used automatic
writing as a method of understanding patients who were not
able to communicate by ordinary means. Part Two describes
some strange coincidences associated with experiments in
automatic writing. Illustrated; 261-item bibliography. 3.
L-C-U.
        IJP 8:154-55 (Win. 1966); JASPR 25:478-86 (Nov.
1931); JSPR 27:30-32 (Feb. 1932).

40 Prince, Walter Franklin. The case of Patience Worth:
        A critical study of certain unusual phenomena. Bos-

ton: Boston Society for Psychic Research, 1927. 509p
OP

When he was Research Officer of the Boston Society
for Psychic Research, the author investigated the literary
communications from "Patience Worth" received by Pearl
Curran. He interviewed not only Mrs. Curran but many of
the people who knew her or had been involved in the case.
The results of his investigation are recorded here. Included
is a section in which he deals with the question whether
trickery on the part of Mrs. Curran was involved, or whether
subconsciously she could have obtained the information trans-
mitted via the ouija board. He analyzes the communications
themselves, indicating how they reflect Patience's character-
istic style. He discusses the criticisms of other investigators and summarizes the theories offered to account for the
case. Bibliographic footnotes. 3. L-C-U.
PSPR 36:573-76, Pt. 103 (1926).

41 Vogt, Evon Z., and Hyman, Ray. Water witching U.S.A.
    Chicago: University of Chicago Press, 1959. 248p
    $7.00
    This is a critical survey of dowsing by an anthropolo-
gist (Vogt) and a psychologist (Hyman). The data upon which
the book is based were gathered to answer the question "Why
does water witching continue to be practiced in the United
States?" (p. 11). Unfortunately the authors' negative bias
predetermined their conclusion: the evidence for dowsing is
not evaluated; rather, it is arbitrarily assumed that dowsing
is superstition. As such, the book reports the folklore of
it. Nevertheless, there is much material included on automatisms. Chapter 5 is a critique of "talking" horses such
as Clever Hans (30) and Lady Wonder. It also contains information on Chevreul's pendulum and Faraday's study of
table-turning. Illustrated; 112-item bibliography. 2. L-C-U.
    JASPR 53:147-55 (Oct. 1959); JP 23:274-77 (Dec.
1959); JSPR 40:260-65 (Mar. 1960).
    Am. Anthropol. 62:1126 (Dec. 12, 1960); Am. J. Psychol.
72:653-54 (1959); Am. Sociol. Rev. 24:739 (Oct. 1959); Booklist 55:589 (July 1, 1959); Christ. Cent. 76:1191 (Oct. 14,
1959); J. Am. Folklore 73:64 (Jan. -Mar. 1960); Libr. J. 84:
1275 (Apr. 15, 1959); MidwestFolklore 10:47 (Spr. 1960);
Nation 188:500 (May 30, 1959); Sat. Rev. 42:43 (June 13,
1959).

42 Wright, Theon. The open door: A case history of auto-
    matic writing. New York: John Day, 1970. 352p
    $7.95

This book is about the author's parents, who began to experiment with automatic writing in 1899 when spiritualism was still "respectable." This continued for 70 years and involved various members of three generations of the Wright family. Although disillusioned with the physical phenomena of spiritualism, the Wrights increasingly turned to the philosophy of life expressed in the messages they received. In Part I "spirit" communications and the problem of survival are discussed. Part II, which forms the bulk of the book, is concerned with how the "door" opened and the content of the writing. The final part discusses the dialogue that can take place by means of automatic writing and the significance of the messages received. Illustrated; bibliography by chapter at the end of the book (57 items). 2. M-L-C-U.
Libr. J. 95:4272 (Dec. 15, 1970).

CRITICISMS

Since the beginnings of organized psychical research (1882), psi phenomena and the methods of investigating them have been under constant critical attack, as would be expected in the case of such a controversial subject. A summary of the earlier criticisms is presented by Prince. A full range of the stances for and against (but mainly against) psychical research is given in The case for and against psychical belief. Hansel's book is the most recent, the most widely read, and covers the entire field of parapsychology. Hall limits himself to a critical discussion of physical mediumship (The spiritualists) and poltergeist/haunting cases (New light on old ghosts).

Additional books with material on criticisms: Exposures of the methods of fraudulent mediumship are given by Abbott (94) and Carrington (96). Hard-nosed, critical views of psi phenomena are found throughout Dingwall and Langdon-Davies (156) and Eysenck (192), and in selections in Schmeidler (59), Gudas (159), and a Parapsychology Foundation Proceedings (175). Well-known cases of apparitions, hauntings, and poltergeists are criticized in The haunting of Borley Rectory (73) and Four modern ghosts (74). The most extensive survey of the early criticisms of quantitative ESP research is found in ESP-60 (57). Criticisms of the survival evidence are presented by Hart (251), Lamont (255), and

Murphy (257).

43   Flew, Antony G. N.   A new approach to psychical re-
         search.   London: Watts, 1953.   161p OP
         This is a critical survey of psi phenomena, and es-
pecially of the survival hypothesis, by a British philosopher.
His aim is twofold: first, to satisfy the layman's curiosity
about the nature of psychical research; and second, to apply
the methods of linguistic analysis to the concepts of psychical research.   The latter is a distinctive contribution, especially in the chapter entitled "Describing and explaining."
Of special interest are two critical appendices, one on the
Moberly/Jourdain case of so-called retrocognition reported
in An adventure, and one on Dunne's "serialism" theory
which he proposed for precognition.   Bibliography at the end
of each chapter (69 items); bibliographical references incorporated in the text; bibliographic footnotes; name index.   2.
M-L-C-U.
         JASPR 48:78-80 (Apr. 1954); JP 18:130-32 (June
1954); JSPR 37:280-88 (Mar.-Apr. 1954).
         ChurchQ.Rev. 155:186-87, No.3 (1954).

44   Hall, Trevor H.   New light on old ghosts.   London:
         Duckworth, 1965.   142p £1.25;   Hollywood-by-the-Sea,
         Fla.: Transatlantic, 1965. $6.75
         The author, a perennial critic of psychical research
and amateur magician, approaches psychical research from
the viewpoint of one interested in the vagaries of human
testimony and the psychology of deception.   In this book he
attempts to find normal explanations for some classical poltergeist and haunting cases (among them the Wesley poltergeist, the Borley Rectory case, and the Cock Lane ghost),
and for the levitation phenomena of D. D. Home.   Hall adds
a new chapter in his retelling of the relationship between
the medium Florence Cook and William Crookes (45).   Illustrated; bibliographic footnotes; index.   1.   A.
         JSPR 44:94-106 (June 1967).
         Libr.J. 91:3963 (Sept. 1, 1966); Spectator, p230,
Feb. 25, 1966; TimesLit.Suppl., p1203, Dec. 23, 1965.

45   Hall, Trevor H.   The spiritualists: The story of Flor-
         ence Cook and William Crookes.   New York: Garrett/
         Helix, 1963.   188p $4.50   (Orig. publ. by Duckworth
         in 1962. OP)
         The British medium Florence Cook has been held by
many to be the most powerful materialization medium of all

time.   She produced a "spirit form, " calling itself Katie
King, which was said to be as solid as a living person and
capable of walking about freely.   Florence was actively
sponsored by Sir William Crookes, the famous physicist, who
had many private sittings with her and published his findings.
On the basis of both contemporary records and new data
which he found, Hall concludes that the "weight of the evidence appears to show that Florence Cook's mediumship was
... shamelessly fraudulent ... [and] that William Crookes
became her accomplice..." (p.170).   Few books in the field
of psychical research have engendered as much heated controversy as this biography of Florence Cook and her family,
as attested to by the reviews and correspondence in the professional parapsychological journals.   Illustrated; bibliographic footnotes; index.   2.   M-L-C-U.
        IJP 5:203-12 (Spr. 1963); JASPR 57:215-26 (Oct.
1963); JP 27:123-37 (June 1963); JSPR 41:372-77 (Sept. 1962).
        NewStatesman 64:260 (Aug. 31, 1962); Tablet 216:1017
(Oct. 27, 1962); TimesLit. Suppl., p512, July 13, 1962.

46 Hansel, C. E. M.   ESP: A scientific evaluation.   Intro-
        duction by E. G. Boring.   New York: Scribner's,
        1966.   263p $10.00; $2.45 (pap)
        A skeptical psychologist offers criticisms of the en-
tire field of psychical research, including detailed analyses
of specific modern experimental investigations.   He especially attacks the work of J. B. Rhine carried out when he was
at Duke University and that of S. G. Soal in England, but
he also deals with other quantitative work and with mediumship (the Fox sisters, Palladino, Margery, Mrs. Piper, and
Mrs. Leonard).   Hall's aim is not to establish that trickery
actually occurred, but only that in certain key investigations
it could have.   41-item glossary; bibliography by chapter at
the end of the book (178 items); "Suggestions for further
reading" (20 items); index.   2.   A.
        JASPR 61:254-67 (July 1967); JP 31:76-82 (Mar. 1967);
JSPR 44:217-32 (Mar. 1968).
        Am. J. Clin. & Exp. Hypn. 16:133-34 (1968); Am. J. Clin.
Hypn. 11:60 (1968/69); Am. J. Psychiat. 123:502-04 (1966/67);
Am. J. Psychol. 79:662-64 (1966); Am. Sci. 54:339A (Aut.
1966); BookWeek, p4, June 12, 1966; Br. J. Psychiat. 114:
653-58 (1968); Br. J. Stat. Psychol. 12:170-71 (1959); Bull.
MenningerClin. 31:318 (1967); Child&Fam. 6:93-95 (1967);
Commonweal 84:646 (Sept. 30, 1966); Contemp. Psychol. 12:
1-3 (Jan. 1967); Contemp. Rev. 211:111 (Aug. 1967); Int. J.
Clin. & Exp. Hypn. 16:133-34 (1968); J. Am. Med. Assoc. 198:
153-54 (Oct. 31, 1966); J. Am. Psychoanal. Assoc. 16:146-78

(1968); J.Nerv.&Ment.Dis. 145:84-86 (1967); Kirkus 34:348
(Mar. 15, 1966); Libr.J. 91:2505 (May 15, 1966); Ment.Hyg.
51:149 (1967); N.Y.Rev.Books 6:27 (May 26, 1966); N.Y.
TimesBookRev. 71:14 (July 17, 1966); NewStatesman 73:374
(Mar. 17, 1967); Psychiat.&Soc.Sci.Rev. 1:7-11 (1967); Sci.
Books 2:85 (Sept. 1966); Science 153:1089 (Sept. 2, 1966);
TimesLit.Suppl., p196, Mar. 9, 1967; Va.Q.Rev. 42:clxv
(Aut. 1966).

47 Murchison, Carl A. (ed.). The case for and against
        psychical belief.   Ann Arbor, Mich.: University Mi-
        crofilms, xerocopy, OP No. 13,940. 365p $15.50
        (Orig. publ. by Clark University in 1927. OP)
        This collection of pro and con papers is an outgrowth
of a symposium held at Clark University in 1926. The contributions are arranged according to the attitude expressed
toward the existence of psi. Papers in the first group are
by those who were "convinced of the multiplicity of psychical
phenomena" (Lodge, Doyle, Bond, Crandon, Austin, and De-
land.) Part Two represents those who were "convinced of
the rarity of genuine psychical phenomena" (McDougall,
Driesch, W. F. Prince, and Schiller). Two contributions
are contained in Part Three: "unconvinced as yet" (Coover
and Murphy). Part Four, "antagonistic to the claims that
such phenomena occur," contains papers by Jastrow and
Houdini. Illustrated; bibliographic footnotes. 2. L-C-U.
        JASPR 21:241-48 (Apr. 1927) and JASPR 21:301-12
(May 1927); JSPR 24:104-07 (July 1927).

48 Prince, Walter Franklin. The enchanted boundary:
        Being a survey of negative reactions to claims of
        psychic phenomena, 1820-1930. Boston: Boston So-
        ciety for Psychic Research, 1930. 348p OP
        This pioneer work reports on the first large-scale
attempt to appraise the criticisms of psychical research and
to assess their quality and cogency. The negative remarks
of 111 persons are considered. The first part of the book
reviews criticisms in 40 books, articles, and letters from
1820 to 1930. The second part is an analysis of 71 replies
given to Prince by prominent men and women who were
asked to assess whether "the notion that some process of
gaining knowledge, at present not isolated and explained by
science, was involved" in the circumstances of a hypothetical case typical of those studied by psychical research.
Bibliographic footnotes; index. 3. L-C-U.
        PSPR 39:415-18, Pt.118 (1931).

49   Rawcliffe, D. H.   Occult and supernatural phenomena.
       Foreword by Julian Huxley.   New York: Dover, 1971.
       551p $3.50 (pap)   (Orig. publ. by Ridgway in 1952
       under title The psychology of the occult, hardcover
       ed., and by Dover in 1959 under title Illusions and
       delusions of the supernatural and the occult. pap OP)
       This book was written to repulse "the ever advancing
tide of supernatural belief which present-day psychical research keeps in motion" (p.12).   Much of the material
covered is not strictly parapsychological (e.g., dissociation,
hysteria, hypnotism), but many topics discussed are relevant
to psychical research, among them out-of-the-body experiences, scrying, automatisms, mediumship, unorthodox healing, physical phenomena (a chapter on Palladino), spontaneous
psi phenomena, and quantitative ESP experiments (including
a chapter on the work of S. G. Soal).   There is also a
chapter on theories entitled "The logic of telepathy."   Illustrated; 203-item glossary; 26-page bibliography.   2.   M-L-
C-U.
       JASPR 47:125-27 (July 1953); JP 16:146-48 (June
1952); JSPR 36:624-27 (May-June 1952).

50   Tanner, Amy E.   Studies in spiritism.   Introduction by
       G. Stanley Hall.   New York: Appleton, 1910. 408p
       OP
       The author, a psychologist and special assistant to G.
Stanley Hall at Clark University, collaborated with him in
investigations of spiritism, especially as reflected in the
work of the S. P. R.   Tanner personally investigated, with
Hall, the mediumship of Mrs. Piper and concluded that her
phenomena were evidence only of secondary personality.
They also examined the trance state, the mediumship of
Mrs. Verrall and Mrs. Holland, the cross correspondences,
and the evidence for telepathy.   The author concludes that
the alleged facts of psychical research are illusory and those
who accept them do so primarily to serve the human need to
believe.   26-item glossary; 42-item bibliography.   3.   L-U.
       JASPR 5:1-98 (Jan. 1911); PSPR 25:90-108, Pt. 62
(1911).
       A. L. A. Booklist 7:159 (Dec. 1910); Dial 49:384 (Nov.
16, 1910); Lit. Dig. 41:947 (Nov. 19, 1910); Nation 91:554
(Dec. 8, 1910); N. Y. TimesSat. Rev. 15:661 (Nov. 26, 1910).

EXPERIMENTAL PSYCHICAL RESEARCH

In this category are reports of quantitative ESP experiments, surveys of the experimental literature, and theoretical writings aimed at explaining or facilitating experimental research. For reviews of the literature, ESP-60 and Rao's book are companion volumes; both are essential for anyone interested in doing research and as reference tools. Rhine and Pratt's Parapsychology belongs in every collection, as does the book by Thouless. Schmeidler and McConnell and Soal and Bateman are both classics and provide valuable accounts of landmark experiments; the latter is also important because it represents the modern British approach. For an all-around collection of papers with a pro-con format, the book edited by Schmeidler is essential. Also of value because of the individual contributions described are Carington, Rhine's Extrasensory perception, Sinclair, and Ullman and Krippner.

Additional books with material on experimental psychical research: A number of books deal with experimental parapsychology in general or contain actual experimental reports. These are Edmunds (158), McConnell (166), Murphy (168), Pratt (174), J. B. Rhine (176), Tyrrell (182, 183), West (185), and L. E. Rhine (236). Older experiments are described by Osty (109) and Gurney, Myers, and Podmore (229). Critical, although not always negative, views of experimental parapsychology are given in Hansel (46), the Ciba Foundation symposium (88), Gudas (159), and Eysenck (192). Rose (35) describes ESP and PK experiments with Australian aborigines. Accounts of PK experiments are also given by Forwald (187) and L. E. Rhine (188). Experiments stressing the psychology of psi phenomena are found in Cavanna (6), Jones (13), McCreery (167), Mangan (194), Rosenthal (196), Rush (197), Schmeidler (198), and in several Parapsychology Foundation Proceedings (18, 19, 89, 92).

51 Carington, Whately. Telepathy: An outline of its facts, theory, and implications. New York: Gordon Press, 1972. 176p $7.95 (Orig. publ. by Methuen in 1945 under this title and by Creative Age in 1946 under title Thought transference. OP)
    This book by one of England's outstanding experimental parapsychologists is divided into three parts. The first is a review of the various types of evidence for telepathy; it

provides an excellent survey of the work on both spontaneous
and experimental psi, with emphasis on the latter. The objections to the telepathic hypothesis are also considered.
Part Two presents Carington's "association theory of telepathy, " which is one of the most fruitful ever offered. The
final section outlines the implications of telepathy for psychology in general, the survival problem, religion, and social
systems.   77-item bibliography; bibliographic footnotes; index.   2.   L-C-U.
        JASPR 40:152-62 (July 1946); JP 10:141-44 (June 1946);
PSPR 47:275-76, Pt.169 (1942).
        Nature 155:619 (May 26, 1945).

52 Rao, K. Ramakrishna. Experimental parapsychology: A
        review and interpretation, with a comprehensive bibli-
        ography.   Springfield, Ill.: Thomas, 1966. 255p $9.50
        This volume surveys all aspects of experimental para-
psychology from 1940 through 1965.   The areas covered are
the existence of psi; the subject in psi tests; the target in
its relation to the subject; experimenter, test conditions, and
methods; the psychology of psi; some parapsychological
theories; and parapsychology and the nature of man.   There
is a summary after each section.   52-item glossary; 1251-
item bibliography; name index; subject index.   3.   M-L-C-U.
        IJP 9:192-95 (Aut. 1967); JASPR 61:280-81 (July 1967);
JP 30:259-62 (Dec. 1966); JSPR 44:188-89 (Dec. 1967).
        Am.J.Psychother. 22:113-15 (1968); Br.J.Med.Psychol.
40:191-92 (1967); Br.J.Psychol. 58:183-84 (1967); Contemp.
Psychol. 12:95-96 (Feb. 1967); J.Am.Psychoanal.Assoc. 16:
146-78 (1968); J.Nerv.&Ment.Dis. 145:84-86 (1967); Psychiat.
Dig. 28:33-34 (1967); Psychoanal.Rev. 69:145-46 (1969);
TimesLit.Suppl., p903, Sept. 25, 1966.

53 Rhine, J. B. Extrasensory perception. Rev. ed.
        Foreword by William McDougall. Introduction by
        Walter Franklin Prince. Boston: Branden, 1964.
        240p $2.75 (pap) (Orig. publ. by the Boston Society
        for Psychic Research in 1934. Hardcover ed. OP)
        This is the first account of the early ESP card-guess-
ing experiments at Duke University.   Included are reports of
work with several high-scoring subjects, among them Hubert
Pearce and Charles E. Stuart.   Still very relevant today is
Rhine's discussion of the psychological and physiological conditions favoring success in ESP testing.   He is more expli-
cit on this important topic here than in any of his later
books.   Contains a new chapter, "From the author in 1964, "
which is a useful survey of progress made in 30 years.

Illustrated; "New annotated 10-item bibliography"; index. 2.
A.
      JASPR 65:117-18 (Jan. 1971); PSPR 43:24-37, Pt.139
(1935).
      BostonEve. Trans., p2, Aug. 4, 1934; Contemp. Psy-
chol. 11:58-60 (Feb. 1966); N.Y. TimesBookRev., p50, Sept.
12, 1965; Nature 134:308 (Sept. 1, 1934).

54   Rhine, J. B. (ed.). Progress in Parapsychology. Dur-
      ham, N.C.: Parapsychology Press, 1971. 315p $7.00
      This is a collection of 23 papers originally presented
at review meetings held at the Institute of Parapsychology of
FRNM and selected for novel features involved. Many of
the papers have been published in full in parapsychological
journals, particularly the Journal of Parapsychology (329)
but for the purposes of this book were made less technical.
They are arranged in five sections: 1/new approaches to
psi experimentation, 2/psychokinesis, 3/factors in psi test
performance, 4/the main lines of continuity in psi research,
and 5/parapsychology in perspective. Each section is preceded by a preface by the editor, who also provides an introduction entitled "Dimensions of progress." Included is a
tribute to William McDougall for his contributions to parapsychology. Appendices present statistical methods for
evaluating various kinds of experimental results, instructions
for generating precognition targets, etc. Illustrated; 45-
item glossary; bibliography at the end of some papers (75
items); name index; subject index. 2. M-L-C-U.
      JASPR 66:215-21 (Apr. 1972); JP 35:144-48 (June
1971); JSPR 46:239-43 (Dec. 1971); PR 2:17-18 (Nov.-Dec.
1971).
      Choice 8:1513 (Jan. 1972); Contemp. Psychol. 17:123-
24 (Mar. 1972); Libr.J. 96:2330 (July 1971).

55   Rhine, J. B. The reach of the mind. New York: Peter
      Smith, 1972. 235p $4.00; New York: Morrow, 1971. $1.95
      (pap) (Orig. publ. by Sloane in 1947. Hardcover ed. OP)
      This book describes the steps taken at the Duke Para-
psychology Laboratory to establish experimentally the existence and some characteristics of telepathy, clairvoyance,
precognition, and psychokinesis. Discusses how normal psi
is and its consequences for human relations. There is a
chapter on the acceptance of the reality of ESP and PK, and
one on the prospects for the practical application of psi.
Illustrated; "additional reading" (11 items); index. 2. A.
      JASPR 42:36-38 (Jan. 1948); JP 11:222-26 (Sept. 1947);
and JP 14:214-21 (Sept. 1950); JSPR 34:183-85 (Feb. 1948).

Booklist 44:45 (Oct. 1, 1947); Chic. SundayBookWeek, p5, Sept. 14, 1947; Choice 8:915 (Sept. 1971); Kirkus 15:325 (June 15, 1947); Libr. J. 72:1031 (July 1947); N.Y. Her. Trib. WklyBookRev., p22, Oct. 19, 1947; N.Y. TimesBookRev., p34, Nov. 2, 1947; NewRepub. 117:25 (Dec. 15, 1947); New Yorker 23:102 (Sept. 20, 1947); SanFranc. Chron., p17, Nov. 16, 1947; Sat. Rev. 30:27 (Nov. 8, 1947); Sch. & Soc. 66:367 (Nov. 8, 1947); Wis. Libr. Bull. 43:147 (Nov. 1947).

56 Rhine, J. B., and Brier, Robert (eds.). Parapsychology today. New York: Citadel, 1968. 286p $6.00
This is a collection of 22 papers originally delivered at three review meetings held at FRNM. The book is intended for students and laymen as well as for research workers, and its purpose is to give a representative picture of current parapsychology, especially of the types of experiments being conducted. Most of the papers appeared in the Journal of Parapsychology, but for the purposes of the book they were trimmed down and made less technical. They are arranged in the following groups: new methods in psi research; the effects of the test situation on psi; the psychology of psi testing; current views of parapsychology; and the significance of parapsychology today. Illustrated; 48-item glossary; bibliography at the end of some papers (36 items); name index; subject index. 2. M-L-C-U.
JASPR 64:111-17 (Jan. 1970); JP 33:77-81 (Mar. 1969); JSPR 45:179-82 (Dec. 1969).
Am. J. Psychiat. 126:911-12 (1969/70); Am. J. Psychol. 83:304-05 (1970); Booklist 65:1192 (July 1, 1969); Libr. J. 93:4303 (Nov. 15, 1968); Psychiatry 33:134-36 (1970); Psychosom. Med. 31:569-70 (1969).

57 Rhine, J. B., and others. Extrasensory perception after sixty years: A critical appraisal of the research in extrasensory perception. Foreword by J. B. Rhine. Boston: Branden, 1966. 483p $5.95 (Orig. publ. by Holt in 1940. OP)
This is the "bible" of experimental parapsychology. It covers the period from 1882 to 1940, with emphasis on the ESP research at Duke University starting in 1927. The authors' purpose was to "survey everything that is of importance to know in deciding whether ESP occurs, and what it is like if it does occur" (p. v). In four parts, the first discusses mathematical and experimental methods, describes the tests in detail, and considers the counterhypotheses to the results obtained. The second presents criticisms of the research and a rebuttal to them. The third is concerned

with the nature of ESP: its incidence, conditions affecting it,
modes of response, and its physical and psychological relationships. The final part discusses unsolved problems and
presents a general overview of the subject. There are 19
appendices, most of them devoted to descriptions of statistical methods used in ESP research. Appendix 17 gives in
tabular form the conditions and results of all published ESP
experiments (1882-1939), and criticisms of the research are
summarized in terms of alternative hypotheses in Appendix
19. Illustrated; 42-item glossary; 361-item bibliography;
name index; subject index. 3. A.
     JASPR 34:266-68 (Aug. 1940); JSPR 44:42 (Mar.
1967); PSPR 46:265-70, Pt. 163 (1940).

58   Rhine, J. B., and Pratt, J. G. Parapsychology: Fron-
     tier science of the mind. Rev. ed. Springfield, Ill.:
     Thomas, 1962. 224p $6.00 (Orig. publ. by Thomas
     in 1957. OP)
     Conceived as a textbook, this work presents "a sur-
vey of the field, the methods, and the facts of ESP and PK
research" (title page). The methodology of basic research
is stressed. Part I is a survey of the present knowledge
about psi, its types, and its relation to other fields. Part
II is a presentation of testing techniques, including a discussion of the basic procedures, methods of scoring, and statistical evaluation; it also contains an important chapter on the
psychological requirements for successful psi testing. There
is a list of "Some significant events in the development of
parapsychology" (40 items), and eight tables for evaluating
test results. Illustrated; 58-item glossary; bibliography at
the end of each chapter (109 items); "additional reading" at
the end of each chapter (120 items); name index; subject index. 3. A.
     JASPR 52:117-20 (July 1958); JP 21:296-304 (Dec.
1957); JSPR 39:249-51 (June 1958).
     Am. J. Psychiat. 115:842-43 (1958/59); Br. J. Educ.
Psychol. 28:299 (1958); Bull. MenningerClin. 22:114 (1958);
Contemp. Psychol. 3:295-96 (Oct. 1958); J. PastoralCare 12:
252-53 (1958); Psychoanal. Q. 27:278-79 (1958).

59   Schmeidler, Gertrude R. (ed.). Extrasensory perception.
     New York: Atherton, 1969. 166p $7.95; $2.95 (pap)
     This is an "Atherton controversy" book, a series
aimed at college students in which both sides of a controversial subject are presented through an Introduction and the
selection of articles by a scholar in the field. The choice
of editor in this case is an excellent one as Schmeidler has

guided many graduate students in psi research. She provides an overview of the subject: its phenomena, methods,
and findings. Two negative and seven affirmative selections
from the literature follow and she comments on each. Six
of the affirmative papers are experimental reports. One
negative paper deals with a specific piece of research, the
Pearce-Pratt series, and is followed by Rhine and Pratt's
defense. The second negative paper is a general critique
of current parapsychology. Bibliography at the end of each
paper (149 items); index. 2. A.
        JASPR 64:443-49 (Oct. 1970); JP 33:267-73 (Sept.
1969).
        Am. J. Psychiat. 127:145-46 (Feb. 1971); Choice 7:303-
04 (Apr. 1970); Contemp. Psychol. 17:141-42 (Mar. 1972); J.
Mark. Res. 7:541 (1970); Libr. J. 94:4442 (Dec. 1, 1969);
Percept. Cogn. Dev. 5:1321 (1969).

60 Schmeidler, Gertrude R., and McConnell, R. A. ESP
    and personality patterns. Introduction by Gardner
    Murphy. New Haven: Yale University Press, 1958.
    136p OP
This book is primarily an account of one of the most
significant series in parapsychology, the "sheep-goat" experiments carried out over a nine-year period by the senior
author. The authors say that "the subject matter of the book
divides into three parts. Chapters 1 and 2 are introductory,
and 3 through 5 present our major findings" (p. viii). Chapter 6 describes work undertaken by eight other investigators
to test the sheep-goat hypothesis; of these, six obtained con-
firmatory results. The third part deals with general personality correlates of ESP success, with chapters on the
Rorschach test, experiments with cerebral concussion patients, and frustration in relation to ESP. In Chapter 10
the authors answer the frequently-asked question, How common is ESP? In the final chapter they discuss their tenta-
tive conclusions and make suggestions for further research.
71-item bibliography; index. 3. A.
        JASPR 52:151-53 (Oct. 1958); JP 22:220-22 (Sept.
1958); JSPR 40:73-79 (June 1959).
        Contemp. Psychol. 3:295-96 (Oct. 1958); J. Ment. Sci.
105:1127 (1959).

61 Sinclair, Upton. Mental radio. Rev. 2d ed. Introduc-
    tion by William McDougall. Preface by Albert Ein-
    stein. With a report by Walter Franklin Prince.
    Springfield, Ill.: Thomas, 1962. 237p $8.50; New
    York: Macmillan, n. d. $1.95 (pap) (Orig. publ. by

the author in 1930. OP)
In this volume Upton Sinclair describes his efforts to
transmit pictures telepathically to his wife, Craig, and outlines the development of her psychic abilities. Illustrations
of his target drawings and her responses are reproduced.
Chapter 21 is especially valuable as it contains Craig's
memorandum on how she developed her psi ability, with her
recommendations for what to do and what pitfalls to avoid.
In an important supplement to this edition, W. F. Prince
gives an account of his efforts to determine the validity of
these and other psi experiments with pictures.   (This material was originally published in Bulletin XVI of the Boston
Society for Psychic Research, Apr. 1932.) Illustrated. 1.
A.
JASPR 24:426 (Sept 1930); and JASPR 65:113-17 (Jan.
1971); PSPR 39:343-46, Pt.116 (1931).
Bookman 72:xv (Oct. 1930); N.Y. Her. Trib. Books,
p15, July 6, 1930; N.Y. TimesBookRev., p20, June 15, 1930;
St. LouisLibr. Bull. 28:229 (Oct. 1930); SpringfieldRepub.,
p5e, July 6, 1930; Survey 64:448 (Aug. 1930); TimesLit.
Suppl., p548, July 3, 1930.

62 Soal, S. G., and Bateman, F. Modern experiments in
     telepathy. Introduction by G. E. Hutchinson. New
     Haven: Yale University Press, 1954. 425p OP
This book accomplishes two purposes. First, it
offers a detailed account of the better experimental work in
ESP from 1883 to 1953, which serves as an excellent introduction for the serious student who wants to review the
quantitative evidence.   Second, it provides the most complete
record there is of Soal's important experimental work with two
British high-scoring ESP subjects, Basil Shackleton and
Gloria Stewart.   The authors tell how these subjects were
discovered and describe the experiments in detail.   Of
special interest is the work with different agents and some
long-distance experiments.   There is a useful general survey
of their data.   Various aspects of the scientific approach to
ESP research are given in several appendices.   Illustrated;
bibliography by chapter at the end of the book (199 items);
index. 3. M-L-C-U.
JASPR 49:80-83 (Apr. 1955); JP 18:245-58 (Dec.
1954); JSPR 38:21-28 (Mar. 1955).
Am. J. Psychother. 11:446-48 (1957); Bull. Menninger
Clin. 19:108 (1955); HibbertJ. 53:304 (Apr. 1955); J. Gen.
Psychol. 52:337-39 (1955); J. Ment. Sci. 101:183-84 (1955);
Manch. Guard., p4, Oct. 26, 1954; N.Y. TimesBookRev.,
p16, Feb. 27, 1955; Sci. Am. 193:116-17 (Oct. 1955); Times

Lit. Suppl., p809, Dec. 10, 1954.

63 Thouless, Robert H. Experimental psychical research.
        Foreword by C. A. Mace. Santa Fe, N. M.: Gannon,
        1969. 148p $5.00 (Orig. publ. by Penguin in 1963.
        OP)
        This book was written to provide a general view of
experimental parapsychology. Although Thouless refers to
most of the major experiments, examining their aims,
methods, and results, he does so in order to illustrate the
application of the experimental method to the study of psi
rather than merely to review the results. In many respects
this is a useful handbook on how to conduct psi experiments.
In addition to detailed descriptions of all the major types of
tests, there are important chapters on how to judge the significance of results, how to draw inferences from data, and
on controls for parapsychological experiments. Some of the
problem areas of the field are outlined. "Suggestions for
further reading" (10 items); 48-item bibliography; index. 2.
A.
        JASPR 59:172-78 (Apr. 1965); JP 28:51-56 (Mar.
1964); JSPR 42:248-50 (Mar. 1964).
        Br. J. Psychol. 55:244 (1964); J. Am. Psychoanal. Assoc.
16:146-78 (1968).

64 Thouless, Robert H. From anecdote to experiment in
        psychical research. London: Routledge and Kegan
        Paul, 1972. 198p £3.00; $10.00
        Begun as a revision of the author's Experimental
psychical research (63), this is a new book in its own right,
following a different plan and much longer. It is intended
for those who are already familiar with other areas of scientific research. Thouless' purpose is not to summarize
the whole field, but "to demonstrate experimental psychical
research as a living field achieving some interesting results
and holding the promise of achieving far more in the future"
(p. ix). He writes about the application of the scientific
method to the data of psychical research with ample illustrations from the literature. He reviews criticisms and has
two chapters on the "patterns of ESP." He gives detailed
descriptions of all the major tests in chapters on precognition, psychokinesis, and survival (in which he outlines the
"cipher" test which he himself designed). He discusses experimental precautions, estimating significance, drawing inferences from data, and experimental design. Illustrated;
bibliography at the end of each chapter (130 items); bibliographic footnotes; index. 2. A.

JP 36:233-36 (Sept. 1972); JSPR 46:164-67 (Sept.
1972); PR 3:17-18 (Nov.-Dec. 1972).

65 Tischner, Rudolf. Telepathy and clairvoyance. 2d ed.
    Trans. by W. D. Hutchinson. Introduction by Eric J.
    Dingwall. New York: Harcourt, Brace, 1925. 227p
    OP (Orig. publ. in German in 1921 under title Uber
    Telepathie und Hellsehen)
One of the volumes in the International Library of
Psychology, Philosophy, and the Scientific Method, this book
by a German ophthalmologist and parapsychologist was
described by Hans Driesch as "the best experimental work
we have on this subject" (p. viii). This pays tribute to the
fact that although Tischner grew up in the "golden age" of
psychical research when mediums were the prime subject of
study, he was one of the first to study psi in the laboratory,
and it was he who coined the term "extrasensory perception."
This volume is a record of his experiments on telepathy and
clairvoyance. He also discusses the theories that have been
offered to explain psi phenomena, and includes a survey of
the German literature on psychical research. Illustrated;
bibliographic footnotes. 2. L-U.
    PSPR 33:437-38, Pt. 86 (1922).
    Discovery 6:273 (July 1925).

66 Ullman, Montague, and Krippner, Stanley. Dream
    studies and telepathy: An experimental approach.
    New York: Parapsychology Foundation, 1970. 119p
    (Parapsychological Monographs No. 12) $3.00 (pap)
    (Available only from the Foundation)
The senior author has had a long-standing interest in
telepathic dreams, beginning with observations he made while
in the private practice of psychoanalysis, and kindled by exploratory studies he carried out in cooperation with the A.S.
P.R. and the Parapsychology Foundation. In 1962 he established the Dream Laboratory at Maimonides Medical Center and the junior author is its director. The first part of
their monograph describes the early pilot studies, while the
latter half presents the results of the laboratory's investigations of ESP in dreams using the Rapid Eye Movement monitoring technique. This book provides an inside view of some
of the most interesting ESP experimentation going on at the
present time. Illustrated; bibliographic footnotes. 2. L-C-
U.
    JASPR 65:364-68 (July 1971); JP 34:249-50 (Sept.
1970); JSPR 45:415-18 (Dec. 1970).
    Am. J. Clin. Hypn. 14:131-32 (1971/72); J. Nerv. &Ment.

Dis. 152:373-74 (1971).

67 Vasiliev, L. L. Experiments in mental suggestion. (No
        trans. named.) Church Crookham, Hampshire, Eng.:
        Institute for the Study of Mental Images, 1963. 178p
        OP (Orig. publ. in Russian in 1962 under title
        Eksperimentalnye issledovanya myslennovo vnushenya)
        This is a translation of the work of one of Russia's
major contributors to parapsychology. It gives an account
of his experiments with hypnotized subjects on the telepathic
suggestion of motor acts, transmission of visual imagery
and sensations, and suggestions at a distance for falling into
hypnotic sleep. Sometimes considerable distances were involved. There is an interesting chapter entitled "Some psychological aspects of mental suggestion." Although Vasiliev
began his experiments believing that telepathy is mediated
electromagnetically, his results when the subject was isolated in a Faraday chamber show that this hypothesis is un-
tenable. Illustrated; bibliography by chapter at the end of
the book (159 items). 2. L-U.
        IJP 5:464 (Aut. 1963); JASPR 58:216-21 (July 1964);
JP 28:138-40 (June 1964); JSPR 42:229-47 (Mar. 1964).

68 Vasiliev, L. L. Studies in mental telepathy. (No trans.
        named.) New York: CCM Information Corporation,
        1971. 141p $12.00 (pap) (Orig. publ. in Russian in
        1962 under title Vnushenye na rasstoyanii)
        This is a Transdex book, a series of xerocopies of
foreign titles translated by the U.S. government; they are
made to order and are available from CCM Information Corporation. (Although these Transdex books may not be in
Books in Print since they are photocopies produced at need,
they can never be said to be out of print.) This is the only
one of Vasiliev's three books translated into English which
is still available. In it he discusses and compares spontaneous and experimental telepathy, physiology and psi, favorable experimantal conditions, and anpsi. He also
describes his own experiments in long-distance suggestion
and offers an electromagnetic hypothesis to explain these
phenomena. Illustrated; bibliographic references included in
the text. 3. L-U.
        IJP 5:95-104 (Win. 1963); JP 27:50-55 (Mar. 1963).

69 Warcollier, René. Experimental telepathy. Trans. by
        Josephine Gridley. Ed. and abridged, with a fore-
        word by Gardner Murphy. Boston: Boston Society for
        Psychic Research, 1938. 296p OP

Warcollier was a pioneer of French parapsychology.
This book is a collection of his previously published theoretical papers and reports on his qualitative experiments using
drawings as targets, plus some previously unpublished material. Few parapsychologists have been more concerned
with the modus operandi of the telepathic process than Warcollier. He discusses the conditions necessary for success,
analyzes the process of sending and receiving, and ties these
in with normal psychology. Illustrated; 22-item glossary;
bibliographic footnotes. 2. L-C-U.
        JASPR 17:228-31 (Apr. 1923); JSPR 21:124-26 (July
1923) and JSPR 31:130-37 (Nov.-Dec. 1939).

70 Warcollier, René. Mind to mind. (E. K. Schwartz,
        ed.) Enl. ed. Introduction by Gardner Murphy.
        New York: Macmillan, 1963. 127p $.95 (pap) (Orig.
        publ. by Creative Age in 1948. Hardcover ed. OP)
        This book describes ESP experiments with drawings
conducted by the author, who was primarily interested in the
dynamic principles involved in the telepathic communication
of free material. The importance of this work lies in its
elucidation of the laws of normal and abnormal perception
which also seem to apply to telepathy. The range of this
correlation is illustrated by listing the relevant chapter headings: Parallelism, Latency, Analysis, Synthesis, Syncretism,
Movement, Prägnanz, Emotional factors, and Imagination.
Illustrated; 50-item glossary; bibliography by chapter at the
end of the book (61 items); 6-page bibliography; name index;
subject index. 1. M-L-C-U.
        JASPR 42:112-14 (July 1948); JP 12:218-19 (Sept.
1948).
        N.Y. TimesBookRev., p12, Apr. 11, 1948; SanFranc.
Chron., p20, July 18, 1948; Sat.Rev. 31:28 (Apr. 24, 1948).

HAUNTINGS AND POLTERGEISTS

The books under this heading are for the most part
concerned with both hauntings and poltergeist phenomena.
The full range of these phenomena is probably best illustrated
by MacKenzie, while the basic book on poltergeists is Owen's
and on hauntings, Salter's. Four modern ghosts is valuable
because of its critical approach to the problems involved and
its delineation of the precautions which should be taken in

studying such cases.

Additional books with material on hauntings and poltergeists: A number of haunting and poltergeist cases are
described by Lang (33, 232), Myers (100, 170), MacKenzie
(234), and Baird (242). Summaries of several papers on
these phenomena given at the Conference on Spontaneous
Phenomena in 1955 are given in Proceedings of four conferences (91). There are long descriptions and discussions
of hauntings and poltergeists in Johnson (163, 216), Podmore
(173), and Salter (264). Zorab has a section on each in his
bibliography (211). Criticisms of some classic poltergeist
and haunting cases can be found in Hall (44).

71 Bennett, Ernest W.   Apparitions and haunted houses: A
     survey of evidence.   Foreword by W. R. Matthews.
     Ann Arbor, Mich.: Gryphon Books, 1971. 396p $15.00
     (Orig. publ. by Faber in 1939. OP)
     The author's avocation was the investigation of haunted
houses. The purpose of this book "is to present a survey of
the evidence furnished ... by reliable witnesses in regard to
what are commonly known as apparitions or ghosts, and the
various hypotheses which may be put forward to meet the
admitted facts" (p. xiii). Since the work of Gurney, Myers,
and Podmore (229) had dealt exhaustively with phantasms of
the living, Bennett considered primarily cases of phantasms
of the dead, selecting 54 of the best-authenticated S. P. R.
cases and adding 50 new ones of his own. Special features
are the large number of collective cases, a chapter on animal apparitions, and one on apparitions of inanimate objects.
In the final chapter he presents theories that might account
for apparitions. Bibliographic footnotes; index. 2. M-L-
C-U.
     JASPR 33:345-46 (Nov. 1939); JSPR 31:113-14 (Sept.-
Oct. 1939).

72 Carrington, Hereward, and Fodor, Nandor.   Haunted
     people: Story of the poltergeist down the centuries.
     New York: New American Library, 1951. 225p $.75
     (pap) (Orig. publ. under this title by Dutton in 1951
     and by Rider in 1953 under title The story of the
     poltergeist down the centuries. Hardcover eds. OP)
     Carrington, an author and psychical researcher,
wrote Part I of this book and Fodor, a psychoanalyst, Part
II. Carrington's half contains an historical review of poltergeist phenomena, including summaries of 375 typical cases.

The last three chapters are each devoted to a famous poltergeist case. Part II consists of Fodor's attempt to apply psychoanalysis to the study of poltergeists on the theory that
there is a sexual basis for these manifestations. In addition
to a general exposition of his theories, Fodor applies them
to several well-known poltergeist cases. Bibliographic footnotes; index. 2. S-M-L-C-U.
    JASPR 46:118-20 (July 1952); JSPR 37:101-05 (May-
June 1953).
    Kirkus 19:628 (Oct. 15, 1951); Libr.J. 76:2000 (Dec.
1, 1951); N.Y.Her.Trib.WklyBookRev., p6, Jan. 20, 1952.

73 Dingwall, Eric J., Goldney, K. M., and Hall, Trevor
    H. The Haunting of Borley Rectory. London: Duck-
    worth, 1955. 181p £1.25
    Published under the auspices of the S.P.R., this is
a critical "investigation of an investigation." It is by three
conservative and cautious psychical researchers and deals
with one of the most publicized of modern British polter-
geists--that of Borley Rectory--and with its investigation by
Harry Price. They had access not only to the extensive
printed material on the case, but also to the even more
voluminous unpublished records. Both are quoted heavily in
the book, especially the latter. The authors reach a verdict
counter to that held by Price. In addition, they offer some
generalizations as to how purported psychic occurrences
should be appraised and the kinds of evidence required before they can be accepted as fact. Illustrated; bibliographic
footnotes; index. 2. M-L-C-U.
    JASPR 50:66-70 (Apr. 1956); JSPR 38:249-64 (June
1956); PSPR 55:66-175, Pt201 (1969).

74 Dingwall, Eric J., and Hall, Trevor H. Four modern
    ghosts. London: Duckworth, 1958. 111p OP
    The authors, experienced investigators known for
their critical cast of mind, intend this book "to assist students to evaluate material submitted to them for scrutiny
and to obtain useful results when dealing with actual cases
which they are called upon to investigate" (p. 9). Dealing
specifically with hauntings and poltergeists, they aim "to
give the reader not only a general idea of the kind of problems he has to face but also some actual case histories in
the examination of which he will learn what errors to avoid
and how to meet some of the many difficulties which he will
most certainly encounter" (p. 9). In the Introduction they
present an overview of where the investigation of poltergeists
and hauntings stands today, and then go on to examine in

detail four well-known cases (Yorkshire Museum ghost,
Harry Price and Rosalie, the Runcorn poltergeist, and the
Ousedale haunt). Illustrated; bibliographic footnotes; index.
2. A.
        IJP 2:105-09 (Win. 1960); JASPR 53:75-77 (Apr. 1959);
JSPR 39:288-89 (Sept. 1958).

75 Flammarion, Camille. Haunted houses. Trans. by E.
        Fournier d'Albe. Detroit: Gale, 1971. 328p $15.00
        (Orig. publ. in English by Appleton in 1924, OP, and
        in French in 1923 under title Les maisons hantées)
        Flammarion, the French astronomer, was also a pio-
neer psychical researcher. First to use the word "psychic,"
he wrote several books on psychical research, the last of
which was Haunted houses. The first chapter is on "experimental proofs of survival." In the remainder of the book he
deals with haunting phenomena, beginning with the various
forms they take. There is a section on poltergeist phenomena (which he denotes as "phenomena not attributable to the
dead") and on "spurious haunted houses." A number of
specific haunting cases are described in detail. He concludes with an examination of the possible causes of hauntings. Bibliographic footnotes. 2. L-U.
        Booklist 21:6 (Oct. 1924); BostonEve. Trans., p4,
Dec. 24, 1924; Lit. Rev., p950, Aug. 9, 1924; N.Y. Times
BookRev., p12, July 27, 1924; Repr.Bull. 17:13 (May-June
1972); St. LouisLibr. Bull., p366, Nov. 1924; Sat. Rev. 1:6
(Aug. 2, 1924); Spectator 131:1052 (June 28, 1924); Times
Lit. Suppl., p375, June 12, 1924; TheWorld, p6e, July 6,
1924.

76 MacKenzie, Andrew. The unexplained: Some strange
        cases of psychical research. Introduction by H. H.
        Price. London: A. Barker, 1966. 180p £1.25; New
        York: Abelard, 1968. $5.95; New York: Popular Li-
        brary, 1970. 173p $.75 (pap)
        This volume offers another collection of well-authenti-
cated spontaneous phenomena, especially apparitions, haunts,
and poltergeists (including an account of the famous Seaford,
Long Island, case). The materials are taken from the serious parapsychological periodical literature, mostly British.
Most of the cases have never appeared in book form before;
the few that have, such as the Cheltenham ghost and the
Versailles case, were selected because new material on
them is presented. In many instances MacKenzie includes
his own firsthand observations. An appendix gives a history
of the S. P. R. Bibliographic references incorporated in the

text; index. 1. M-L-C.
JSPR $\overline{4}4$:38-41 (Mar. 1967); PR 1:17-18 (Sept.-Oct. 1970).
Booklist 66:1356 (July 15, 1970); Libr.J. 95:2270 (June 15, 1970).

77 Owen, A. R. G. Can we explain the poltergeist? New York: Garrett/Helix, 1964. 436p $8.50
The author points out that the aim of the first half of this book ("Spurious poltergeists and perhaps some others" and "Some genuine poltergeists") is different from that of the latter ("Powers and limitations of the poltergeist" and "Interpretation"). He says: "The former is concerned strictly with establishing the reality of some poltergeists. The latter takes this as settled and adopts as its themes the physical powers of the poltergeist, and its implications for physical, psychological, and psychic science" (p. 3). This is a thorough survey of the range of poltergeist phenomena, the psychology of poltergeists, and the various theories that have been offered to explain them. Bibliography at the end of most chapters (329 items); list of cases cited after most chapters (433 cases). 3. M-L-C-U.
IJ$\overline{P}$ 7:103-06 (Aut. 1965); JASPR 60:191-95 (Apr. 1966); JP 29:207-09 (Sept. 1965); JSPR 43:93-97 (Mar. 1965).
Libr.J. 89:3761 (Oct. 1, 1964); Nation 199:358 (Nov. 16, 1964).

78 Salter, W.H. Ghosts and apparitions. London: G. Bell, 1938. 138p OP
This is part of a very useful series published by G. Bell in which experts in the field deal with specific types of psi experiences and illustrate them by examples taken from the files of the S.P.R. The examples in the present volume have been selected to shed light on the different aspects of ghosts and apparitions, which the author breaks down into apparitions seen in dreams, those seen in the waking state, hauntings in the form of apparitions, and hauntings in the form of poltergeists. He compares these "true" experiences with the characteristics of the traditional "ghost story." 33-item glossary; bibliographic references incorporated in the text. 2. A.
$\overline{J}$ASPR 33:27-32 (Jan. 1939); JSPR 30:305-06 (Dec. 1938).

79 Thurston, Herbert. Ghosts and Poltergeists. Edited, with an introduction by J. H. Crehan. Chicago: Regnery, 1954. 372p OP

This is a collection of articles on poltergeists by a
Catholic priest. Thurston gives a general view of the phenomena and then cites many cases. He ends with an assessment of the evidence, which he finds large in quantity and
high in quality. He also deals with exorcism and points out
that although the Catholic Church, in its rites of exorcism,
has made provision for dealing with persons possessed by
evil spirits, none has been made for places, such as are often associated with poltergeist activity, nor hauntings in
which a deceased person or persons are purportedly involved.
Bibliographic footnotes; index. 1. M-L-C-U.
JASPR 49:38-40 (Jan. 1955); JSPR 37:311 (May-June
1954).
Cathol. World 179:79 (Apr. 1954); Chic. SundayTimes,
p6, Apr. 18, 1954; Christ. Cent. 71:585 (May 12, 1954);
Commonweal 60:126 (May 7, 1954); N. Y. Her. Trib. BookRev.,
p15, Mar. 28, 1954; N. Y. TimesBookRev., p18, Apr. 18,
1954; NewStatesman&Nation 47:377 (Mar. 20, 1954); SanFranc.
Chron., p21, Mar. 15, 1954; TimesLit. Suppl., p413, June
25, 1954.

HISTORIES AND HISTORICAL WORKS

This group contains two types of books: histories of
psychical research (or aspects of it) and works which express
points of view on the subject held by historic figures in the
field. In the former category the most useful is the book
by Gauld. In the latter, the collections of James' and
McDougall's writings are recommended. Ebon's book also
contains much historical information about psychical research.

Additional books with material on histories and historical works: Material on various historical aspects of psychical research is contained in Carrington (155), Knight's anthology (164), Somerlott (180), and Sudre (181). Historical
material on the heyday of spiritualism and the "golden age"
of mediumship is covered in Dingwall's Abnormal hypnotic
phenomena (9), the biography of Mrs. Piper (110), Brown
(223), Fornell (224), Gutteridge (225), and Podmore (228).
The history of the Duke Parapsychology Laboratory and its
successor, FRNM, is given by Rhine (176). Much historical
information is contained in the entries in the Biographical
dictionary of parapsychology (200) and in Encyclopaedia of

psychic science (201).

80 Baird, Alexander T. Richard Hodgson: The story of a
    psychical researcher and his times. Foreword by
    Ernest N. Bennett. London: Psychic Press, 1949.
    310p £. 37½ (pap)
    Although one of the major pioneers of psychical re-
search, Richard Hodgson never published anything in book
form. The present biography, although written primarily
for laymen and not always accurate as to dates and references, is still the fullest record of Hodgson's work outside
his own writings in hard-to-find psychical research periodicals. Although he started out as a skeptic, his attitude
changed during the major research of his career: the investigation of the mediumship of Mrs. Piper. This book is
not only a record of Hodgson's life and investigations, but
also of the climate of the times in which he lived. Frontispiece; bibliographic footnotes; index. 2. L-U.
        JASPR 44:125-26 (July 1950); JP 14:222-23 (Sept.
1950); JSPR 35:311-12 (Sept.-Oct. 1950).

81 Ebon, Martin. They knew the unknown. New York:
    World, 1971. 285p $6.95; New York: New American
    Library, 1972. $1.25 (pap)
    This is a compilation of the psychic experiences of
nearly 30 persons famous in other fields from the time of
Socrates to the present. It was written to compensate for
"the incapacity of standard biographers to integrate psychic
subject matter into their accounts" (p. xi). In each case
Ebon provides a biographical background, tells how interest
in psi was triggered, how pursued, and the effect this interest and the experiences themselves had on the person
written about. Writers (novelists, poets, playwrights) pre-
dominate. No living persons are included. Bibliographic
references incorporated in the text; "Additional reading"
(65 items); name index. 1. A.
        JASPR 66:336-39 (July 1972); JP 35:300-01 (Dec.
1971); PR 2:18 (Nov.-Dec. 1971).

82 Gauld, Alan. The founders of psychical research. New
    York: Schocken, 1968. 387p $10.00
    After summarizing the beginnings of spiritualism in
the United States and Great Britain, the author concentrates
on the initiation of serious psychical research beginning with
the early investigations centering around the Sidgwicks and
leading to the organization of the S.P.R. Gauld presents de-

tailed accounts of the lives, motivations, and researches of
the Society's pioneers, among them Frederic W. H. Myers,
Edmund Gurney, and Henry and Eleanor Mildred Sidgwick.
Highlighted is the work on phantasms of the living and of the
dead, physical phenomena (especially that of Palladino), mental mediums (especially Mrs. Piper and Mrs. Thompson),
and the theories of Myers.   Appendix A offers an annotated
list of early S. P. R. thought-transference experiments and
Appendix B contains quotations from critics of Mrs. Piper.
Bibliographic footnotes; index.   2.   M-L-C-U.
          JASPR 63:203-05 (Apr. 1969); JP 32:267-72 (Dec.
1968); PSPR 55:341-67, Pt205, (1972).
          Contemp. Psychol. 14:125 (Feb. 1969); Libr. J. 93:
3569 (Oct. 1, 1968); Manch. Guard. 98:10 (May 23, 1968);
NewStatesman 75:516 (Apr. 19, 1968); TimesLit. Suppl., p938,
Sept. 5, 1968; VictorianStud. 13:234-35 (Dec. 1969).

83 Le Clair, Robert C. (ed.).   The letters of William
        James and Théodore Flournoy.   Foreword by Gardner
        Murphy.   Madison: University of Wisconsin Press,
        1966. 252p $10. 00
          Approximately a third of the letters here collected
are about James' and Flournoy's deep interest in psychical
phenomena, mainly mediumship and automatisms.   Most of
these letters are in Chapter 3, the longest in the book, entitled "Progress in psychical research, 1901-1905, " although
there are references to the subject scattered throughout the
book.   Among the topics they discuss are Mrs. Piper,
Hélène Smith, James' Varieties of religious experience, and
F. W. H. Myers' Human personality and its survival of
bodily death.   Frontispiece; bibliographic footnotes; index.
2.   L-U.
          JASPR 63:95-99 (Jan. 1969); JP 32:265-67 (Dec. 1968).
          Am. Notes&Queries 5:46 (Nov. 1966); Choice 3:1083
(Jan. 1967); Christ. Sci. Monit., p11, Oct. 6, 1966; Contemp.
Psychol. 12:430 (Aug. 1967); N. Engl. Q. 40:476 (Sept. 1967);
TimesLit. Suppl., p24, Jan. 12, 1967.

84 Lodge, Oliver J.   Past years: An autobiography.   New
        York: Scribner's, 1931. 364p OP
          Two major interests dominated the life of Sir Oliver
Lodge, physics and psychical research, and he was a recognized leader in each field.   He became active in psychical
research in 1884, first in telepathy, and then in mediumship.
Approximately a fourth of his autobiography is devoted to
psychical research matters, beginning with his acquaintance
with Edmund Gurney even before the S. P. R. was founded.

Step by step Lodge reviews the experiences and events which
gradually convinced him of the truth of survival. Of considerable interest is his account of his personal relationships
with many of the notable persons connected with the early days
of psychical research: the Sidgwicks, Gurney, Myers, and
Richet. Lodge also describes his work with Palladino. Illustrated; bibliographic references incorporated in the text.
2. L-U.

      Booklist 28:347 (Apr. 1932); BostonEve. Trans., p2,
Mar. 12, 1932; Christ. Cent. 49:259 (Feb. 24, 1932); Homi-
leticRev. 104:14-16 (July 1932); N. Y. Her. Trib. Books, p7,
Feb. 14, 1932; N. Y. TimesBookRev., p5, Feb. 21, 1932;
Nature 129:74 (Jan. 16, 1932); NewRepub. 71:242 (July 13,
1932); NewStatesman&Nation 2:684 (Nov. 28, 1931); Outlook
160:193 (Mar. 1932); Rev. Revs. 85:9 (Apr. 1932); Sat. Rev.
8:696 (Apr. 30, 1932); SpringfieldRepub., p7e, Feb. 14,
1932; Survey 68:156 (May 1, 1932); TimesLit. Suppl., p927,
Nov. 26, 1931; Wis. Libr. Bull. 28:199 (June 1932).

85 Murphy, Gardner, and Ballou, Robert O. (eds.). Wil-
     liam James on psychical research. New York: Kelley,
     1970. 339p $12.50; New York: Viking, 1969. $1.95
     (pap) (Orig. publ. by Viking in 1960. Hardcover ed.
     OP)

This is a collection of James' writings, including
correspondence, on psychical research topics. Arranged in
seven sections, the first contains his review of Planchette,
by Epes Sargent. Section II, General Statements, includes
his S. P. R. presidential address and the important essay,
"What psychical research has accomplished." Part III contains writings on clairvoyance, levitation, and out-of-the-
body experiences. The fourth section is devoted to Mrs.
Piper and the fifth to F. W. H. Myers. Section VI is entitled "Religion and the problems of the soul and immortality." The last section consists of "The final impressions of
a psychical researcher." Gardner Murphy provides an informative introduction and concluding chapter. Frontispiece
(hardcover ed.); bibliographic footnotes; index. 2. M-L-C-
U.

      IJP 3:96-101 (Spr. 1961); JASPR 56:102-08 (Apr.
1962); JP 25:59-62 (Mar. 1961); JSPR 41:82-83 (June 1961).
      Contemp. Psychol. 6:149 (May 1961); HibbertJ. 60:74
(Oct. 1961); Libr. J. 85:3089 (Sept. 15, 1960); NewStatesman
62:126 (July 28, 1961); Spectator, p236, Aug. 18, 1961;
SpringfieldRepub., p40, Oct. 23, 1960.

86   Van Over, Raymond, and Oteri, Laura (eds.).   William
       McDougall, explorer of the mind: Studies in psychical
       research.   Foreword by Eileen J. Garrett.   Intro-
       duction by J. Wainwright Evans.   New York: Garrett/
       Helix, 1967. 319p $8. 50.
     This is a compilation of McDougall's writings relevant
to parapsychology.   Part One contains papers on psychical
research in general and on its importance, including "A plea
for psychical research, " "The need for psychical research, "
his S. P. R. presidential address, and "Psychical research as
a university study. "   Part Two, mainly on mediumship, includes his writings on automatisms, hallucinations, multiple
personality, trance, "Margery" (the Boston physical medium),
and fraudulent mediums.   The third part deals with hypnosis,
suggestion, and the subliminal self.   Part Four consists of
the final chapter, entitled "Animism, " from his book Body
and mind.   Frontispiece; bibliographic footnotes; index.   3.
M-L-C-U.
       IJP 10:217-18 (Sum. 1968); JP 32:60-66 (Mar. 1968);
JSPR 44:414-15 (Dec. 1968).
       Contemp. Psychol. 13:538 (Oct. 1968).

INTERDISCIPLINARY STUDIES

       In this category are contributions to psychical research
by persons identified with other disciplines who write from
the viewpoint of their special fields of knowledge.   Also included are books dealing with the implications of parapsychology for other fields, and vice versa.   Most of the titles
are technical, being written for the most part by and for professionals.   By the same token, they are highly stimulating
works and would be of great value to students interested in
serious research.   The Ciba Foundation symposium and the
Smythies volume provide interdisciplinary discussions of
parapsychological phenomena, methodology, and implications.
The book edited by Angoff and the Parapsychology Foundation
Proceedings are more theoretical in nature; they both contain
important selections.

       Additional books with material on interdisciplinary
studies: An interdisciplinary approach to parapsychology as
a whole is provided by three Parapsychology Foundation Proceedings (18, 19, 175).   In the symposium edited by Garrett

(249) the main emphasis is on an interdisciplinary approach
to the survival problem. Burt (191) stresses changes in
other disciplines that should alter views of psi phenomena
and vice versa, and Zorab's bibliography (211) has a section
on parapsychology and other disciplines.

87   Angoff, Allan (ed.). The psychic force: Essays in
      modern psychical research from the International
      Journal of Parapsychology. New York: Putnam, 1970.
      345p $7.95
         This is a collection of 22 primarily theoretical papers
from the last decade relating parapsychology to other disciplines such as psychology, psychiatry, medicine, and religion. The papers are arranged under the following headings:
"Parapsychology: The struggle for recognition, " "Mesmerism
and hypnosis, " "Sleep and dreaming, " "Visions and hallucinations, " "Medicine and parapsychology, " "Twins and extrasensory perception, " "Telepathy, " "Creativity as a psychic
force, " and "Reincarnation, survival, and communication
with the dead. " (The International Journal of Parapsychology (340), from which these papers were taken, was published by the Parapsychology Foundation from 1959 to 1968.)
33-item glossary; bibliography by chapter at the end of the
book (239 items); index. 3. L-C-U.
         PR 2:12-14 (Mar.-Āpr. 1971).
         Choice 8:292 (Apr. 1971); Libr.J. 95:3790 (Nov. 1,
1970).

88   Ciba Foundation. Extrasensory perception: A Ciba
      Foundation Symposium. (G. E. Wolstenholme and
      E. C. P. Millar, eds.) New York: Citadel, 1966.
      240p $2.25 (pap) (Orig. publ. by Little, Brown in
      1956. Hardcover ed. OP)
         This book is based on the Ciba Foundation Symposium
held in London in 1955 in which 23 parapsychologists and
representatives from other fields participated. It contains
14 papers together with discussions of them. There are
general papers dealing with the nature of the evidence for
ESP, theories of psi phenomena, and the relation of psi to
other disciplines such as biology, medicine, and psychoanalysis. In addition there are articles on psi among primitive
peoples, ESP among European peasant populations, bird
navigation, homing in pigeons, and pseudo-ESP (stage telepathy). Bibliography at the end of some papers (149 items);
subject index. 3. S-M-L-C-U.
         JASPR 5Ī:76-80 (Apr. 1957); JP 20:197-203 (Sept.

1956); JSPR 38:369-75 (Dec. 1956).
     Br. J. Psychol. 49:79-80 (1958); J. Psychosom. Res. 2:
304 (1957); Sat. Rev. 39:35-36 (Sept. 1, 1956).

89 Proceedings of an international conference on methodol-
     ogy in psi research: Psi favorable states of conscious-
     ness. (Roberto Cavanna, ed.) New York: Parapsy-
     chology Foundation, 1970. 264p $6.50 (Available
     only from the Foundation)
     This book consists of papers and discussions by a
number of parapsychologists, psychiatrists, physicists, and
biologists on the methodology of psi research. It stresses
applications from other experimental sciences to parapsychology. It contains several papers on psi and altered states of
consciousness and one on anpsi. The 21 papers are arranged
under the following headings: Methodology in psi research:
conceptual approaches (5); Methodology in psi research:
technical approaches (7); Experimentation in psi research
(5); and Directions for future studies (4). This volume provides stimulating discussions and much cross-fertilization of
ideas. The background and special interests of the 28 participants are given. Bibliography at the end of most papers
(142 items). 3. L-U.
     JASPR 65:229-33 (Apr. 1971); JP 34:166-70 (June
1970); JSPR 46:184-85 (Sept. 1971).

90 Proceedings of an international conference: Psi factors
     in creativity. (Allan Angoff and Betty Shapin, eds.)
     New York: Parapsychology Foundation, 1970. 220p
     $6.00 (Available only from the Foundation)
     This Parapsychology Foundation conference Proceed-
ings contains 15 papers on various aspects of creativity,
and on the relation between creativity and psi phenomena,
by scientists, writers, artists, and parapsychologists. Although nearly all the papers are relevant to creativity, only
a few deal to any extent with its relation to psi. These
are "Science, creativity, and psi" by Henry Margenau; "Does
creativity open the way for psi phenomena?" by Austin C.
Towle; "Psi and creativity: Some neuropsychological doubts
and discoveries" by W. Grey Walter; "Preconscious process,
ESP, and creativity" by Emilio Servadio; and "Psi phenomena,
psi factors, and the creative process" by Eugenio Gaddini.
Discussions--often valuable and stimulating--are included.
The participants' backgrounds and interests are described.
Bibliography at the end of most papers (190 items). 3.
M-L-C-U.
     JASPR 65:482-88 (Oct. 1971); JP 35:229-32 (Sept.
1971); JSPR 46:185-87 (Sept. 1970).

91 Proceedings of four conferences of parapsychological
       studies. Preface by Eileen J. Garrett. New York:
       Parapsychology Foundation, 1957. 180p $3.00 (Avail-
       able only from the Foundation)
       This volume consists of summaries of 60 papers by
experts in parapsychology and related fields delivered at four
conferences sponsored by the Parapsychology Foundation.
There is a section for each conference with an introduction
summarizing its activities and accomplishments, followed by
three-page abstracts of the papers. The first conference,
held in 1954, was on the philosophical implications of psi,
survival, time, and the mind-body problem. The second,
also held in 1954, was on unorthodox healing (16 papers on
paranormal diagnosis, psychodiagnostic tests of healers, and
the scientific method and unorthodox healing). The third conference, on spontaneous psi, was held in 1955 (13 papers
stressing methodology, the psychology of spontaneous psi,
and poltergeists). The last conference was held in 1956 and
was on psychology and parapsychology (16 papers on psi and
psychoanalysis, psychological variables, and anthropology).
Bibliographic references incorporated in the text. 3. U.
         JASPR 51:115-17 (July 1957); JP 21:304-12 (Dec.
1957).
         J. Nerv.&Ment.Dis. 128:566-67 (1959).

92 Proceedings of the first international conference of para-
       psychological studies. Introduction by Gardner Mur-
       phy. New York: Parapsychology Foundation, 1955.
       136p $3.00 (Available only from the Foundation)
       This is the Proceedings of the first in the series of
interdisciplinary and international conferences sponsored by
the Parapsychology Foundation. Generally known as the
"Utrecht Conference," it was held in 1953. The 78 participants were divided into four working groups at which the
relevant papers were read and discussed. The work of each
group is summarized, followed by one- to four-page summaries of the papers. The group topics and number of papers in each are as follows: Quantitative studies 14; Psycho-
therapeutic and psychoanalytic approach 15; Spontaneous
phenomena and qualitative research 15; and Personality of the
sensitive 5. 3. U.
         JASPR 50:85-86 (Apr. 1956); JP 20:62-66 (Mar. 1956).
         Bull. MenningerClin. 21:81 (1957); Science 118:402
(Oct. 9, 1953).

93 Smythies, J. R. (ed.). Science and ESP. New York:
       Humanities, 1967. 306p $13.00

This volume in the International Library of Philosophy
and the Scientific Method brings together 13 essays by various writers on the evidence for psi phenomena, the place of
psi in the framework of modern science, and its relation to
other areas of study such as biology, anthropology, philosophy, psychology, and psychoanalysis. A number of testable
hypotheses are proposed. Despite some lack of continuity in
the essays, they provide a stimulating "inside" view of the
field and its implications. According to Smythies, the con-
sensus of the authors is "that these phenomena are very
probably valid, that they are important and that we simply
cannot continue to ignore them" (p. vii). Contains a brief
annotated guide to the experimental literature (25 items).
Bibliographic footnotes. 3. M-L-C-U.
    JASPR 62:415-22 (Oct. 1968); JP 32:136-37 (June
1968); JSPR 44:247-50 (Mar. 1968).
    Br. J. Psychiat. 114:658-60 (1968); Br. J. Psychol. 59:
336-37 (1968); Contemp. Psychol. 14:383-85 (July 1969); Mod.
Sch. 47:103-04 (Nov. 1969); Observer, p27, Oct. 8, 1967;
Relig. Stud. 4:297-300 (Apr. 1969); TimesLit. Suppl., p1067,
Nov. 9, 1967.

MEDIUMS AND SENSITIVES

    Most of the books in this section are biographies and/
or accounts of investigations of specific mediums or aspects
of mediumship. Cummins' Swan on a black sea is typical of
many of the mediumistic studies which appeared in the early
S. P. R. and A. S. P. R. publications, but which rarely find
their way into print today. Carrington provides a good introduction to the controversial subject of physical mediumship.
The evaluative method described by Thomas was an important
step in the scientific investigation of mental mediumship.
The autobiographies of Heywood and Leonard and any of those
by Garrett, as well as the biographies of Leonard by Smith
and of Piper by her daughter, are also basic reading.
Flournoy's book is an important contribution to the psychology
of mediumship.

    Additional books with material on mediums and sensi-
tives: A number of books deal with historical mediums and
with mediums and mediumistic activities when spiritualism
was at its peak: Gauld (82), Lodge (84), Brown (223), For-

nell (224), Hardinge (226), and Podmore (228, 261). Books
containing lengthy discussions of individual mediums and
their phenomena are by Baird (80), Le Clair (83), Mc Dou-
gall (86), Besterman (153), Heywood (160), Knight (164),
Smith (179), Somerlott (180), Tyrrell (182, 183), Brown (190),
Pike (260) and Thomas (267). Studies of the personality of
mediums and the modus operandi of mediumistic communications are discussed in Van Over (25), Proceedings of the
First International Conference (92) and of Two conferences
(19), LeShan (129), Bendit (139), Flournoy (146), Broad (154),
Tyrrell (183), Mitchell (195), and Salter (264). The various
phenomena of mediumship are treated extensively in Barrett
(151), Carrington (155), Edmunds (158), Holms (162), Johnson (163), Tyrrell (182), Baird (242), Hart (251), Saltmarsh
(265), and Walker (269, 270). Critical views of mediumship
are offered by Hall (45), Rawcliffe (49), Tanner (50), and
West (185). The most recent book on evaluating mediumistic
material is by Pratt (273).

94 Abbott, David P.   Behind the scenes with the mediums.
       5th rev. ed.   Chicago: Open Court, 1926. 340p OP
       (Orig. publ. by Open Court in 1907. OP)
       The phenomena of mediumship, especially physical
phenomena, are often produced by fraudulent means. For
this reason magicians have attended séances with a view to
exposing mediums and have worked out methods of duplicat-
ing various mediumistic phenomena by trickery, thereby per-
forming a valuable service to psychical research. An excellent exposition of how mediumistic phenomena can be
fraudulently produced is set forth in this book by a magician.
He covers raps and other "spirit sounds," billet reading,
slate writing, materializations, and various fortunetelling
methods. Bibliographic references incorporated in the text;
index. 2. M-L-C-U.
       JASPR 1:492 (Oct. 1907).
       N. Y. TimesSat. Rev. 12:551 (Sept. 14, 1907); Nation
85:212 (Sept. 5, 1907); Rev. Revs. 36:511 (Oct. 1907).

95 Carrington, Hereward.   The American séances with
       Eusapia Palladino.   New York: Garrett/Helix, 1954.
       273p $3.75
       The mediumship of the Italian peasant woman, Eusapia
Palladino, consisted primarily of physical phenomena: lights,
materializations, raps, and movement of objects. Carrington provides an historical summary of the many published
investigations of Eusapia, but the bulk of the book consists

of stenographic records of 31 séances held in the United
States, with Carrington's comments on each. This is the
fullest account available of the American investigations,
which produced the last startling phenomena of her mediumship. Twenty-seven of the séances reported were organized
by Carrington. The remaining four were held at Columbia
University and were arranged by a committee of scientists
from several universities. The book includes comments on
the mediumship, both pro and con, by various prominent
persons. Bibliographic footnotes. 2. L-U.
        JASPR 50:27-33 (Jan. 1956); JSPR 37:387-89 (Nov. -
Dec. 1954).

96 Carrington, Hereward. The physical phenomena of
        spiritualism: Fraudulent and genuine. 3d ed. New
        York: Dodd, Mead, 1920. 426p OP (Orig. publ. by
        Turner in 1907. OP)
        The gist of this book is given on the title page:
"... a brief account of the most important historical phenomena; a criticism of their evidential value; and a complete
exposition of the methods employed in fraudulently reproduc-
ing the same." Carrington felt it was important to expose
the fraudulent practices involved in physical mediumship because he believed that genuine phenomena do occur; so only
could the wheat be separated from the chaff. The book is
divided into two parts, the first and longest being a survey
of fraudulent phenomena, and the second an overview of the
genuine. Illustrated; 14-item glossary; bibliographic footnotes; index. 2. M-L-C-U.
        PSPR 21:392-404, Pt. 55 (1908).

97 Crookes, William. Researches in the phenomena of
        spiritualism. Rev. ed. Manchester: Two Worlds;
        London: Psychic Bookshop, 1926. 147p OP (Orig.
        publ. by James Burnes in 1874. OP) (Included in
        R. G. Medhurst, Crookes and the spirit world. New
        York: Taplinger, 1972. 288p $8.95)
        The experimental reports in this book represent one
of the first attempts to investigate mediumship scientifically;
most of them were originally published in the Quarterly
Journal of Science. From 1870 to 1874 Crookes devoted
himself to the investigation of mediumship, particularly that
of Florence Cook and D. D. Home, devising special apparatus for testing and controlling the phenomena produced.
His reports, however, were not well received by the scientific community. This book contains descriptions of his experiments and their results, and his replies to criticisms

of his work. The revised edition includes an extract from
an address Crookes gave in 1898 before the British Association and an appendix by Arthur Conan Doyle entitled "Independent testimony as to the mediumship of Florence Cook."
Illustrated; bibliographic footnotes; index. 2. U.
     No reviews.

98 Cummins, Geraldine. Swan on a black sea: A study in
        automatic writing: The Cummins-Willet scripts. Rev.
        ed. (Signe Toksvig, ed.) Foreword by C. D. Broad.
        London: Routledge and Kegan Paul, 1970. 168p £2.25;
        New York: Weiser, 1970. $6.50 (Orig. publ. by
        Routledge and Kegan Paul in 1965. OP)
     This book consists primarily of scripts of automatic
writing followed by the editor's notes. The automatist was
Geraldine Cummins (one of England's best known mediums)
and the communications purported to come from the famous
British sensitive (now deceased), "Mrs. Willett" (pseudonym
for Mrs. Coombe-Tennant). Cummins relates how the
scripts began (at which time she had no knowledge of the
communicator's identity), and in a chapter called "The lines
of communication" she discusses the process of mediumistic
communication. The persons involved in the scripts, living
and dead, include some of the major figures in psychical
research: mediums, investigators, and their friends and
relatives. Extremely useful is C. D. Broad's presentation
in chart form of the significant dates in the lives of the
people involved and a synopsis of the main contents of the
scripts. Illustrated. 2. M-L-C-U.
     IJP 8:483-84 (Sum. 1966); JASPR 61:81-84 (Jan. 1967);
JP 30:55-59 (Mar. 1966); JSPR 43:267-70 (Mar. 1966) and
46:75 (Mar. 1971).
     NewStatesman 70:290 (Aug. 27, 1965); Observer, p21,
Aug. 22, 1965; TimesLit.Suppl., p829, Sept. 23, 1965.

99 Dingwall, Eric J. Some human oddities: Studies in the
        queer, the uncanny and the fanatical. Introduction by
        John C. Wilson. New Hyde Park, N.Y.: University
        Books, 1962. 198p OP (Orig. publ. by Home and
        Van Thal in 1947. OP)
     This book presents biographies of six "human oddi-
ties." Although it has only one chapter which seems to be
directly relevant to psychical research (on D. D. Home),
seen from a wider perspective the others have relevance
also. Dingwall says, "The problem underlying the life and
work of D. D. Home can be briefly summed up by saying
that it is the problem of miracles in its most acute form"

(p. 187). The thread running through each biography is this
element of the miraculous and inexplicable, a feature of the
data of psychical research as well. There are six appendices,
each a bibliographic essay on the sources of information on
the subjects of the respective chapters. Illustrated. <u>2</u>. M-
L-C-U.

      JSPR 34:27-28 (Mar.-Apr. 1947).
      Time 80:87 (July 13, 1962).

100   Dingwall, Eric J. <u>Very peculiar people: Portrait</u>
      <u>studies in the queer, the abnormal and the uncanny</u>.
      Introduction by John C. Wilson. New Hyde Park,
      N.Y.: University Books, 1962. 233p OP (Orig. publ.
      by Rider in 1950. OP)
      This volume presents portraits of five lives charac-
terized by "problems so complex and obscure that any real
understanding of them can hardly be said to exist" (Preface).
As in the companion volume (99), only one chapter is devoted to a person acknowledged as being of direct relevance
to psychical research (Eusapia Palladino), but each portrait
provides background material for the study of human nature
so essential to the field. On training for psychical research,
Dingwall says: "The investigator must be something of an
anthropologist, psychologist, and statistician combined. But
above all he must know human beings, and try to understand
... why and how they behave as they do" (p. 207). Each
chapter is followed by a bibliographic essay outlining the
sources of information available on the subject. Illustrated;
name index. 2. M-L-C-U.
      JASPR 44:162-64 (Oct. 1950); JSPR 35:284 (July-Aug.
1950).

101   Feilding, Everard. <u>Sittings with Eusapia Palladino and</u>
      <u>other studies</u>. Introduction by Eric J. Dingwall.
      New Hyde Park, N.Y.: University Books, 1963. 324p
      $10.00
      This book pulls together six papers originally pub-
lished in the <u>Journal</u> and <u>Proceedings</u> of the S.P.R. The
principal paper is a report on a series of sittings in Naples
with the Italian physical medium, Palladino, by Feilding, W.
W. Baggally, and Hereward Carrington. There are five
shorter papers, three by Feilding, one by Baggally, and one
by Baggally and Alice Johnson. The first four describe a
poltergeist found to be fraudulent, two cases of fraudulent
physical mediumship, and a case of "weeping" religious
statutes. In the final paper Feilding reviews the Catholic
attitude toward psi phenomena and discusses the implications

of psychical research for religion and survival after death.
Bibliographic footnotes.   2.   L-U.
          JASPR 59:260-61 (July 1965); JSPR 42:353-60 (Sept.
1964).

102 Flournoy, Théodore.   From India to the planet Mars:
      A study of a case of somnambulism with glossolalia.
      Trans., and with a preface by Daniel B. Vermilye.
      Introduction and concluding chapter by C. T. K.
      Chari.   New Hyde Park, N.Y.: University Books,
      1963. 457p $10.00   (Orig. publ. in French in 1900
      under title Des Indes à la Planète Mars)
          The author, a Swiss psychologist, gives an account
of his investigation of Hélène Smith, whose phenomena included mediumship, somnambulism, reincarnation material,
and glossolalia.   He starts with a biographical sketch, re-
counts the beginnings of her mediumship, and then goes on
to describe in detail the famous "Hindoo" and "Martian"
cycles.   In a final section, "Supernormal appearances," he
discusses physical phenomena, telepathy, lucidity, reincarnation, and spirit messages.   2.   L-U.
          JSPR 43:322-23 (June 1966); PSPR 15:384-415, Pt.38
(1900).
          Dial 29:179-80 (Sept. 16, 1900); Independent 52:1133-
34 (May 10, 1914); Nation 70:463 (June 1914); NorthAm. Rev.
171:734-47 (Nov. 1900); Pop. Sci. Mon. 57:662-63 (Oct. 1900).

103 Garrett, Eileen J.   Adventures in the supernormal: A
      personal memoir.   New York: Garrett/Helix, 1949.
      242p $4.95.   With a foreword by Hugh Lynn Cayce
      and new preface by author, New York: Paperback Li-
      brary, 1968. 175p $.75 (pap)
          In this autobiography Eileen Garrett attempts to pre-
sent "so much of my life as I believe necessary to an understanding of the origin and functioning of supernormal perception" (p.11).   More than her other autobiographies, this
one describes in depth the many aspects of psi in her life.
She tells of the development of her mediumship, ESP experiments, clairvoyance, psychometry, telepathy, precognition,
and PK manifestations.   There is an interesting chapter on
the validity of her controls and one on discarnate entities.
1.   M-L-C-U.
          JASPR 44:81-82 (Apr. 1950).

104 Garrett, Eileen J.   Many voices: The autobiography of
      a medium.   Introduction by Allan Angoff.   New York:
      Putnam, 1968. 254p $6.95; New York: Dell, 1969.

$.95 (pap)

The author's final and most well-rounded autobiographical work, this book covers all aspects and phases of her complex, many-faceted life. In addition to a good explication of her mediumship, she discusses her non-mediumistic activities here more fully than in the other two autobiographies in this section. She describes how she founded the magazine Tomorrow, how she entered the book-publishing business, and the establishment and administration of the Parapsychology Foundation. Index. 1. M-L-C-U.

IJP 10:416-20 (Win. 1968); JASPR 63:202-03 (Apr. 1969); JSPR 44:404-07 (Dec. 1968).

BestSell. 28:165 (July 15, 1968); BookWorld, p5, June 16, 1968; Booklist 65:78 (Sept. 15, 1968); Expos. T. 80: 352 (Aug. 1969); Kirkus 36:434 (Apr. 1, 1968); Libr. J. 93: 1998 (May 15, 1968); Publ. Wkly 193:36 (Apr. 1, 1968).

105 Garrett, Eileen J. My life as a search for the mean-
        ing of mediumship. New York: Oquaga, 1939. 225p
        OP

Eileen Garrett wrote several autobiographical works (see 103, 104) for she was always fascinated by the puzzle of her mediumship. This was the first, written when she was 45, and it is perhaps the most informative and appealing. Because it is a simple, straightforward account of her psychic phenomena--how she experienced them and how they developed--it sheds more light on the "inside" of her mediumship than any of her other books. She describes in detail the role played by Hewat McKenzie in developing her mediumship. Of particular interest are her descriptions of J. B. Rhine's experiments with her at Duke and William Brown's work with her in England when she was under hypnosis. 1. M-L-C-U.

JASPR 33:340-42 (Nov. 1939); JSPR 31:155-56 (Jan.-Feb. 1940).

106 Heywood, Rosalind. ESP: A personal memoir. Intro-
        duction by Sir Cyril Burt. New York: Dutton, 1964.
        224p $5.95; London: Pan Books, 1972, under title
        The infinite hive £.35 (pap) (Orig. publ. by Chatto
        and Windus in 1964 under title The infinite hive.
        Hardcover ed. OP)

This is an autobiography of a well-known English sensitive and investigator. She begins with a discussion of the evidence for ESP and of the mental climate which, when negative, can have an inhibiting effect on a person with psychic tendencies. After summarizing aspects of her child-

hood and adolescence which may have had a bearing on her
psi abilities, she embarks upon the main part of the book
which consists of an account of her experiences. They are
arranged according to type: telepathy, precognition, hand-
reading, "secret music," inner guidance, human and non-
human presences, drug experiences, and veridical dreams.
Throughout the book the author is commendably cautious in
drawing conclusions about the nature of her experiences.
Bibliographic footnotes. 2. A.
     IJP 6:507-09 (Aut. 1964); JASPR 59:178-81 (Apr.
1965); JSPR 42:299-303 (June 1964).
     Fant.&Sci.Fict. 28:58 (Mar. 1965); Observer, p22,
Feb. 6, 1966.

107 Home, Mrs. Daniel Dunglas. D. D. Home: His life
     and mission. Edited, with an introduction by Arthur
     Conan Doyle. London: Kegan, Paul, Trench, Trübner;
     Manchester: Two Worlds; New York: Dutton, 1921.
     230p OP (Orig. publ. by Trübner in 1888. OP)
     Perhaps the most famous physical medium of all
time was Daniel Dunglas Home. This biography by his wife,
Julie de Gloumelinn, is an account of the events in his life
and mediumship. The arrangement of chapters is mainly
geographic, describing for each country the events, seances,
phenomena, and investigation of them, that took place there.
Mrs. Home depended heavily on her husband's correspondence as source materials. This book provides one of the
most complete records of Home's mediumship. Bibliographic
references incorporated in the text. 2. L-U.
     JASPR 15:497-98 (Oct. 1921); JSPR 4:101-16 (July
1889).

108 Leonard, Gladys Osborne. My life in two worlds.
     Foreword by Sir Oliver Lodge. London, Cassell,
     1931. 300p OP
     The author was one of the greatest mental mediums
of all time, and, unlike so many, she was noted for her
willingness to cooperate with investigators. She says of this
autobiography, "it is the knowledge of what spiritualism has
done for me spiritually, mentally, and even physically, that
impels me to try, in this simple book, to show others how
to grasp the truth of personal survival" (p. 3). She presents
some of the evidence that convinced her (and many of her
sitters) of the truth of spiritualism, tells how her mediumistic abilities developed, and describes the many channels
through which they were expressed. She gives instructions
by which others may develop their psychic faculties. Frontis-

piece. 2. M-L-C-U.
JSPR 27:131 (Dec. 1931).

109 Osty, Eugène. Supernormal faculties in man: An experimental study. Trans. by Stanley de Brath. London: Methuen, 1923. 245p OP (Orig. publ. in French
in 1922 under title La connaissance supranormale)
The author was a physician and also a pioneer in
French parapsychology. He says the book has a dual purpose: "To trace the main outlines of the problem of supernormal cognition, and to make a general psychological study
of the conditions under which that study is most fertile;
namely when a person endowed with supernormal faculty ex-
ercises it upon a human personality" (p. vii). He describes
his research on experimental clairvoyance over a 12-year
period. There is a valuable discussion of the psychological
conditions favoring psi phenomena and one on the type of
errors made in psychic functioning. Bibliographic footnotes;
index. 3. L-C-U.
JASPR 18:10-17 (Jan. 1924); PSPR 34:333-35, Pt. 92
(1924).
Bookman 59:345 (May 1924); BostonEve. Trans., p4,
Apr. 12, 1924; N.Y. Her. Trib. Books, p26, July 13, 1924;
Outlook 136:489 (Mar. 19, 1924); Spectator 132:18 (Jan. 5,
1924); TimesLit. Suppl., p27, Jan. 10, 1924.

110 Piper, Alta L. The life and work of Mrs. Piper. Introduction by Sir Oliver Lodge. London: Kegan Paul,
Trench, Trübner, 1929. 204p OP
Leonora E. Piper, probably the greatest medium the
United States has produced, was discovered by William
James. He started out to debunk her, and ended by pro-
claiming her his "one white crow." Extensively tested both
here and in England, detailed reports of her mediumship
can be found in the publications of the A.S.P.R. and S.P.R.
In addition, more material about her exists in book form
than is true of most mediums. Of these, the present one,
written by her daughter, is among the best. After two introductory chapters on mediumship in general and Mrs. Piper's early life, the remainder of the book is devoted to an
account of her mediumship and of the men who investigated
her, primarily William James and Richard Hodgson. Illustrated; bibliographical references incorporated in the text.
2. M-L-C-U.
JSPR 26:9-10 (Jan. 1930).

111   Progoff, Ira.   The image of an oracle: A report on re-
      search into the mediumship of Eileen J. Garrett.
      New York: Garrett/Helix, 1964. 372p $7.50
          The author, a psychotherapist, gives an account of
the many conversations he held with Mrs. Garrett's "controls"--the four figures who spoke through her when she was
in trance. Progoff attempts to find the significance of these
controls for Mrs. Garrett's personality and to shed light on
their true nature. Although he does not give any definitive
answers, some interesting possibilities are explored in this
novel approach to trance mediumship. Verbatim transcripts
of the conversations are presented, together with Progoff's
commentaries on them. Bibliographic footnotes. 2. L-C-U.
          JASPR 59:254-60 (July 1965); JP 29:58-61 (Mar. 1965);
JSPR 43:214-15 (Dec. 1965).

112   Salter, W. H.   Trance mediumship: An introductory
      study of Mrs. Piper and Mrs. Leonard.   Revised by
      Margaret Eastman.   London: Society for Psychical
      Research, 1962. 47p £.25 (pap) (Available only from
      the Society)
          This pamphlet put out by the S.P.R. is an excellent
introduction to mediumship and its scientific investigation.
Although it can be read as an introduction to mediumship in
general, it is primarily a study of mental mediumship, and
within that category, of Stainton Moses, and especially of
Mrs. Piper and Mrs. Leonard. The object of the pamphlet
is to give an account of these mediums as a help to the
reader "intending to study not only their phenomena but the
more general problem of communications claiming to come
from intelligences that have survived the death of the body"
(p. 9). Miss Eastman supplied an "Appendix on the physiology of trance mediumship." Bibliographic references incorporated in the text. 2. S-M.
          JSPR 35:248-49 (May 1950).

113   Smith, Eleanor T.   Psychic people.   New York: Mor-
      row, 1968. 194p $5.95; New York: Bantam, 1969.
      197p $.95 (pap)
          The author presents accounts of the lives and psychic
experiences of 19 persons, mostly mediums. The book was
written for people with little or no acquaintance with the
literature of psychical research. The author says, "Variety
of experience has been the chief criterion in making my selection, and entertainment, not conversion, is my aim" (p.
vi). A chapter is devoted to each of the 19 psychics, among
them D. D. Home, Hester Dowden, Leonora Piper, Pearl

Curran, Geraldine Cummins, and Eileen Garrett. "Selected
reading" (67 items). 1. H-S-M-L.
    JASPR 65:358 (July 1971).
    Cathol. Libr. World 40:144 (Oct. 1968); Kirkus 36:543
(May 1, 1968); Libr. J. 93:2250 (June 1, 1968); Publ. Wkly
193:60 (May 20, 1968).

114 Smith, Susy. The mediumship of Mrs. Leonard. New
     Hyde Park, N.Y.: University Books, 1964. 260p
     $7.50
    This book by a former newspaper reporter whose
main interest is psychical research presents the highlights
of the mediumship of Mrs. Gladys Osborne Leonard, one of
this century's greatest mediums. The author has brought
together many materials scattered in the parapsychological
literature. After introductory chapters about Mrs. Leonard,
her controls, and her sitters, she summarizes the Trou-
bridge-Hall reports, proxy sittings, book tests, word association tests, and direct voice phenomena. There are two
chapters on the nature of mediumistic communication.
Frontispiece; bibliographic footnotes; 71-item bibliography.
2. S-M-L-C-U.
    IJP 7:107-09 (Win. 1965); JASPR 59:90-92 (Jan. 1965);
JSPR 42:416-18 (Dec. 1964).

115 Thomas, John F. Beyond normal cognition: An evalua-
     tive and methodological study of the mental content of
     certain trance phenomena. Foreword by William
     McDougall. Ann Arbor, Mich.: University Microfilms,
     xerocopy, OP No. 53,686. 170p $8.50 (Orig. publ.
     by the Boston Society for Psychic Research in 1937.
     OP)
    The main purpose of this book is to establish that
there are instances of information paranormally obtained in
mediumistic utterances. It was accepted as a doctoral
thesis in the Department of Psychology, Duke University.
It represents a major step in the objective study of the
mental content of mediumistic productions in that Thomas
applied a quantitative method of evaluating each statement
so that the role of chance could be assessed. The medium
involved in the 24 major sittings (22 of them being proxy
sittings) analyzed in detail in the book was Mrs. Leonard;
they were supplemented by 501 additional records made by
different recorders and from different mediums. The role of
fraud and chance are discussed in two chapters; there is
also an interesting chapter on cross correspondences between Mrs. Leonard's material and that of the other mediums.

Thomas provides a summary and an exposition of theories
which might account for the source of the information con-
veyed. Bibliographic footnotes; index. 3. L-C-U.
    JASPR 31:212-13 (July 1937); JSPR 30:148 (Dec. 1937).

OUT-OF-THE-BODY EXPERIENCES

    There is a considerable overlap among the books in
this section. For an extensive overview of the entire subject, Smith's book would be the most useful. The Projection
of the astral body by Muldoon and Carrington offers the best
review of the various types of out-of-the-body experiences.
Green's book is of interest because of its psychological approach; and Crookall's offers more than just a collection of
cases because it ties the experiences in with survival. The
long introduction by Tart enhances the value of the Monroe
book.

    Additional books with material on out-of-the-body ex-
periences: There are sections on out-of-the-body experiences
in Knight (164) and Johnson (216), while their relationship to
mysticism and survival is examined by Vyvyan (184), Crookall (212), Hart (251), and Heywood in Man's concern with
death (268). Broad (154) relates them to dreams. Green
in Lucid dreams (11) has a section on out-of-the-body experiences, as does Tart in On being stoned (24).

116 Crookall, Robert. The study and practice of astral
        projection. Hackensack, N.J.: Wehman, 1961. 234p
        $7.50; New Hyde Park, N.Y.: University Books,
        1966. $7.50 (Orig. publ. by Aquarian in 1960. OP)
        By a British geologist who has intensively studied
out-of-the-body phenomena for several decades, this book
contains 160 firsthand accounts of such experiences and a
discussion of their characteristics. Crookall considers
them as evidence for survival of death. He contrasts "natural, " or spontaneous projections with "forced, " or induced
projections. In a 14-page appendix he reviews the literature
of the subject. Bibliographic references incorporated in the
text; case index. 2. M-L-C-U.
    IJP 5:463-64 (Aut. 1963); JASPR 56:91-96 (Apr. 1962);
JSPR 41:159-61 (Sept. 1961).

Libr.J. 92:247 (Jan. 15, 1967).

117 Fox, Oliver [pseud. for Hugh Colloway]. Astral pro-
     jection: A record of out-of-the-body experiences. In-
     troduction by Ralph Shirley. Foreword by John C.
     Wilson. New Hyde Park, N.Y.: University Books,
     1963. 160p $5.00 (Orig. publ. by Rider in 1939. OP)
         This is one of the first autobiographical accounts of
     out-of-the-body experiences and their characteristics. Fox
     describes how he first experienced being out-of-the-body and
     how it was closely associated with dreams. He tells how he
     learned to exercise some control over his experiences and
     presents several methods for inducing projections. He out-
     lines the dangers and difficulties involved and offers many
     additional insights and observations on the psychology of out-
     of-the-body experiences. He views his experiences within
     a theosophical framework. Bibliographic references incor-
     porated in the text. 1. M-L-C-U.
         JSPR 42:138-40 (Sept. 1963).

118 Green, Celia E. Out-of-the-body experiences. Fore-
     word by H. H. Price. London: published for the In-
     stitute of Psychophysical Research by Hamish Hamil-
     ton, 1968. 144p (Proceedings of the Institute, v. 2)
     £1.75
         This is an analysis of out-of-the-body experiences
     based on the accounts of more than 300 persons who re-
     ported having such experiences and replied to questionnaires
     sent to them in regard to details. Green coins the term
     "ecsomatic" for out-of-the-body experiences and classifies
     them further as either parasomatic, in which "the percipient
     is associated with a seemingly spatial entity with which he
     feels himself to be in the same kind of relationship as, in
     the normal state, he is with his physical body" (p.17); or
     as asomatic, in which "the subject is temporarily unaware
     of being associated with any body or spatial entity at all"
     (p.17). The psychology of these experiences is stressed:
     the circumstances preceding them; what they feel like; re-
     laxation and meditation; paralysis; motor control; time sense;
     and getting "in" and "out." There are four chapters on psi
     and out-of-the-body experiences and one on autoscopy. Bib-
     liographic footnotes; index. 2. L-C-U.
         JASPR 64:219-27 (Apr. 1970); JSPR 45:172-78 (Dec.
     1969).

119 Monroe, Robert A. Journeys out of the body. Intro-
     duction by Charles T. Tart. Garden City, N.Y.:

Doubleday, 1971. 280p $6.95; $1.95 (pap)

A journalist and radio-television executive, the author is one of those rare individuals seemingly capable of having out-of-the-body experiences often and at will. This book contains an account of his experiences: how they developed, how he has experimented with them, and what he has encountered during his "travels." He offers many suggestions for inducing out-of-the-body experiences and presents his theories on their occurrence and significance. Tart's introduction is an excellent and up-to-date survey of the scientific approach to the subject. 14-item bibliography. 1. S-M-L-C-U.

PR 3:15-16 (Mar.-Apr. 1972).
Libr.J. 96:3146 (Oct. 1, 1971).

120 Muldoon, Sylvan, and Carrington, Hereward. The phenomena of astral projection. London: Rider, 1951. 222p £1.05; Hackensack, N.J.: Wehman, n.d. $4.95; New York: Weiser, n.d. $3.75 (pap)

Muldoon knew at firsthand what being out-of-the-body is like, having had many experiences, while Carrington was a writer and psychical researcher. Their combined talents produced this introduction to "astral projection." Part One is a brief history of the notion of an "astral body" and a review of traditional approaches to the subject. Part Two is a collection of cases arranged by the conditions and circumstances inducing astral projections; e.g., drugs, illness, impending death, suppressed emotions, hypnosis, and those occurring spontaneously (sleeping and waking). Illustrated; 54-item bibliography. 2. A.

JASPR 46:161-63 (Oct. 1952) and 65:356-57 (July 1971).

121 Muldoon, Sylvan, and Carrington, Hereward. The projection of the astral body. Rev. ed. London: Rider, 1956. 242p £1.25; Hackensack, N.J.: Wehman, n.d. $4.95; New York: Weiser, n.d. $3.75 (pap) (Orig. publ. by Rider in 1929. OP)

In this book Muldoon, who had had out-of-the-body experiences from the age of 12 on, describes his experiences, the many forms they took, the conditions either favoring or inhibiting them, and offers suggestions for inducing such experiences. Carrington edited the book and provided an introduction in which he reviews the literature and introduces Muldoon to the reader. Illustrated; bibliographic footnotes; index. 1. M-L-C-U.

JASPR 65:356-57 (July 1971).

122   Smith, Susy. The enigma of out-of-body travel. New
         York: Garrett/Helix, 1965. 189p $4.95; New York:
         New American Library, 1968. 157p $.60 (pap)
         This is a general introduction to out-of-the-body ex-
periences with a sound base in the literature of the subject,
but written in popular style. After an introductory chapter,
the author cites several spontaneous cases, followed by a
chapter on "habitual travelers," or those who have repeated
out-of-the-body experiences. There are also chapters on
traveling clairvoyance, the astral body, ESP projections, the
double, and bilocation. The author points to the many similarities among the independent accounts of out-of-the-body
experiences which make "their value en masse almost stag-
gering" (p.16), and offers evidence indicating that they are
much more common than is usually believed. Bibliography
by chapter at the end of the book (98 items); "additional bibliography" (18 items); index. 1. H-S-M-L-C.
         IJP 8:472-77 (Sum. 1966); JASPR 60:393-96 (Oct.
1966); JSPR 43:323 (June 1966).
         Antiq.Bkmn 36:2079 (Dec. 6, 1965).

                    PHILOSOPHY AND PSI PHENOMENA

         In this section are books by professional philosophers
who examine the philosophical implications of psi and also
books in which parapsychologists set forth the philosophical
ramifications of psi or their theories about the why and
wherefore of the paranormal. Both types of authors emphasize the relevance of psi to the mind-body problem. In the
first category titles of note are those by Bergson, Broad,
and Flew. In the second group, Carington and Rhine stand
out. LeShan's monograph is important because he gives suggestions for empirically testing the theory he puts forward.

         Additional books with material on philosophy and psi
phenomena: The Parapsychology Foundation Proceedings (91)
contains summaries of the 14 papers given at the International Philosophic Symposium sponsored by the Foundation in
1954. Broad (154) deals with philosophical points arising in
connection with various psi phenomena. Both Smythies (93)
and Gudas (159) contain several papers on philosophy and
psi. One fourth of Sudre's Parapsychology (181) is concerned
with philosophical problems. Other books in this category

are those by Flew (43), Beloff (189), and Burt (191).   Several authors deal with applications of philosophy to the survival question: Broad (244), Ducasse (246, 247, 248), the book
edited by Garrett (249), Penelhum (259), and Price's essay
in Man's concern with death (268).   In another group are
books by authors who present a philosophy that takes psi
phenomena into account: Carington (51, 245), Barrett (151),
Koestler (165), and Tyrrell (221).

123   Aristotelean Society for the Systematic Study of Philoso-
        phy. Psychical research, ethics, and logic. Pro-
        ceedings. Supplementary vol. 24. New York: Johnson
        Reprint, 1971. 231p $9.20; $7.20 (pap) (Orig. publ.
        by Harrison in 1950. OP)
        The Aristotelean Society, a British philosophical or-
ganization, publishes proceedings of its annual meetings.
The volume for 1950 represents a joint session of the Society with the Mind Association, another British group.
Several of the papers read are concerned with parapsychology, the most important being a symposium entitled "Is psychical research relevant to philosophy?" The participants
were Mrs. M. Kneale, and Drs. R. Robinson and C. W. K.
Mundle. All three papers deal with psychical research and
linguistic philosophy: they examine the terminology of the
field and discuss the problem of how psi phenomena should
be described. Bibliographic footnotes. 3. U.
        JP 15:216-23 (Sept. 1951); JSPR 36:395-401 (Mar.-
Apr. 1951).

124   Bergson, Henri. Mind-energy: Lectures and essays.
        Trans. and with a preface by H. Wildon Carr. New
        York: Holt, 1920. 262p OP (Orig. publ. in French
        in 1919 under title L'Energie spirituelle)
        In Mind-energy, which consists of several lectures
and essays, Bergson deals with psychical research in
greater depth than in any of his other books. Chapter three
is entitled " 'Phantasms of the living' and 'psychical research,' " and is his presidential address to the S. P. R.
All the chapters are relevant to the mind-body problem.
Chapter five is an excellent survey of the literature on
false recognition, or déjà vu, and the theories that have
been offered to explain it. Bibliographic footnotes; index.
2. L-C-U.
        JASPR 15:314 (June 1921).
        Booklist 17:137 (Jan. 1921); BostonEve. Trans., p4,
Sept. 22, 1920; N.Y.EveningPost, p6, Jan. 15, 1921; Out-

look 126:767 (Dec. 29, 1920); TimesLit. Suppl., p715, Nov.
4, 1920.

125 Broad, C. D. Religion, philosophy and psychical re-
       search: Selected essays. New York: Humanities,
       1969. 308p $6.50 (Orig. publ. by Routledge and Ke-
       gan Paul in 1953. OP)
        This volume in the International Library of Psychology,
Philosophy, and the Scientific Method comprises essays by
the British philosopher, C. D. Broad. It is arranged in
three sections: Psychical research; Religion; and Politics.
The longest section is the one dealing with psychical research, which contains five essays. The first deals with
the relevance of psychical research to philosophy. The second is a discussion of normal cognition, clairvoyance, and
telepathy. The third is a critical essay on J. W. Dunne's
serial theory of time. The last two are on the contributions,
respectively, of Henry Sidgwick and Immanuel Kant to psychical research. Analyzed in Essay and general literature
index, v. 4. Bibliographic references incorporated in the
text, name and title index; subject index. 3. L-C-U.
        JASPR 48:56-68 (Apr. 1954); JSPR 37:165-68 (July-
Oct. 1953).
        Ann. Am. Acad. 288:193 (July 1953); Cathol. Libr. World
177:160 (May 1953); Christ. Cent. 70:666 (June 3, 1953);
Manch. Guard., p4, Mar. 20, 1953; NewStatesman&Nation
45:238 (Feb. 28, 1953); TimesLit. Suppl., p6, Feb. 20, 1953
and p321, May 15, 1953.

126 Carington, Whately. Matter, mind and meaning. Pre-
       face by H. H. Price. Freeport, N.Y.: Books for
       Libraries, 1970. 257p $11.00 (Orig. publ. by
       Methuen in 1949. OP)
        This book, on which the author was working just be-
fore he died, represents his final attempt to provide a philosophical framework which would allow for the occurrence of
psi phenomena. The book is primarily on the mind-body
problem in its relation to all the phenomena of psychical research. In his preface Price says that Carington has provided a working philosophy of psi phenomena which, though
leaving many questions unanswered, "may be sufficient for
our needs. It is certainly comprehensive, and it does in-
troduce some kind of intelligible order into the whole field
of 'supernormal' happenings; it also makes [their] relation
to 'normal' ones a good deal less unintelligible than it was"
(p. ix). Analyzed in Essay and general literature index, v.
4. Bibliographic footnotes; index. 3. L-U.

JASPR 44:34-38 (Jan. 1950); JP 14:78-80 (Mar. 1950); PSPR 49:51-52, Pt.177 (1949).

127 Flew, Antony G. N. (ed.). Body, mind, and death.
Introduction by the editor. New York: Macmillan,
1964. 306p $1.95 (pap)
The editor, a British philosopher with a longstanding
interest in psychical research, says that "the present volume
can be characterized as dealing with the question of human
survival and personal immortality, insofar as these are related to questions about the relation of mind to body, and
vice versa" (p.297). It provides an excellent overview of
the philosophical concepts which anyone interested in theoriz-
ing about psi phenomena and/or survival must take into consideration. Essays of special note are "The soul as an
'astral body' " by Tertullian; "On a future life" by Joseph
Butler; "On the immortality of the soul" by David Hume;
"What spiritualist evidence does not establish" by H. F.
Bradley; and "The empirical evidence for personal survival"
by C. J. Ducasse. 10-page bibliographic essay. 3. U.
Interpretation 20:363 (July 1966); Libr.J. 90:653 (Feb.
1, 1965); Rev.Metaphysics 18:780 (June 1965).

128 Langdon-Davies, John. On the nature of man. London: New England Library, 1961. 224p £.17½ (pap)
(Orig. publ. by Secker and Warburg in 1960 under
title Man: The known and unknown. Hardcover ed.
OP)
The author urges scientific openness toward and recognition of the as yet little understood areas of human nature. He points out that science does not have all the
answers and is blind to several areas of human experience,
one being psi abilities. The last half of the book, comprised of four chapters, reviews the facts of psychical research. There is a chapter on telepathy and the present
position of the evidence for its existence. Another chapter
is on "Prayer and communion, " which deals with a scientific
approach to this subject, including the relevance of ESP to
prayer. The last two chapters discuss unorthodox healing
and survival. Bibliographic footnotes; index. 1. M-L-C-U.
JSPR 41:89-90 (June 1961).

129 LeShan, Lawrence. Toward a general theory of the
paranormal: A report of work in progress. Foreword by Henry Margenau. New York: Parapsychology
Foundation, 1969. 112p (Parapsychological Monographs
No. 9) $3.00 (pap) (Available only from the Founda-
tion)

By a research psychologist, this book takes into consideration the data of psychical research (particularly that of
mediumship as expressed in the writings of Eileen Garrett,
with whom LeShan worked closely), mysticism, and theoretical physics to outline a testable theory of reality which has
a place for psi phenomena.   He calls it the "individual reality" (IR) theory and in Chapter VI he lists 10 generally-
agreed upon statements about the nature of psi and shows how
the IR theory is either consistent with them or at least not
inconsistent.   Next he offers seven ways of testing the IR
theory empirically, i.e., to predict new data.   Theoretically
and experimentally this book is a fruitful source of ideas
about psi.   97-item bibliography.   2.   L-C-U.
        JASPR 64:343-47 (July 1970); JP 33:276-77 (Sept.
1969); JSPR 45:247-48 (Mar. 1970).
        MainCurr. 26:64 (Nov.-Dec. 1969).

130   Rhine, J. B.   New world of the mind.   New York:
        Morrow, 1971. 339p $2.50 (pap) (Orig. publ. by
        Sloane in 1953. OP)
        This is an attempt to determine if discoveries about
psi phenomena have revealed a "new world"; that is, an outlook that "changes distinctly and profoundly the way we look
at the world we already know; when it exerts a permanent
influence on our way of life" (p.x).   The author summarizes
the experimental findings of parapsychology and shows how
these facts have a bearing on the natural sciences, medicine,
religion, and the conduct of life.   Bibliography by chapter at
the end of the book (102 items); index.   2.   M-L-C-U.
        JASPR 48:156-65 (Oct. 1954); JP 18:43-51 (Mar. 1954);
JSPR 38:28-29 (Mar. 1955).
        Booklist 50:178 (Jan. 1, 1954); Christ.Cent. 71:208
(Feb. 17, 1954); Kirkus 21:651 (Sept. 15, 1953); Libr.J. 78:
1930 (Nov. 1, 1953); N.Y.TimesBookRev., p6, Dec. 27,
1953; NewYorker 29:102 (Jan. 23, 1954); Sat.Rev. 37:55
(Feb. 13, 1954); SpringfieldRepub., p5c, Aug. 8, 1954;
Time 62:53-54 (Dec. 7, 1953); Wis.Libr.Bull. 50:21 (Jan.
1954).

131   Smythies, J. R. (ed.).   Brain and mind: Modern con-
        cepts of the nature of mind.   New York: Humanities,
        1965. 272p $8.50
        A volume in the International Library of Philosophy
and the Scientific Method, this is a collection of papers on
the mind-body problem by nine contributors, mainly philosophers and psychologists.   Of special importance is the inclusion of Oxford philosopher H. H. Price's "Survival and

the idea of 'another world, ' " originally published in S. P. R.
Proceedings. Also of relevance to psi are "The identity
hypothesis: A critique, " by the University of Edinburgh psychologist, John Beloff, and "Minds, matter and bodies, " by
C. J. Ducasse, the American philosopher. In "Mind and
matter, " the Oxford philosopher Antony Quinton touches on
psychical research in passing. Each paper is followed by
brief remarks from some of the other contributors, sometimes with the author's reply, which enhances the value of
the book. Bibliographic footnotes; index. 3. M-L-C-U.
        JASPR 61:163-69 (Apr. 1967); JP 32:137-39 (June
1968); JSPR 43:434-36 (Dec. 1966).
        Am. J. Orthopsychiat. 37:803-06 (1967); Br. J. Psychiat.
113:806-08 (1967); Brain 89:391-96 (1966); Choice 3:783 (Nov.
1966); Contemp. Psychol. 12:37-38 (Jan. 1967); Int. Philos. Q.
7:181 (Mar. 1967); Philos. Books 7:30 (May 1966); Philos. Q.
16:382 (Oct. 1966); Philos. Rev. 76:246 (Apr. 1967); Rev.
Metaphysics 19:820 (June 1966); TimesLit. Suppl., p915, Oct.
6, 1966.

PRECOGNITION AND RETROCOGNITION

        It has often been pointed out that psi phenomena
transcend time and space; however, the usual definitions of
psi and of its basic components, ESP and PK, stress space
rather than time. The books in this section deal with the
transcendence of psi over our usual experiences of the future
(in precognition) and the past (in retrocognition). Not much
has been written about the latter, partly because it is very
difficult to rule out normal explanations when dealing with
the past, and partly because no experiments have been de--
vised to test it. Ellwood's anthology is the first book in
the field to deal exclusively with retrocognition. Ebon's is
of value for its coverage of many diversified types of precognitive phenomena, while Lyttelton's and Saltmarsh's books
are classic collections of spontaneous precognition cases.
Dunne presents a quasi-experimental method for inducing
precognitive dreams. Unfortunately, except for a few chapters in Ebon's book, no titles in this section deal with the
quantitative investigation of precognition.

        Additional books with material on precognition and
retrocognition: Precognition in mediums and sensitives is

covered in Garrett (103), Heywood (106), Smith (114), and,
as regards Mrs. Leonard's newspaper tests, in Thomas
(267). General chapters on precognition can be found in
Flew (43), Edmunds (158), Johnson (163), Murphy (168),
Pierce (172), Pratt (174), Richet (177), Ryzl (178), and
Somerlott (180). Spontaneous precognition is stressed by
Devereux (140), MacKenzie (234), and L. E. Rhine (237)
and experimental precognition by J. B. Rhine (55), Soal and
Bateman (62), Thouless (63, 64) and Smith (179). A survey
emphasizing the religious implications of precognition and
retrocognition is given by Tyrrell (182) and Johnson (163,
216). An investigation testing Dunne's method of inducing
precognitive dreams (see above) is described by Besterman
(153). A negative assessment of the evidence for precognition is expressed by Podmore (173). Several papers stressing time and psi phenomena are summarized in the Proceedings of four conferences (91).

132   Barker, J. C.   Scared to death: An examination of
        fear, its causes and effects. London: Muller, 1968.
        182p £1.30; New York: Dell, 1969. 158p $.60 (pap)
        The author, a British physician, presents data indi-
cating that apparently healthy individuals can die from fright
alone. He also gives an account of what he calls the "pre-
disaster syndrome," or "the possibility that some persons
[appear] to act like human seismographs in advance of major
calamities" (p.145). He discusses the problem of "intervention"--the possibility of changing the future by altering one's
behavior in response to a premonition. And he postulates
the opposite--the fulfillment of predictions by means of suggestion or, in the absence of normal means of communication, by some form of psi. 54-item bibliography. 1. M-
L-C-U.
        JASPR 64:347-50 (July 1970); JSPR 45:17-21 (Mar.
1969).

133   Dunne, J. W.   An experiment with time.   5th ed.
        London: Faber, 1939. 254p £.90 (pap); 3d ed. New
        York: Hillary, 1958. $4.00, $1.50 (pap) (Orig. publ.
        by Macmillan in 1927. Hardcover ed. OP)
        This is a description by a British aeronautical en-
gineer of the methods he devised for inducing and taking note
of dreams about events occurring at a distance or that are
to take place in the future. Many examples are provided
and analyzed, mostly Dunne's own experiences, but those of
others are also included. He presents his theory of "serial-

ism" to account for such phenomena, together with his replies to criticisms of the theory. He makes a number of
interesting suggestions on how to remember dreams and how
to recognize precognitive elements in them. Bibliographic
references incorporated in the text; index. 2. M-L-U.
    JASPR 21:454-74 (Aug. 1927); JSPR 24:119-23 (Oct.
1927) and JSPR 28:270-74 (July 1934).
    Booklist 24:6 (Oct. 1927); and 34:302 (Apr. 15, 1938);
BostonEve. Trans., p4, May 28, 1927; Christ. Cent. 55:209
(Feb. 16, 1938); Churchman 152:17 (Aug. 1938); Discovery
10:168-70 (May 1929); Forum 98:312 (Dec. 1937); J. Philos.
24:690 (Dec. 8, 1927); LivingAge 332:1122 (June 15, 1927);
N. Y. TimesBookRev., p16, Oct. 16, 1927; Nation 125:233
(Sept. 7, 1927); Nature 119:847 (June 11, 1927); NewRepub.
52:49 (Aug. 31, 1927); NewStatesman 28:761 (Apr. 2, 1927);
Outlook 146:259 (June 22, 1927); Sat. Rev. 4:61 (Aug. 20,
1927) and 17:6 (Feb. 26, 1938); Sat. Rev. [Lond.] 143:602
(Apr. 16, 1927); Spectator 138:600 (Apr. 2, 1927) and 138:
Suppl. 651 (Apr. 9, 1927); TimesLit. Suppl., p659, Sept. 29,
1927.

134 Ebon, Martin. Prophecy in our time. New York: New
     American Library, 1969. 240p $.75 (pap); Alhambra,
     Cal.: Borden, 1971. $2.50 (pap) (Orig. publ. by
     World in 1968. Hardcover ed. OP)
    This is a collection of instances of spontaneous and
experimental precognition, including several current examples
as well as historical cases. The subjects of some of the
chapters are the Titanic disaster, Edgar Cayce, Jeane Dixon,
Hitler's prophets, Croiset's chair experiments, the cargo
cults, Freud, Jung, psychiatry and psi phenomena, and laboratory precognition. Of interest is a chapter on prophetic
methods in modern economics because, in the author's words,
"forecasting techniques in this field are closer to traditional
oracular methods than is commonly realized" (p. 229). 84-
item bibliography; index. 1. A.
    JASPR 63:99-104 (Jan. 1969); JP 32:224-26 (Sept.
1968).
    Am. Imago 28:79-83 (Spr. 1971); BestSell. 27:478
(Mar. 15, 1968); Libr. J. 93:1006 (Mar. 1, 1968).

135 Ellwood, Gracia Fay. Psychic visits to the past: An
     exploration of retrocognition. New York: New Ameri-
     can Library, 1971. 176p $.75 (pap)
    This book by a writer with a special interest in para-
psychology brings together a number of articles and parts of
books on the subject of retrocognition. She gives examples

in three categories: "walk-in" (in which the percipient
seemingly steps into the past); memories of alleged former
incarnations; and psychometry, or object-reading. There
are 15 chapters devoted to specific examples, most of them
cases of the first type, arranged chronologically from 1642
to 1963. The author provides introductory and concluding
chapters. This is the first collection to be compiled on the
topic of retrocognition. Illustrated; 64-item bibliography.
2. A.
      No reviews.

136 Lyttelton, Edith. Some cases of prediction: A study.
       London: G. Bell, 1937. 160p OP
       This book is a collection of precognitive cases ob-
tained in response to a BBC radio broadcast request. The
cases are arranged in four categories according to the hypothesis most likely to explain them: coincidence, straightforward telepathy, complicated telepathy, and true precognition. This arrangement makes the book an instructive introduction to the study of precognition and the difficulties
involved in determining whether or not it has occurred in
any given case. Bibliographic footnotes. 2. M-L-C-U.
       JASPR 33:349-50 (Nov. 1939); JSPR 30:190 (Mar.
1938).

137 Priestley, J. B. Man and time. New York: Dell,
       1968. 319p $1.25 (pap) (Orig. pub. by Doubleday.)
       In this outstandingly illustrated book on the nature of
time, Priestley examines man's images of time in Part I and
his ideas about it in Part II. Part III is largely composed
of Priestley's report on hundreds of letters dealing with unusual time experiences which he received following an appeal on a BBC television program in 1963. A number of
them contained personal experiences which he divides into
three groups: 1/"examples, outside dreaming, of what I
called the influence of the future on the present" (p.192);
2/clearly stated precognitive dreams; and 3/less clearly
stated precognitive dreams, premonitions, hunches that came
true, and other odd time experiences. He cites examples
from the letters plus accounts from other sources to illustrate various aspects of time and the paranormal. The remainder of the book is devoted to theories about time, including those of Dunne, Ouspensky, Nicoll, and Priestley
himself. Illustrated; bibliographic references incorporated
in the text; index. 2. A.
       JASPR 60:180-87 (Apr. 1966); JP 30:120-30 (June
1966); JSPR 43:31-39 (Mar. 1965).

BookWeek, p1, Dec. 20, 1964; Christ.Cent. 81:1534
(Dec. 9, 1964); Christ.Sci.Monit., p3B, Dec. 3, 1964; Ken-
yonRev. 27:364 (Spr. 1965); Libr.J. 89:4338 (Nov. 1, 1964);
N.Y.Her.Trib.WklyBookRev., p1, Dec. 20, 1964; N.Y.Rev.
Books 3:15 (Jan. 28, 1965); N.Y.TimesBookRev., p54, Dec.
6, 1964; NewStatesman 68:656 (Oct. 30, 1964); NewYorker
40:244 (Nov. 7, 1964); Spectator, p748, Nov. 27, 1964;
TimesLit.Suppl., p951, Oct. 22, 1964.

138 Saltmarsh, H. F. Foreknowledge. London: G. Bell,
      1938. 120p OP
     This book on precognition is another in the "Psychical
Experiences" series published by Bell. It is based on a
study of the S.P.R. case collection which Saltmarsh had already published in the Society's Proceedings. In sifting
through the archives he found 281 cases meeting his criteria;
they are set forth in the second chapter. He summarizes a
number of representative examples of the various forms precognitive experiences take. There are two chapters on alternative explanations to precognition--telepathy, autosuggestion,
subliminal knowledge and inference therefrom, hyperesthesia,
illusions of memory, and chance coincidence. He describes
metaphysical theories offered to account for precognition,
notably those of Dunne, Broad, H. H. Price, and Du Prel.
In the final chapter he points out the implications of precognition. 33-item glossary; bibliographic references incorporated in the text. 2. M-L-C-U.
     JASPR 33:127-28 (Apr. 1939); JSPR 31:41-42 (Mar.
1939).

PSYCHIATRY AND PSI PHENOMENA

     For the individual or library with a limited budget,
the books to pick in this category are Devereux and Eisenbud. (The former is the best source for Freud's views on
the paranormal as well as those of many other analysts.)
Flournoy provides a good pre-psychoanalytic view of psi,
with emphasis on mediumship. Ehrenwald's writings, especially New dimensions of deep analysis and Telepathy and
medical psychology, are also essential reading. Jaffé's
book on Jung is in some respects a better introduction to
Jung's views on psi than his own book.

Additional books with material on psychiatry and psi
phenomena: A number of papers on psychiatry and/or psychoanalysis and psi appear in the Parapsychology Foundation
Proceedings (18, 91, 92) as well as in The psychic force (87),
the interdisciplinary Ciba Foundation symposium (00), and
the Smythies anthology (93). At a more popular level, Ebon
(134) has several chapters on psychiatry and psi phenomena.
Psychiatry and the psychology of sensitives is dealt with by
Progoff (111) and by Eisenbud (186). Fodor (72) applies
psychoanalysis to poltergeist phenomena and Jung (231) ties
his own psi experiences in with his system of analytic psychology.

139 Bendit, Laurence J.   Paranormal cognition: Its place
        in human psychology. London: Faber, 1944. 79p OP
        The substance of this volume is an emended version
of a thesis accepted by the Department of Medicine of Cambridge University in fulfillment of the requirements of the
degree of Doctor of Medicine. A practicing psychiatrist,
the author deals with the question of psi experiences in the
therapeutic setting in general and, in particular, with the
psychological problems peculiar to persons with pronounced
psychic ability. Rather than denying the gift, he offers suggestions for learning to accept, live with, and use unusual
sensitivities. He also discusses the psychology of the psi
process as experienced by the psychic individual. Bibliographic references incorporated in the text; 15-item bibliography. 2. U.
        JASPR 38:228-30 (Oct. 1944); JP 9:52-55 (Mar. 1945);
JSPR 33:68-99 (May-June 1944).
        Nature 154:192 (Aug. 12, 1944).

140 Devereux, George (ed.).   Psychoanalysis and the occult.
        New York: International Universities Press, 1971.
        448p $12.00; $3.95 (pap) (Orig. publ. by Internation-
        al Universities Press in 1953. OP)
        The editor, an ethnopsychiatrist, is interested in re-
ports of psi from the sociocultural and psychological point
of view. This volume is a collection of papers from the
professional literature dealing with psychoanalytic studies of
psi phenomena. Section I contains an historical survey of
the field by J. Eisenbud and a methodological review by
Devereux himself. Section II consists of papers by Freud,
while Section III is comprised of papers by seven other psychoanalytic pioneers. Three papers on the Hollós-Schilder-
Servadio controversy make up Section IV and 12 papers on

the Eisenbud-Pederson-Krag-Fodor-Ellis controversy Section
V. Both controversies make lively and stimulating reading.
Section VI, "New contributions," consists of papers by W.
H. Gillespie and S. Rubin. The final section contains a pa-
per by Devereux entitled "The technique of analyzing 'occult'
occurrences in analysis." 204-item bibliography; index. 3.
L-C-U.
        JASPR 48:113-18 (July 1954); JP 18:125-30 (June 1954);
JSPR 37:235-43 (Jan.-Feb. 1954).
        Contemp. Psychol. 16:670 (Oct. 1971).

141 Ehrenwald, Jan.   Neurosis in the family and patterns
        of psychosocial defense: A study of psychiatric epide-
        miology. New York: Harper & Row, 1963. 203p OP
        The author, a psychoanalyst, has had a long-standing
interest in parapsychology. This book is addressed primarily to analysts and offers three hypotheses which incorporate
psi phenomena: The first deals with therapeutic communication in which what Ehrenwald terms "telepathic leakage" can
occur. The second proposes that patterns of sick interpersonal relationships are sometimes shared or imitated by
means of psi. Finally, he points out that a telepathic factor
may be involved in the origin of paranoid delusions. Illustrated; bibliography at the end of each chapter (149 times);
index. 3. L-U.
        IJP 6:255-56 (Spr. 1964); JASPR 58:298-301 (Oct.
1964).
        Am. J. Orthopsychiat. 34:595-96 (1964); Arch. Gen.
Psychiat. 10:320 (1964); Bull. MenningerClin. 28:5152 (1964);
Int. J. Psychoanal. 46:268-70 (1965); J. ChildPsychol. &Psychiat.
5:157-59 (1964); J. Nerv. &Ment. Dis. 141:125 (1965); J. Psychosom. Res. 7:304 (1963/64); Psychiatry 27:86-7 (1964); Psychoanal. Rev. 51:676-77 (1964/65); Psychosom. Med. 26:295-96
(1964); Psychosomatics 7:197 (1966).

142 Ehrenwald, Jan.   New dimensions of deep analysis: A
        study of telepathy in interpersonal relationships.
        New York: Grune and Stratton, 1955. 316p OP
        In this book, his second on psi and psychoanalysis,
the author pursues in great detail as well as depth the psychology of the telepathic process. Part One is a review of
cases of telepathy and precognition in the psychoanalytic situation, occurring mostly in dreams. In Part Two he offers
a theory of the function of psi at different levels of consciousness. He includes a considerable amount of material
on psi in the family situation. Finally, in Part Three he
shows how considering the psi hypothesis in the analytic

situation can facilitate the therapeutic process.   Illustrated;
28-item glossary; 138-item bibliography; index.   <u>3</u>.   M-L-
C-U.
        JASPR 49:161-63 (Oct. 1955); JP 18:258-71 (Dec.
1954); JSPR 37:349-52 (July-Oct. 1954).
        Am. J. Psychother. 10:381 (1956); Psychoanal. Q. 25:
110-11 (1956).

143   Ehrenwald, Jan.   <u>Psychotherapy: Myth and method. An</u>
        <u>integrative approach.</u>   New York: Grune and Stratton,
        1966. 212p $8.50
        In this book the author proposes that modern psycho-
therapies, even though they undoubtedly achieve cures, are
nevertheless based on myth; i. e., on hypothetical constructs
rather than on empirical facts.   There are references to
psi throughout the book, especially in a chapter entitled
"Parapsychology, or testing the limits of myth" in which
Ehrenwald points out the relevance of psi to an understanding of the therapeutic setting; and in the chapter "What triggers the existential shift?", in which he uses illustrations
from parapsychology as well as other disciplines.   Bibliography at the end of most chapters (225 items); index.   <u>3</u>.
L-C-U.
        IJP 10:93-96 (Spr. 1968); JASPR 61:278-80 (July 1967).
        Am. J. Psychoanal. 28:214-16 (1968); Am. J. Psychother.
22:113 (1968); Bull. MenningerClin. 31:126 (1967); Contemp.
Psychol. 13:104-05 (Feb. 1968); Individ. Psychol. 4:33-34
(1966/67); Int. J. Clin. & Exp. Hypn. 17:74-76 (1969); Ment. Hyg.
51:307-08 (1967); Psychiat. & Soc. Sci. Rev. 2:24-25 (1968);
Psychoanal. Q. 37:304-05 (1968); Psychoanal. Rev. 55:323-27
(1968/69); Psychol. Rec. 17:569 (1967); Rev. Exist. Psychol. &
Psychiat 8:66-67 (1968).

144   Ehrenwald, Jan.   <u>Telepathy and medical psychology.</u>
        Foreword by Gardner Murphy.   New York: Grune and
        Stratton, 1966. 212p $8.50   (Orig. publ. by Norton
        in 1948. OP)
        In this book the author reviews the evidence for tele-
pathy and goes into the personal dynamics of telepathic communication, stressing projective mechanisms, unconscious
needs, and the inclusion of telepathically-received information in dreams and waking associations.   He systematically
presents his theory of the development of telepathic powers
as a compensation for a biological defect or, as he terms
it, a "minus function."   In several chapters he shows how
telepathy can be used to shed light on certain psychiatric
disorders.   He also shows how psychiatric principles can

aid in understanding the psychology of mediums and sensitives. 37-item glossary; 100-item bibliography; name index.
2. L-C-U.
   JASPR 42:72-77 (Apr. 1948); JP 12:219-20 (Sept.
1948); JSPR 34:211-15 (Mar.-Apr. 1948).
   NewStatesman&Nation 35:158 (Feb. 21, 1948); San
Franc.Chron., p19, Apr. 18, 1948; Sat.Rev. 31:27 (Apr. 24,
1948).

145 Eisenbud, Jule. <u>Psi and psychoanalysis: Studies in the</u>
   <u>psychoanalysis of psi-conditioned behavior.</u> New York:
   Grune and Stratton, 1970. 359p $12.75
   The author sets forth the hypothesis that the usual
data of analysis (symptoms, dreams, associations, actions)
can be psi-conditioned, and stresses that to fully understand
analysis and the analytic relationship the psi hypothesis must
be taken into account. Numerous examples are provided
from the author's practice and his theory of psi-conditioned
behavior is applied to life outside analysis and to the scientific world view. There is a good explication of psi symbolism. One of the most intriguing chapters is entitled "The
psychic pathology of everyday life." 332-item bibliography;
index. 3. M-L-C-U.
   JP 35:292-96 (Dec. 1971); PR 3:25-26 (Jan.-Feb.
1972).
   Am.J.Psychiat. 127:161-62 (Mar. 1971); Psychoanal.
Rev. 59:150-52 (Spr. 1972).

146 Flournoy, Théodore. <u>Spiritism and psychology</u>. Trans.
   and abridged with an introduction by Hereward Carrington. New York: Harper, 1911. 343p OP (Orig.
   publ. in French in 1890 under title <u>Métapsychique et</u>
   <u>psychologie</u>)
   Flournoy was one of the first to recognize the need
for relating psi phenomena and depth psychology. Although
he was convinced of the genuineness of mediumistic phenomena, he did not feel that they supported the spiritistic
hypothesis. Rather, he viewed them as creations of the
subconscious imagination of the medium. This book consists of an examination of the phenomena of mediumship
with a view to outlining the range of human psychic ability
which he saw as essential before attributing "the inexplicable
residue of ... mediumship to the intervention of the discarnate or to other occult entities" (p. 302). Illustrated; bibliographic footnotes; index. 2. L-C-U.
   JASPR 7:303 (May 1913).
   Dial 51:399 (Nov. 16, 1911); Lit.Dig. 43:872 (Nov. 11,

1911); Outlook 99:881 (Dec. 9, 1911).

147 Freud, Sigmund. Studies in parapsychology. (Philip
     Rieff, ed.) Introduction by Philip Rieff. New York:
     Macmillan, 1963. 125p $.95 (pap) (Collected papers,
     v.10)
         In his introduction, Philip Rieff, who is skeptical
about psi, writes of that side of Freud that shared this
skepticism. Rieff makes some constructive remarks in relating parapsychology to mysticism and in suggesting that
parapsychology be studied sociologically. The contributions
of Freud which Rieff feels deal with psi are "The uncanny"
1919, "Dreams and telepathy" 1922, and "A neurosis of
demonical possession in the seventeenth century" 1923.
Devereux (140) includes only one of these in his section on
Freud's parapsychological papers, together with five additional ones. Bibliographic footnotes. 3. L-C-U.
         IJP 6:379 (Sum. 1964); JASPR 65:354-55 (July 1971).

148 The Interpretation of nature and the psyche. Synch-
     chronicity: An acausal connecting principle, by C. G.
     Jung; The influence of archetypal ideas on the scien-
     tific theories of Kepler, by Wolfgang Pauli. Trans.
     by R. F. C. Hull. Princeton: Princeton University
     Press, 1955. 247p $3.00 (Orig. publ. in German
     in 1952 under title Naturerklärung und Psyche)
         Jung's essay is an exposition of his views on psi
phenomena, which he saw as instances of what he termed
"synchronicity." There is a review of the literature concerning forerunners of the idea of synchronicity. He presents his views on meaningful coincidences and acausality.
He also reports on his unusual astrological experiment in
which his theory was put to test with interesting results.
In the companion essay by Pauli further examples of acausality are given from modern physics. Illustrated; bibliographic footnotes; index. 3. M-L-C-U.
         JASPR 48:27-32 (Jan. 1954); JP 20:59-62 (Mar. 1956);
JSPR 37:26-35 (Jan.-Feb. 1953).
         Am.J.Psychiat. 113:669-70 (1956/57); J.Anal.Psychol.
1:209-10 (1955/56); J.PastoralCare 12:197 (Fall 1958).

149 Jaffé, Aniela. From the life and work of C. G. Jung.
     Trans. by R. F. C. Hull. New York: Harper & Row,
     1971. 137p $8.50; $3.25 (pap) (Orig. publ. in Ger-
     man in 1968 under title Aus Leben und Werkstatt von
     C. G. Jung)
         Jung was interested in a vast array of seemingly un-

related facts and experiences, yet to him they were connected
by his theory of the archetypes. This book by Aniela Jaffé,
his secretary during the last six years of his life, contains
four chapters, the longest of which is entitled "Parapsychology: Experience and theory." In it she describes Jung's life-
long interest in psi, his own spontaneous experiences, and
his work with mediums (his doctoral dissertation was about
some mediumistic experiments he had conducted). She also
attempts an explication of his theory of synchronicity, by
which he explained psi. This exposition is noteworthy for
its simplified presentation of Jung's own writings, which to
many seem obtuse and obscure. Bibliographic footnotes. 3.
M-L-C-U.

     JASPR 66:339-41 (July 1972); JP 28:67 (Mar. 1964).
     Libr. J. 97:76 (Jan. 1, 1972).

150 Schwarz, Berthold E. Parent-child telepathy: Five
    hundred and five possible episodes in a family. New
    York: Garrett/Helix, 1971. 241p $7.95
    Subtitled "A study of the telepathy of everyday life,"
this is a record of apparent telepathic communication between
the author, a psychiatrist, his wife, and their two young
children. In three parts, the first provides the background
material on ESP in children and on the Schwarz family.
Part Two contains the record of the psi experiences. Along
with a factual account of each episode, the author points out
the inter- and intra-personal dynamics apparently involved.
The final section consists of his observations of meaningful
patterns in the experiences. There is an appendix consisting
of tables which illustrate various aspects of the experiences
such as interpersonal variables. Bibliography at the end of
Parts I and III (84 items). 2. M-L-C-U.

     JASPR 67:105-07 (Jan. 1973); JSPR 46:43-45 (Mar.
1972).
     Libr. J. 97:206 (Jan. 15, 1972).

PSYCHICAL RESEARCH IN GENERAL

    For sound and reasonably up-to-date surveys under-
standable to laymen, the following are recommended: Dingwall and Langdon-Davies, Heywood (160), Johnson, Knight,
Pratt, and Somerlott. More advanced coverage of the same
areas is offered by Edmunds, McConnell, Murphy, Sudre,

the Tyrrell books, and West.   The Parapsychology Foundation Proceedings (175) has a number of articles reviewing contemporary psychical research.   The most recent information is provided by Koestler.   Earlier surveys of the subject still of value because of their broad coverage of the phenomena of psychical research (many of which are not dealt with in the more modern books) are Barrett (152), Carrington, Driesch, and Myers.

Additional books with material on psychical research in general: There are a number of books which give a brief overview of the subject: Langdon-Davies (128), Beloff (189), Eysenck (192), and Thouless (219).   Works with a critical approach are Flew (43), Murchison (47), and Prince (48). Altogether negative is Hansel (46).   Historical approaches are found in Lang (33), Tischner (65), Gauld (82), James (85), McDougall (86), Podmore (228), and Hyslop (254). Overviews of experimental parapsychology are provided in Rao (52), Rhine (55), Rhine and Brier (56), Rhine and others (57), Rhine and Pratt (58), Schmeidler (59), and Soal and Bateman (62).   The relation of parapsychology as a whole to other scientific disciplines is stressed in the Ciba Foundation symposium (88) and in Smythies (93); and to philosophy and religion in Angoff (87), Rhine (130), Johnson (216), and Smith (218).   Three reference works dealing with the entire subject are the Biographical dictionary of parapsychology (200), Encyclopaedia of psychic science (201), and Bibliography of parapsychology (211).

151   Barrett, W. F.   On the threshold of the unseen: An examination of the phenomena of spiritualism and of the evidence for survival after death.   2d rev. ed. New York: Dutton, 1971. 336p OP (Orig. publ. by Kegan Paul in 1908 under title On the threshold of a new world of thought. OP)
        The author, a well-known British physicist, was investigating psi phenomena as early as 1863 and in 1876 he presented a paper on "thought-transference" to the British Association.   In the present volume he presents his most mature views on the entire range of phenomena studied in psychical research.   Part 1 is on opinions and attitudes toward the subject.   The second part deals with various physical phenomena.   In Part 3 he discusses evidence, theories, and problems of mediumship.   Parts 4 and 5 are mainly on the mental phenomena of mediumship and their implications, particularly for survival.   The philosophical

and religious implications of psi are covered in the final
section. Bibliographic footnotes; index. 2. L-U.
    JSPR 17:14-16 (Jan. 1915).
    Athenaeum, p406, Aug. 1917; HibbertJ. 16:172 (Oct.
1917); N.Y. TimesBookRev. 22:281 (July 29, 1917); Spectator
118:612 (June 2, 1917); TimesLit.Suppl., p251, May 24,
1917 and p280, June 14, 1917.

152 Barrett, William F. Psychical research. New York:
        Holt, 1911. 255p (Home University Library of Modern
        Knowledge, No. 2) OP
    This is one of the earliest introductory outlines of
psychical research. It surveys the main lines of work
carried on by the S.P.R. and summarizes the results. After an introductory chapter on science and superstition, the
subjects covered are: Automatisms such as dowsing, crystal-
gazing and automatic writing; telepathy; hypnosis and psi;
phantasms of the living and the dead; veridical dreams;
clairvoyance; hauntings and poltergeists; physical phenomena;
and survival after death. This book is of interest as one
of the first maps made of the territory of psychical research
when that land was still new. 21-item annotated bibliography;
index. 2. A.
    JSPR 15:148-50 (Nov. 1911).
    A.L.A.Booklist 8:224 (Apr. 1912); Spectator 108:236
(Feb. 10, 1912).

153 Besterman, Theodore. Collected papers on the para-
        normal. New York: Garrett/Helix, 1968. 455p
        $12.50
    This book reprints 27 of Besterman's papers on psy-
chical research. There are a number of general articles
dealing with topics ranging from anthropology and psi to
theosophy and Madame Blavatsky; from reincarnation to the
clairvoyance of Swedenborg and Ossowiecki. The bulk of
the book is on mediumship, mental and physical. There is
a large section on book tests with Mrs. Leonard, and on
the work of Mrs. Piper, Eva C., Margery, Karl Kraus,
Mirabelli, and other mediums. Of special interest are "The
psychology of testimony in relation to paraphysical phenomena, "
and "Report of an inquiry into precognitive dreams, " in
which Besterman describes his attempts to replicate the
work of J. W. Dunne. Illustrated; bibliographic footnotes;
index. 3. L-C-U.
    JP 32:273-75 (Dec. 1968); JSPR 44:407-10 (Dec. 1968).

154   Broad, C. D.   Lectures on psychical research.   New
        York: Humanities, 1962. 450p $15.00
        A volume in the International Library of Philosophy
and Scientific Method, this book is based on the Perrott
Lectures given by Broad at Cambridge in 1959 and 1960,
plus additional material from published and unpublished
sources.   There is an introduction on the nature, relationships, and methods of psychical research.   The first main
section of the book contains three chapters on the card-
guessing experiments of Rhine, Soal, and Tyrrell.   The
second section comprises six chapters on various aspects
of spontaneous psi, including dreams, out-of-the-body experiences, and collective and reciprocal hallucinations.   The
final section includes a general discussion of trance phenomena and a description of the work of four well-known sensitives: Mrs. Leonard, Mrs. Willett, Mrs. Warren Elliott,
and Swedenborg.   There is a 43-page epilogue on human
personality and survival.   Bibliographic references incorporated in the text; bibliographic footnotes; name and title index; subject index.   3.   L-C-U.
        JASPR 58:66-71 (Jan. 1964); JP 27:210-14 (Sept.
1963); JSPR 42:71-78 (June 1963).
        NewStatesman 65:51 (Jan. 11, 1963); Philos.&Phenom-
enol.Res. 24:561-66 (June 1964); Philos.Rev. 73:412-15
(July 1964); Sci.Am. 209:171 (Nov. 1963); TimesLit.Suppl.,
p20, Jan. 11, 1963.

155   Carrington, Hereward.   The story of psychic science
        (psychical research).   New York: Ives Washburn,
        1931. 399p OP (Orig. publ. by Rider in 1930. OP)
        The main topics that this book deals with are the
historical antecedents of psychical research, the rise of
modern spiritualism, psychology and psychical research,
mediumistic phenomena, and the relation of psi to the arts
and sciences.   A list is given of the principal contents of
the Proceedings of the A.S.P.R. and S.P.R., and of the
Bulletins of the Boston S.P.R.   There is also a detailed
chart of the psychic sciences, legitimate and illegitimate,
which is helpful in sorting out the wheat from the chaff.
Illustrated; 12-page bibliography listed under broad subject
headings; index.   2.   A.
        JSPR 26:141-42 (Nov. 1930).

156   Dingwall, Eric J., and Langdon-Davies, John.   The
        unknown--Is it nearer?   New York: New American
        Library, 1956. 160p $.75 (pap) (Also available as
        a xerocopy from University Microfilms.   Order by

OP no. 2566. $13.20)

This introductory survey of psi phenomena is primarily critical. The authors discuss spontaneous psi experiences, laboratory ESP, automatisms, apparitions and haunted houses, poltergeists, mediumship, and survival. Throughout the book they point out the large amount of "fraud, careless observation, ignorance of scientific method and rules of evidence, and sheer silliness" (p.158) that has been involved in the foregoing areas. However, in the final brief chapter they present a residue of sound material that cannot be explained away. Bibliographic footnotes; index. 1. A.

JASPR 50:128-29 (July 1956); JP 20:135 (June 1956); JSPR 38:270-71 (June 1956).

Contemp. Psychol. 1:292 (Oct. 1956).

157 Driesch, Hans. <u>Psychical research: The science of the supernormal.</u> Trans. by Theodore Besterman. Foreword by Sir Oliver Lodge. London: G. Bell, 1933. 176p OP (Orig. publ. in German in 1932 under title <u>Parapsychologie</u>)

The author hoped that this book would show "those who want to work in the field of psychical research ... how ... the reality of the facts [is] to be determined, and [how] ... a particular theoretical explanation [is] to be chosen" (p.xi). He deals extensively with the necessity for precautions and with the many possibilities for deception in both observations and experiments. He then examines the problems involved in specific areas of psychical research and concludes with a survey of theories in the field. Bibliographic footnotes; index. 2. M-L-C-U.

JASPR 28:54-55 (Feb. 1934); JSPR 28:159 (Dec. 1933).

158 Edmunds, Simeon. <u>Miracles of the mind: An introduction to parapsychology.</u> Springfield, Ill.: Thomas, 1965. 204p $7.75

The author describes the full range of phenomena investigated in parapsychology, including telepathy, clairvoyance, precognition, mediumship, unorthodox healing, and survival. The chapter entitled "The 'higher phenomena' of hypnotism" is a thorough survey of hypnosis and psi phenomena. Chapter 9 provides a good overview of modern experimental parapsychology. There are two chapters on the psychology of testimony and its fallibility. Illustrated; bibliography at the end of each chapter (361 items); index. 2. M-L-C-U.

JASPR 61:87-89 (Jan. 1967); JP 30:53-54 (Mar. 1966); JSPR 43:371-72 (Sept. 1966).

Contemp. Rev. 208:167 (Mar. 1966); Psychoanal. Rev.
56:146-47 (1969).

159 Gudas, Fabian (ed.).   Extrasensory perception.   New
      York: Scribner's, 1961. 141p OP
      This book is one in the series of Scribner research
anthologies dealing with sources for and methods of preparing
term papers.   After an introduction to the subject of ESP
by the editor, 25 selections are presented, chronologically
arranged.   Much of the early material is not very useful as
it is primarily concerned with witchcraft.   But thereafter a
good controversial presentation emerges which contrasts the
positive position (Rhine, Thouless, and Soal and Bateman)
with the negative position (Jastrow, Skinner, and Boring).
The philosophical ramifications of psi are brought out by
Broad, Joad, and Ducasse.   There is a brief biographical
section on each author.   Gudas concludes with "Suggested
topics for controlled research" and "Suggested sources and
topics for library research," which should prove useful for
students.   Bibliographic references at the end of a few selections (46 items).   1.   A.
      JASPR 56:96-101 (Apr. 1962); JP 25:226-29 (Sept.
1961).

160 Heywood, Rosalind.   The sixth sense: An inquiry into
      extrasensory perception.   Rev. ed.   London: Pan
      Books, 1971. 268p £.35 (pap) (Orig. publ. by Chatto
      and Windus in 1959 under this title and by Dutton in
      1961 under title Beyond the reach of sense.   Hard-
      cover eds. OP)
      This introduction to the phenomena of psychical re-
search stresses qualitative experiments, mediumship, and
survival research.   The author is not only an investigator
and frequent contributor to the parapsychological literature;
she has also had many personal psi experiences, and this
"inside view" allows her to paint a more intimate portrait
of the phenomena of psychical research than most books in
this category.   There is an interesting appendix, "Some explanations and hypotheses," which presents the thoughts on
psi held by physical scientists, psychologists, philosophers,
and a biologist.   Bibliographic footnotes; index.   2.   A.
      IJP 2:101-04 (Win. 1960); JASPR 53:156-60 (Oct.
1959); JP 23:273-74 (Dec. 1959); JSPR 40:140-42 (Sept. 1959).
      Booklist 57:624 (June 15, 1961); Bookmark 20:209
(June 1961); Books&Bkmn 11:75 (Mar. 1966); Br.J. Stat.
Psychol. 12:170-71 (1959); Can. Forum 39:189 (Nov. 1959);
Can. Psychiat. Assoc. J. 5:247-50 (1960); Contemp. Psychol.

7:104-06 (Mar. 1962); J. Am. Folklore 73:64 (Jan. -Mar. 1961);
J. Ment. Sci. 106:1594-95 (1960); Kirkus 29:93 (Jan. 15, 1961);
Libr. J. 86:2113 (June 1, 1961); NewStatesman 57:698 (May
16, 1959); Philosophy 35:166 (Apr. 1960); SanFranc. Chron.,
p27, June 25, 1961; Sat. Rev. 44:15 (Apr. 1, 1961); Times
Lit. Suppl., p245, Apr. 24, 1959.

161   Heywood, Rosalind.   Telepathy and allied phenomena.
        Rev. and expanded by Renée Haynes.   London: Society
        for Psychical Research, 1967. 30p £.25 (pap) (Orig.
        publ. by the S. P. R. in 1948. OP) (Available only
        from the Society)
        This pamphlet is a compact summary of the evidence
for and characteristics of ESP.   It is one of a series
written at the request of the S. P. R. Council for the purpose
of bringing the public reliable information on the subject.
The specific topics covered are telepathy, veridical hallucinations and dreams, clairvoyance, precognition, and psychometry. 53-item bibliography. 1. H-S-M.
        JSPR 34:215 (Mar. -Apr. 1948).

162   Holms, A. Campbell.   The facts of psychic science
        and philosophy collated and discussed.   Foreword by
        Leslie Shepard.   New Hyde Park, N. Y.: University
        Books, 1969. 512p $7.95 (Orig. publ. by Kegan
        Paul in 1925. OP)
        In this encyclopedic compendium the author attempts
to draw together all the facts about psi phenomena.   The
book is strongest on the subject of mediumship and its manifestations, but only the very early quantitative experiments
are touched upon.   Of particular interest are various chapters on automatic writing and drawing; direct writing, drawing, and painting; ouija board; and psychometry.   Several
chapters are devoted to physical phenomena, including fire
tests, the passage of matter through matter, apports, and
transfiguration.   There is a section on unorthodox healing.
An appendix gives rules for forming "spirit circles." Bibliographic footnotes; name index; subject index. 2. L-C-U.
        No reviews.

163   Johnson, Raynor C.   Psychical research: Exploring the
        supernatural.   New York: Funk and Wagnalls, n. d.
        174p $1.75 (pap) (Orig. publ. by English Universi-
        ties Press, 1955. OP)
        This introductory overview of psychical research is
based mainly on material originally appearing in the S. R.
Journal and Proceedings.   The author, a physicist interested

in the implications of psi, says he wrote the book "for the
ordinary thoughtful person who has not a great deal of time
for reading but would like to understand what psychical research is all about and why I regard its implications and its
future as of such importance" (p.vii).   There are chapters
on clairvoyance and telepathy; precognition and retrocognition;
psychometry, PK and poltergeists, materializations, apparitions and hauntings; and mediumship and survival.   The last
chapter is entitled "The importance of psychical research."
Bibliographic references incorporated in the text; index.   1.
A.
        JSPR 38:220-21 (Mar. 1956).
        Am. J. Psychiat.   114:475-76 (1957/58); Bull. Menninger
Clin. 21:77-78 (1957); Concor. Theol. Mon. 28:785-86 (Oct.
1957); Contemp. Psychol. 1:364-65 (Dec. 1956); J. Bible&Relig.
25:91-92 (Jan. 1957).

164 Knight, David C. (ed.).   The ESP reader.   New York:
        Grosset and Dunlap, 1969. 432p $5.95
        This anthology is intended to help the reader to deep-
en and enlarge his acquaintance with the original source materials of psychical research.   There are a number of broad
subject categories, each illustrated by selections from the
literature.   The editor provides an introduction to each section and selection.   The categories are historical mediums
(Home, Palladino, Piper, Eva C.); spontaneous psi (30
cases); modern mediums and psychics (Leonard, Ford, Garrett, Cayce, Hurkos, Dixon); ouija board and planchette;
automatic writing; out-of-the-body experiences; survival and
the experience of death; and reincarnation.   The concluding
selection is F. W. H. Myers' "High possibilities."   86-item
glossary; 59-item bibliography; index of 49 principal cases.
1. A.
        Libr. J. 95:2170 (June 1, 1970).

165 Koestler, Arthur.   The roots of coincidence.   With a
        postscript by Renée Haynes.   London: Hutchinson,
        1972. 159p £2.00; New York: Random, 1972. $5.95
        In the realm of science writing Koestler is an intel-
lectual goad to both sluggish and closed minds.   In this book
he awakens the former and opens the latter by tying the findings of parapsychology in with those of theoretical physics.
His thesis is that "the unthinkable phenomena of ESP appear
somewhat less preposterous in the light of the unthinkable
propositions of modern physics" (p.11-12).   He discusses
various theories, including Kammerer's "seriality" and
Jung's "synchronicity," and has much to say about "meaning-

ful coincidences." He concludes by stressing the importance
of psychical research. The postscript by Haynes is on spontaneous psi and was added at Koestler's suggestion to balance
his concentration on experimental parapsychology. Bibliography by chapter at the end of the book (126 items); 116-
item bibliography; name index. 2. M-L-C-U.

JSPR 46:91-93 (June 1972); PR 3:11-12 (May-June
1972).

Libr.J. 97:2741 (Sept. 1, 1972); Listener 87:187 (Feb.
10, 1972); N.Y.Rev.Books 19:23 (Sept. 1972).

166 McConnell, R. A. ESP curriculum guide. New York:
Simon and Schuster, 1971. 128p $4.95; $1.95 (pap)
The author prepared this curriculum guide "for se-
condary-school and college teachers of psychology, biology,
and general science who may wish to teach extrasensory perception and related topics, either briefly or as a formal
course unit, or who may have occasion to recommend the
purchase of library materials for student projects on this
subject" (p. 9). The book is geared to the four areas in
which McConnell sees the educational challenge of ESP to
lie: "In the use of the scientific method, in the nature of
scientific controversy, in the unknown psychological conditions necessary for the production of ESP, and in its philosophic implications" (p. 9). It contains a syllabus for use in
teaching parapsychology, an annotated list of the 16 "most
important" books in print on the subject, and detailed instructions for conducting ESP and PK experiments and evaluating their results. Name index; subject index. 2. · A.

JASPR 66:408-14 (Oct. 1972); JP 36:150-55 (June
1972); JSPR 46:42-43 (Mar. 1972); PR 3:16 (Mar.-Apr. 1972).

Choice 9:285 (Apr. 1972); Contemp.Psychol. 17:405
(July 1972); Libr.J. 96:2525 (Aug. 1971).

167 McCreery, Charles. Science, philosophy and ESP.
Foreword by H. H. Price. London: published for the
Institute of Psychophysical Research by Hamish Hamilton, 1969. 199p (Proceedings of the Institute, v.3)
£2.25 (Orig. publ. by Faber in 1967. OP)
This is a research-oriented book which stresses physical phenomena, repeatability, and conditions favoring success
in testing psi. The first half is an introduction to the field
in which he reviews some outstanding investigations of the
past; in the second half he offers a testable theory for psi.
Both informative and provocative is the discussion of altered
states of consciousness and the psychology of the psi process.
McCreery recommends the use of the EEG in connection with

the study of psi. 38-item glossary; bibliography by chapter
at the end of the book (200 items); name index; subject index.
2. M-L-C-U.
    IJP 10:304-07 (Aut. 1968); JASPR 65:110-12 (Jan.
1971); JP 32;139-41 (June 1968),
    Br.J. Psychiat. 114:658-60; Br.J. Psychol. 10:304-07
(1968); Libr.J. 93:2670 (July 1968); TimesLit.Suppl., p966,
Oct. 12, 1967.

168   Murphy, Gardner (with Laura A. Dale). Challenge of
       psychical research: A primer of parapsychology.
       New York: Harper & Row, 1961. 297p $6.50; $1.95
       (pap)
       In Harper's "World Perspectives" series, the purpose
ot this book is to "show what psychical research is by giving
documented examples of the kinds of data available in relation to a few main kinds of problems, selecting from the
classics and the near-classics of the field" (pp.5-6). Spontaneous psi is illustrated by some cases investigated by the
A.S.P.R., two dreams of W. F. Prince, and an experience
occurring during psychoanalysis reported by Ehrenwald. Under experimental telepathy the work of Warcollier, Brugmans,
and Carington is presented. The Pearce-Pratt series,
Schmeidler's sheep-goat research, and the Anderson-White
classroom experiments are excerpted in the section on experimental clairvoyance. Under precognition is Soal's work
with Shackleton, while psychokinesis is illustrated by Dale's
A.S.P.R. experiment and Forwald's placement work at Duke.
The section on survival features long excerpts from three
well-known cross correspondences. Murphy's comments before and after each selection are particularly instructive.
He also provides an introduction and a final evaluative summary, with a section on "What does psychical research include and exclude?" Illustrated; bibliographic footnotes; index. 2. A.
    IJP 3:77-87 (Win. 1961); JASPR 55:122-25 (July 1961);
JP 25:219-23 (Sept. 1961); JSPR 41:73-79 (June 1961).
    Am.J.Psychol. 75:709 (1962); Aust.J.Psychol. 14:85
(1962); Br.J.Psychol. 52:400 (1961); Bull. MenningerClin. 25:
209 (1961); Contemp.Psychol. 7:14-15 (Jan. 1962); J.Am.
Psychoanal.Assoc. 16:146-78 (1968).

169   Myers, Frederic W. H. Human personality and its
       survival of bodily death. Introduction by Gardner
       Murphy. New York: Longmans, Green, 1954. 2v.
       OP (Orig. publ. by Longmans, Green in 1903. OP)
       This is a major classic of psychical research. Any
of the two-volume editions or one-volume abridgements (170)

is worth reading, but this one has been selected because it
contains Gardner Murphy's sensitive and informative introduction. A classic of psychology as well, in this massive
work Myers has provided an encyclopedic survey of the
range of human experiences. He deals with multiple personality, dissociation, genius, sleep, hypnotism, sensory
and motor automatisms, phantasms of the dead, trance, possession, and ecstasy. Extensive appendices (nearly two
thirds of each volume) consist primarily of illustrative cases
documenting statements made in the text. 123-item glossary;
bibliographic footnotes; index. 3. A.
        JASPR 49:42-44 (Jan. 1955); JP 19:52-57 (Mar. 1955);
PSPR 18:22-61, Pt. 46 (1903).
        Arena 30:193-99 (Aug. 1903); Athenaeum 1:276-77
(Feb. 28, 1903) and Athenaeum, p78, Jan. 16, 1920; Atl.
Mon. 92:126-28 (July 1903); Bookman[Lond.] 23:236-38 (Mar.
1903); Dial 69:201 (Aug. 1920); HibbertJ. 2:44-64 (Oct. 1903);
Independent 55:1249-53 (May 28, 1903); Outlook 125:281 (June
9, 1920); Quar.Rev. 198:211-29 (July 1903); SpringfieldRepub.,
p11a, June 20, 1920.

170 Myers, Frederic W. H. <u>Human personality and its sur-</u>
        <u>vival of bodily death.</u> (Abridged and ed. by Susy
        Smith.) Foreword by Aldous Huxley. New Hyde Park,
        N.Y.: University Books, 1961. 416p $10.00
        In her preface the editor writes: "... Myers' monu-
mental study has often, and with justification, been referred
to as a classic. Unfortunately, voluminous classics are
widely praised but rarely read. The present edition is an
abridgement of the original two-volume 1,360 page work,
prepared to make its major content more readily accessible
to the modern reader" (p. 9). She presents a concise version of the arguments and cases in Myers' original work
(169), covering altered states of consciousness, automatisms,
phantasms of the dead, and trance phenomena. Much of the
corroboratory material used in authenticating the cases in
the original edition has been omitted, and the extensive appendices incorporated in the text. Bibliographic references
incorporated in the text; index. 2. A.
        JASPR 56:56-59 (Jan. 1962); JSPR 41:155-56 (Sept.
1961).
        Contemp. Psychol. 7:106 (Mar. 1962).

171 Omez, Reginald. <u>Psychical phenomena.</u> Trans. by
        Renée Haynes. London: Burns and Oates, 1958.
        144p OP (Orig. publ. in French in 1956 under title
        <u>Supranormale ou surnatural</u>?)

This is an introductory survey of psychical research
written by a Catholic priest for Catholics. (It is v. 36 of
the Twentieth century encyclopedia of Catholicism.) It contains an historical survey emphasizing Continental work; a
review of the phenomena and methods of investigating them;
and a section on parapsychology and religion, including
miracles. Omez defines the attitude of the Catholic Church
toward psi phenomena. In Chapter 4 he assesses contemporary opinions on the evidence for automatisms, various
physical and mental phenomena, and astrology. The scientific status of parapsychology is dealt with in the final chapter. "Select bibliography" (21 items); bibliographic references
incorporated in the text. 2. L-C-U.
        JASPR 54:171-74 (Oct. 1960); JP 23:68-70 (Mar. 1959);
JSPR 40:81-82 (June 1959).

172   Pierce, Henry W. Science looks at ESP. New York:
        New American Library, 1970. 144p $. 75 (pap)
        The author of this introduction to parapsychology is a
science writer. Quality is not sacrificed as the major areas
of study are described in laymen's terms. Where possible
Pierce has used illustrations and examples from his own experience. Among the topics he deals with are repeatability
in psi experiments, the significance of psi for our views of
human nature, hypnosis and psi, out-of-the-body experiences,
reincarnation, Soviet parapsychology, and science writers
and parapsychology. 18-item bibliography. 1. H-S-M.
        No reviews.

173   Podmore, Frank. Studies in psychical research. New
        York: Putnam, 1897. 458p OP
        In this book Podmore records his observations on a
wide variety of subjects, among them spiritualism, theosophy,
poltergeists, physical phenomena, ghosts and haunted houses,
experimental and spontaneous telepathy, precognition, automatism and the subconscious, and possession. Therefore
this is a good introduction to the varied phenomena studied
by psychical research. Of special relevance today, when
the public seems ready to believe almost anything without
questioning, is Podmore's critical gift. In each chapter he
stresses the pitfalls to be avoided and spells out the counterhypotheses that must be ruled out before any given phenomenon can be attributed to psi. Bibliographic footnotes; index.
3. M-L-C-U.
        PSPR 13:604-09, Pt. 33 (1898).
        Critic 32[n. s. 29]:400 (June 18, 1898); Dial 24:147
(Mar. 1, 1898); Nation 65:362 (Nov. 4, 1897); Spectator 79:

892-93 (Dec. 18, 1897).

174   Pratt, J. Gaither.   Parapsychology: An insider's view
        of ESP.   Rev. ed.   New York, Dutton, 1966.   300p
        $5.95   (Orig. publ. by Doubleday in 1964. OP)
        A "parapsychological autobiography" in which the
author tells how he became interested in the field as a graduate student at Duke University and what it was like to grow
up with the ESP experimentation there.   Of special interest
is his firsthand account of the landmark Pearce-Pratt and
Pratt-Woodruff experiments.   He tells how PK was first investigated at Duke by throwing dice and reviews the work
that followed there and at other centers.   Pratt was one of
the main investigators of the Herrmann poltergeist case (Seaford, Long Island) and he provides a full account of it.   In
other chapters he reviews the evidence for precognition and
survival of death.   There is a chapter on anpsi in general,
including the results of his experiments with the dog Chris,
and one on homing in pigeons.   The concluding chapter is on
the importance of parapsychology.   "Suggestions for further
reading" (8 items); index.   1.   A.
        IJP 7:203-08 (Spr. 1965); JASPR 58:293-98 (Oct.
1964); JP 28:135-36 (June 1964); JSPR 42:360-63 (Sept. 1964).
        BookWeek, p10, July 26, 1964; J. Am. Psychoanal.
Assoc. 16:146-78 (1968); Libr. J. 89:1100 (Mar. 1, 1964);
N. Y. Rev. Books 3:15 (Oct. 8, 1964); N. Y. TimesBookRev.,
p18, Jan. 1, 1967; Psychoanal. Rev. 56:145-47 (1969/70);
Psychosomatics 7:265 (1966); Punch 249:361 (Sept. 8, 1965);
Sci. Books 3:3 (May 1967); TimesLit. Suppl., p71, Jan. 28,
1965.

175   Proceedings of an international conference.   A century
        of psychical research: The continuing doubts and af-
        firmations.   (Allan Angoff and Betty Shapin, eds.)
        New York: Parapsychology Foundation, 1971.   212p
        $6.00   (Available only from the Foundation)
        This is an anthology of 15 papers by professionals
from a number of disciplines: psychology, psychiatry, physics, and parapsychology.   Most participants had either engaged actively in psychical research or had some acquaintance
with the literature and were thus in a position to assess the
scientific status of the field over the past century.   Information is given concerning the participants' backgrounds and
special interests.   The volume also includes discussions of
the papers as well as the opening and closing remarks of
the chairman, Emilio Servadio.   Stressing both pros and
cons, this is an eclectic survey of where parapsychology

stands in the early 1970s. Bibliography at the end of six
papers (74 items). 3. L-C-U.
    JASPR 66:329-36 (July 1972); JP 35:290-92 (Dec.
1971); JSPR 46:38-40 (Mar. 1972).

176 Rhine, J. B., and associates. Parapsychology from
     Duke to FRNM. Durham, N.C.: Parapsychology
     Press, 1965. 121p $2.50 (pap)
    This volume commemorates the formation in 1962 of
the Foundation for Research on the Nature of Man (FRNM)
and, in the following year, its research unit, the Institute
of Parapsychology, which gradually took over the work of
the Duke University Parapsychology Laboratory. Two papers combine to give an interesting history of the early research conducted by Rhine and his associates at Duke, while
reports by six "students in training" in the Laboratory indicate the trend of more recent research. The current scientific status and prospects of parapsychology are dealt with
extensively. A description of the organization and aims of
FRNM is given in an appendix. 2. L-U.
    JASPR 60:285-89 (July 1966); JSPR 43:367-70 (Sept.
1966).
    Libr.J. 91:119 (Jan. 1, 1966).

177 Richet, Charles. Thirty years of psychical research:
     Being a treatise on metapsychics. Trans. by Stanley
     de Brath. New York: Macmillan, 1923. 646p OP
     (Orig. publ. in French in 1922 under title Traité de
     métapsychique)
    This book is a summary of Richet's investigations and
conclusions on various aspects of psychical research. In
four parts, the first is a general introduction to psychical
research, which he termed "metapsychics." The second
part is on "subjective metapsychics" or "cryptesthesia" (the
term he used to cover telepathy, clairvoyance, and precognition). The third section is on "objective metapsychics,"
or physical phenomena such as movement of objects, materializations, and levitation. He also includes here bilocation
and hauntings. His conclusions are given in the fourth section. He hoped to find a physiological basis for psi phenomena and could not accept the possibility of survival after
death. Illustrated; bibliographic footnotes; name index. 2.
L-C-U.
    JASPR 17:589-622 (Nov. 1923) and 18:155-69 (Mar.
1924); JSPR 21:139-43 (Oct. 1923); PSPR 34:70-106 (1924).
    BostonEve.Trans., p2, June 16, 1923; Cathol.World
118:131 (Oct. 1923); HibbertJ. 22:501-14 (Apr. 1924); Lit.

Rev., p17, Sept. 8, 1923} N.Y.TimesBookRev., p6, June 17, 1923; N.Y.Trib., p18, July 1, 1923; TimesLit.Suppl., p566, Aug. 30, 1923.

178 Ryzl, Milan. Parapsychology: A scientific approach.
      New York: Hawthorn, 1970. 216p $7.95
      The author, a Czechoslovak parapsychologist now liv-
ing in the United States, provides an introduction to parapsychology which differs from many of the other books listed in
this section in that it gives more coverage to European work.
There is an historical section and one on newer developments.
There are chapters on laboratory investigations of ESP, Soviet parapsychology, physical phenomena, precognition, and
theories about psi phenomena. He concludes with a chapter
on the future application of psi. "Suggested readings" (23
items); index. 2. L-U.
      JASPR 65:227-29 (Apr. 1971); JP 34:234-38 (Sept.
1970); JSPR 46:64-68 (Mar. 1971); PR 2:11-12 (Mar.-Apr.
1971).

179 Smith, Alson J. (ed.). The psychic source book. In-
      troduction by Pitirim A. Sorokin. New York: Crea-
      tive Age, 1951. 442p OP
      This anthology provides a good sample of the litera-
ture of psychical research. In four parts, the first contains
four papers illustrating the scope of the field. Part Two
consists of examples of the types of experience with which
psychical research deals, e.g., ecstasy and inspiration;
mediumship and trance; telepathy, clairvoyance, and precognition; and automatisms. The third part is on experiments
and the selection ranges from Gurney, Myers, and Podmore
to J. B. Rhine. The concluding section is an overview and
summary. An appendix includes letters on the importance
of parapsychology from Rhine and Sorokin, and biographical
descriptions of 46 persons associated with psychical research.
99-item glossary; 298-item bibliography; subject index. 2.
M-L-C-U.
      JASPR 46:38-41 (Jan. 1952); JSPR 36:627-28 (May-
June 1952).

180 Somerlott, Robert. "Here, Mr. Splitfoot": An informal
      exploration into modern occultism. New York: Viking,
      1971. 311p $7.50
      This is a popular account of spiritualism and psychi-
cal research, written in response to the current wave of
interest in the "occult." Somerlott takes the position that
although much of what sparks this interest has no basis in

fact, there is a residue of truth to be found in the literature
of psychical research, and he endeavors to make known to
today's seekers this heritage of the past.   He covers mediumship, spirit photography, hauntings and poltergeists, crystal-
gazing, and precognition.   There is a final chapter on recent work.   This is a readable introduction to many of the
major names and cases of psychical research.   Illustrated;
44-item bibliography; index.   1.   A.
        JASPR 66:221-26 (Apr. 1972); JP 35:150-53 (June
1971); PR 2:8 (July-Aug. 1971).
        America 124:385 (Apr. 10, 1971); Atlantic 227:113
(Mar. 1971); Libr.J. 96:645 (Feb. 15, 1971).

181   Sudre, René. Parapsychology.   Trans. by Celia E.
        Green. New York: Citadel, 1960. 412p OP (Orig.
        publ. in French in 1956 under title Traité de para-
        psychologie)
This survey differs from most of the books in this
section because European, and especially French, work is
emphasized.   Part One is a general history and survey of
the field; Part Two is a review of psychological phenomena;
Part Three covers physiological and physical phenomena; and
Part Four deals with philosophical problems, among them
the spiritistic interpretation of psi, which Sudre rejects.
His main concern is to establish that "parapsychology is
simply a natural science." Bibliographic footnotes; name
index. 3. L-U.
        IJP 3:102-04 (Win. 1961); JASPR 56:87-90 (Apr.
1962); JP 21:314 (Dec. 1957); JSPR 39:87-88 (June 1957).
        Aust.J. Psychol. 13:135-36 (1961); Psychoanal.&Psy-
choanal.Rev. 48:125-26 (1961).

182   Tyrrell, G. N. M.   The personality of man: New facts
        and their significance.   Harmondsworth, Eng.: Pen-
        guin, 1947. 295p OP
In this book, which has become a minor classic of
psychical research, we have one of the broadest introductions to the field and still one of the best.   Tyrrell begins
with a description of the "higher reaches of personality,"
culminating in genius, inspiration, and mysticism.   He suggests that the questions they raise may be answered by the
methods and findings of psychical research.   He covers the
laboratory research of Rhine, Carington, Hettinger, and
Soal.   There follows a section on telepathy and precognition,
and their implications.   In a section on mediumship he discusses the case of Patience Worth, the cross correspondences,
Mrs. Willett, various French mediums, and the Mexican hyp-

notic subject, Senora Z.   There are sections on physical
phenomena and on survival.   He relates psychical research
to psychology, philosophy, and religion, and considers its
significance for the future of man.   Bibliographic footnotes;
101-item bibliography (arranged under broad subject headings); index.   2.   A.
       JASPR 42:40-42 (Jan. 1948); JP 11:313-15 (Dec. 1947);
JSPR 34:98-100 (Sept. 1947).

183   Tyrrell, G. N. M.   Science and psychical phenomena.
       New York: Harper, 1938. 379p OP
       Tyrrell had a grasp of the need to investigate psi ex-
perimentally and also the vision to see the theoretical implications of the data thus obtained.   He wrote this book to inform the general public of "the true importance of the subject, its seriousness and strictly scientific basis" (p.xv).
In Part I he presents many cases of spontaneous psi and discusses the evidence they provide for telepathy, clairvoyance,
and precognition.   Part II is concerned with experimental
ESP, reviewing the most important research conducted between 1882 and 1938.   In Part III he deals with the significance of the evidence, including a section on "the prevailing
attitude towards psychical phenomena."   Part IV is on mediumistic trance, with chapters on Mrs. Piper, Mrs. Leonard,
book tests, and the cross correspondence.   Part V deals
with the theoretical aspects of trance phenomena; a chapter
on the survival problem and one on psychical research and
religion are included in this section.   Bibliographic footnotes;
index.   2.   A.
       JASPR 32:22-24 (July 1938); PSPR 45:127-30, Pt.155,
(1938).
       BostonEve. Trans., p1, Apr. 15, 1939; Contemp.
Psychol. 2:106 (Mar. 1962); Manch.Guard., p9, May 24,
1938; Nature 143:223 (Feb. 11, 1939); TimesLit.Suppl.,
p811, Dec. 24, 1938.

184   Vyvyan, John.   The case against Jones: A study of psy-
       chical phenomena.   London: James Clarke (for the
       Churches Fellowship for Psychical and Spiritual
       Studies), 1966. 220p £1.25; Greenwood, S.C.: Attic
       Press, n.d. $4.50
       The "Jones" of the title is the renowned Freudian,
Ernest Jones, who held that disbelief in the independent existence of "mental beings" is the single most important criterion of a well-balanced mind.   Vyvyan summarizes the
findings of psychical research, which he believes refute
Jones' position.   He especially considers the evidence for

and implications of out-of-the-body experiences, precognition,
mediumistic communications, psychometry, deathbed visions,
and the cross correspondences. He concludes that the data
suggest "a series of extensions of consciousness, each with
its own field, is the pattern to which speculative reason, and
psychical and mystical experiences would seem to point" (p.
213). Bibliographic footnotes; 55-item bibliography; index.
2. M-L-C-U.
        TimesLit. Suppl., p915, Oct. 6, 1966.

185 West, Donald J. Psychical research today. New York:
        Hillary, 1956. 144p $3.00 (pap) (Orig. publ. by
        Duckworth in 1954; rev. ed., 1962. OP)
        The author, a psychiatrist, has made a number of
important contributions to the experimental literature of
parapsychology. In this book he offers a survey of the
phenomena studied by psychical research and in each case
discusses the evidence. The emphasis throughout is on research. There is a chapter on spontaneous psi and one on
theories of the paranormal. Three chapters are devoted to
mediumship, including the ESP abilities of mediums, and
three on experimental parapsychology. Worth noting is
Chapter 8, "Fresh light on some old beliefs, " in which he
discusses phenomena that cannot easily be assessed: dowsing, anpsi, haunts and poltergeists, and stage telepathy. Illustrated; bibliography at the end of each chapter (128 items);
index. 2. A.
        JASPR 49:40-42 (Jan. 1955); JP 18:203-05 (Sept. 1954);
JSPR 37:348-49 (July-Oct. 1954).
        Am. J. Psychiat. 112:863-64 (1955/56); Am. J. Psychol.
68:692-93 (1955); J. Ment. Sci. 101:413 (1955).

PSYCHOKINESIS

        Psychokinesis, the latest form of psi to be studied
under laboratory conditions, has not been written about extensively in book form. For this reason all three titles
listed below are important: Rhine's as the first general survey, Eisenbud's because of the unprecedented breadth of his
investigation of psychic photography, and Forwald's for its
record of the most extensive experimental PK work ever
carried out.

Additional books with material on psychokinesis: An
account of the early PK work at Duke is provided by Rhine
(55). Examples of outstanding PK experiments are given in
Murphy (168) and in Pratt (174). A section on PK stressing
its philosophical and religious implications is provided by
Johnson (163). Good surveys of the methods and findings of
experimental PK are in the Rhine-Pratt textbook (58) and in
Thouless (64). A combined discussion of spontaneous and
experimental PK is given by L. E. Rhine (236) and in Progress in parapsychology (54).

186 Eisenbud, Jule. The world of Ted Serios: "Thoughto-
 graphic" studies of an extraordinary mind. New York:
 Paperback Library, 1969. 367p $.95 (pap) (Orig.
 publ. by Morrow in 1967. Hardcover ed. OP)
 The author, a well-known psychoanalyst, gives a fast-
moving account of his investigation of the psychic photography
of Ted Serios who, by no known normal means, imprinted
mental images on photographic film. Eisenbud took Serios
into his own home for two years and actively sought the par-
ticipation of fellow scientists at the University of Colorado
in extensive studies of Serios. A total of 25 persons took
part in the experiments described in the book. Eisenbud reports on a variety of experimental conditions. He also analyzes the personality of Serios, offering suggestions as to
the "how" and "why" of what he is. There are 150 photographs of Serios' work. Illustrated; 145-item bibliography;
index. 2. A.
 JASPR 62:193-216 (Apr. 1968); JP 31:297-300 (Dec.
1967); JSPR 44:260-65 (Mar. 1968).
 Am. J. Clin. Hypn. 10:143 (1967/68); Behav. Sci. 13:
326-28 (1968); BookWeek, p5, Apr. 23, 1967; Books&Bkman
13:31 (July 1968); BooksToday 4:5 (May 21, 1967); Choice 4:
1053 (Nov. 1967); Contemp. Psychol. 12:572 (Nov. 1967); J.
Am. Psychoanal. Assoc. 16:146-78 (1968); J. Am. Soc. Psychosom. Dent. 14:135-38 (1967); Kirkus 34:1215 (Nov. 15, 1966);
Libr. J. 92:248 (Jan. 15, 1967); Listener 79:740 (June 6,
1968); N. Y. TimesBookRev., p38, May 14, 1967; Natl. Obs.
6:21 (Apr. 17, 1967); NewStatesman 75:689 (May 24, 1968);
Psychoanal. Rev. 55:655-61 (1968/69); Va. Q. Rev. 43:132
(Sum. 1967).

187 Forwald, Haakon. Mind, matter, and gravitation: A
 theoretical and experimental study. New York: Parapsychology Foundation, 1970. 72p (Parapsychological
 Monographs No. 11) $3.00 (pap) (Available only from

the Foundation)

This is a summary by a man who achieved success
in quantitative PK experimentation over a longer period than
any other subject. In it he describes his work over 20 years
with PK placement tests which he conducted with himself as
subject. He was able to repeat his results in several laboratories in the United States with observers present. Forwald
also offers theories to account for his results based on the
physical characteristics of the dice and the role of gravitation as a link in the interaction between mind and matter.
Of special interest is his discussion of the physical and psychological aspects of successful PK experimentation. Bibliographic footnotes. 3. L-C-U.

JASPR 65:223-27 (Apr. 1971); JP 34:242 (Sept. 1970).

188 Rhine, Louisa E.   Mind over matter: Psychokinesis.
New York: Macmillan, 1970. 402p $7.95; $1.95 (pap)

This is the first book-length general survey of the
evidence for and characteristics of psychokinesis. The author, wife of J. B. Rhine, describes at first hand how the
quantitative investigation of PK using dice began at the Duke
Parapsychology Laboratory, and the many experiments there
and in other research centers which followed. All types of
PK experimentation are treated, their results and implications evaluated. Physiological, psychological, and other
variables are discussed. There are several chapters on
spontaneous PK and on theories concerning PK. Bibliographic footnotes; index. 2. A.

JASPR 65:360-64 (July 1971); JP 34:164-66 (June
1970); JSPR 46:138-40 (June 1971); PR 1:8 (Nov.-Dec. 1970).
Contemp. Psychol. 16:540 (Aug. 1971); Libr.J. 95:
2170 (June 1, 1970).

PSYCHOLOGY AND PSI PHENOMENA

Although by definition parapsychological phenomena are
"beyond" or outside academic psychology, as a form of human behavior they can be viewed as an aspect of psychology.
A number of the books below deal with a theoretical view of
man's nature which encompasses what we know from both
psychology and parapsychology. The most important of these
are Beloff and Burt. Mitchell presents an older view of the
relation between human personality and psi phenomena. Seve-

ral of the titles relate personality variables to psi: Mangan
reviews the published research in this area, while Schmeidler's monograph is a summary of her own findings on ESP
and personality dynamics as indicated by the Rorschach test.
The monograph by Rush offers provocative suggestions for
psi experiments based on various aspects of human psychological functioning.

    Additional books with material on psychology and psi
phenomena: Some titles cover psi in relation to various
forms of altered states (as studied by psychology): Oesterreich (34) and several Parapsychology Foundation Proceedings
(18, 89, 90). Others are concerned with psi and only one form
of altered state such as dreaming (11, 13, 66), hypnosis (9, 67),
drugs (19), and out-of-the-body experiences (118). Consideration of the entire range of phenomena which concern both
psychology and psychical research is provided by Carrington
(155), Myers (169, 170), and Tyrrell (182). Van Over (25),
McDougall (86), and Tyrrell (221) discuss theories of human
personality which take psi into account. Several books present data on psi and various personality variables as
measured by psychological tests: Rao (52), Progress in
parapsychology (54), Parapsychology today (56), Schmeidler
and McConnell (60), and two Parapsychology Foundation Proceedings (91, 92). Some authors have written at length on
the psychology of the psi response itself: Rhine (53), Rhine
and Pratt (58), Warcollier (69, 70), LeShan (129), McCreery
(167), and Sidgwick (239). The psychology of PK phenomena
is examined by Eisenbud (186) and L. E. Rhine (188). Finally, the psychology of mediums and sensitives is dealt
with in several papers in the Utrecht Conference Proceedings
(92), by Osty (109), Progoff (111), Bendit (139), Flournoy
(146), and Broad (154).

189 Beloff, John. The existence of mind. New York: Cita-
        del, 1965. 263p $1.95 (pap) (Orig. publ. by MacGib-
        bon in 1962. OP)
        In this book the author, a British psychologist, pre-
sents his views on the place of mind in psychology and on
the implications of parapsychology. Actually a work of philosophical psychology, it is a discussion of the mind-body
problem and a defense of dualism in the following controversial areas of psychology (each represented by a chapter):
Behaviorism, perception, thought, action, personal identity,
and (chapter 7) the paranormal. The latter is both an evaluation of the evidence for psi and a consideration of its

implications. Beloff concludes that "in the long run the case
for dualism is likely to stand or fall with the success or
failure of parapsychology" (p. 297). There is an appendix to
this chapter in two sections: The evidence for the paranormal, and General reading (11 items). Bibliography at the
end of each chapter (315 items: 46 in Chapter 7); name index. 2. M-L-C-U.
        IJP 6:373-77 (Sum. 1964); JP 27:252-57 (Dec. 1963);
JSPR 41:43-37 (Dec. 1962).
        N.Y.TimesBookRev. 70:51 (Sept. 12, 1965); Philos.Q.
15:27 (July 1965); Rev. Metaphysics 19:804 (June 1966).

190 Brown, William. Science and personality. Foreword
        by Sir Oliver Lodge. College Park, Md.: McGrath,
        1972. 258p $15.00 (Orig. publ. by Yale University
        Press in 1929. OP)
        Originally presented as the Terry Lectures, the author,
a British psychiatrist, viewed this book as a sequel to his
Mind and personality. It contains considerably more material on psychical research than does the former, although
Brown says he hesitated to include it, finally doing so because "as a scientist I feel that these phenomena of apparently supernormal (or at least unusual) mental power are worthy
of the closest scientific investigation, and have an important
bearing on the question of survival" (Preface). In addition
to two chapters on personality and psychical research and an
appendix which is a verbatim report of a sitting he had with
the medium, Mrs. Osborne Leonard, there is material of
relevance to psi in the discussion throughout the book on the
mind-body problem. Bibliographic footnotes; index. 2. L-
U.
        JSPR 26:35-37 (Feb. 1930).
        BostonEve.Trans., p2, June 5, 1929; N.Y.Evening
Post, p6m, Aug. 3, 1929; Nature 123:901 (June 15, 1929);
NewStatesman 33:446 (July 13, 1929); Spectator 142:709 (May
4, 1929); TimesLit.Suppl., p430, May 30, 1929.

191 Burt, Cyril. Psychology and psychical research. Lon-
        don: Society for Psychical Research, 1968. 109p £.50
        (pap) (Available only from the Society)
        This monograph consists of the paper which Burt, the
distinguished British psychologist, delivered to the S.P.R.
as its Seventeenth Frederic W. H. Myers Memorial Lecture.
He points out that psi phenomena are regarded as "paranormal" simply because they do not fit into the antiquated doctrine of materialistic monism. "Once we have ceased to accept this as the essential basis for 'normal' science, there

is no longer any ground ... for describing the phenomena investigated in psychical research as 'paranormal' " (p. 7).   He
outlines in detail the proper subject matter of psychology,
with specific reference to the data of psychical research.
He makes three points: 1/Changes in psychology, neurophys-
iology, and other fields are making psi more credible, 2/these
new views will help provide a scientific theory to account for
psi, and 3/the goals of psychical research should be modi-
fied in view of these findings from other fields.   Bibliographic footnotes; index. 3. L-C-U.
        No reviews.

192 Eysenck, H. J.   Sense and nonsense in psychology.
        Harmondsworth, Eng.: Penguin, 1957. 349p $1.25;
        £.35 (pap)
        The purpose of this book, says the author, a well-
known British psychologist, is to pick a few aspects of psychology about which a lot of nonsense is talked, "to sort out
the chaff from the wheat, and to put before the reader the
facts as well as the speculations, the sense as well as the
nonsense, which have grown up around these topics" (p. 11).
One of the topics dealt with is psychical research in a
chapter rather too narrowly titled "Telepathy and clairvoyance. " In it Eysenck sets forth the areas studied, types of
proof offered, and pitfalls to be avoided.   He describes
some data of observation and experiment that are difficult
to explain away, with emphasis on the major quantitative experimental efforts of recent times.   He also reviews the
main criticisms of the work.   "Recommended further reading" (8 items); bibliographic references incorporated in the
text. 2. A.
        IJP 1:117-20 (Sum. 1959); JASPR 52:78 (Apr. 1958).
        Aust. J. Psychol. 9:195 (1957); Br. J. Psychol. 49:82
(1958); Contemp. Psychol. 2:244-45 (Sept. 1957); Eugen. Rev.
50:63 (1958/59); Occup. Psychol. 32:69-70 (1958).

193 Hudson, Thomson J.   The law of psychic phenomena:
        A working hypothesis for the systematic study of the
        vast potential of man's mind.   New York: Weiser,
        1972. $6.50.   With an introduction by Jack H. Hol-
        land, Chicago: Hudson-Cohan, 1970. 221p $2.95 (pap)
        (Orig. publ. by McClurg in 1894. Hardcover ed. OP)
        Hudson was one of the first to propose a comprehen-
sive theory of psi that took into account all the phenomena,
but rejected the spiritualist hypothesis of communication
with the dead.   He is primarily concerned with the role
which suggestion plays in drawing upon and channeling the

evolving aspects of human nature.   He includes psi phenomena as part of the farther reaches of human personality and
offers valuable hints regarding conditions favoring or inhibiting suggestion, many of which are also relevant to psi.   This
was one of the most successful books of the 19th century
(47 printings) and it has influenced the thinking of some present-day parapsychologists.   Frontispiece; bibliographic footnotes.   3.   L-C-U.
        PSPR 9:230-34, Pt. 24 (1893).
        Arena 13:177-84 (July 1895); Dial 14:359-61 (June 16,
1893); Pop. Sci. 45:562-63 (Aug. 1894).

194   Mangan, Gordon L.   A review of published research on
        the relationship of some personality variables to ESP
        scoring level.   New York: Parapsychology Foundation,
        1958. 62p (Parapsychological Monographs No. 1) $1.75
        (pap) (Available only from the Foundation)
        This is a concise, technical review of quantitative
studies on the relation of ESP scoring level and various personality and attitude variables.   The variables considered
are intelligence, interest ratings, introversion-extraversion,
expansion-compression, adjustment ratings (obtained from
questionnaires), combinations of personality correlates, attitudes of belief, combination of Rorschach adjustment ratings
with attitudes of belief, combinations of seven Rorschach
signs with attitudes of belief, reactions to frustration, and
value-ratings.   57-item bibliography.   3.   L-C-U.
        JASPR 65:356 (July 1971); JP 23:141-42 (June 1959).

195   Mitchell, T. W.   Medical psychology and psychical re-
        search.   London, Methuen, 1922. 244p OP
        Much of this book by the British physician and psy-
chologist, T. W. Mitchell, was originally published in a
number of papers in the S. P. R. Proceedings.   His main
purpose is to describe "those branches of Medical Psychology which have thrown most light on the problems of Psychical Research" (p. v).   He deals primarily with hypnotism,
hysteria, and--extensively--with multiple personality, about
which he was an acknowledged expert.   The volume contains
his important paper "The appreciation of time by somnam-
bules. "   This book is of particular interest for the light it
sheds on the psychology of mediumship.   Bibliographic footnotes; index.   3.   L-U.
        PSPR 33:673-75, Pt. 88 (1923).
        Lit. Rev. , p567, Mar. 31, 1923; N. Y. TimesBookRev. ,
p18, Apr. 8, 1923; Spectator 130:64 (Jan. 13, 1923).

196 Rosenthal, Robert. Experimenter effects in behavioral
     research. New York: Appleton-Century-Crofts, 1966.
     464p $8.25
       This book, by a Harvard psychologist specializing in
the social psychology of psychological research itself, is included here because it deals with a variable--experimenter
effects--which must be taken into consideration by all the
behavioral sciences, including parapsychology. Moreover,
parapsychology may be the science that best illustrates the
unwitting influence of the experimenter on his results because there is evidence that they can be influenced even when
the experimenter is at a distance from the subject and the
latter has no normal knowledge of the experimenter's wishes
and ideas concerning the outcome of the experiment. Rosenthal includes examples from the parapsychological literature
to illustrate some of his points. 21-page bibliography; name
index; subject index. 3. L-C-U.
       JASPR 63:303-07 (July 1969).
       Am. J. Psychol. 81:120-21 (1968); Am. Sociol. Rev. 33:
459-60 (1968); Aust. J. Psychol. 19:279-80 (1967); Cathol.
Psychol. Rec. 6:55-59 (1968); Choice 4:916 (Oct. 1967); Contemp. Psychol. 13:5-7 (Jan. 1968); Manpower&Appl. Psychol.
2:83 (1968); Psychol. Rec. 17:544 (1967); Psychol. Rep. 19:
339 (1966).

197 Rush, Joseph H. New directions in parapsychological
     research. New York: Parapsychology Foundation,
     1964. 61p (Parapsychological Monographs No. 4) $1.75
     (pap) (Available only from the Foundation)
       This monograph by a physicist who has long been in-
volved in parapsychology sets forth his ideas concerning the
way psi operates. In the first chapter he elaborates on the
associative tendencies of psi phenomena. In the second he
comments on the implications of information theory and their
possible application to problems of parapsychology. He next
discusses the associative facilitation of psi phenomena by the
sensorimotor situation in which they are embedded. He concludes with a discussion of methods for training subjects and
ways of inducing detached states. Some actual experimental
designs are presented. 56-item bibliography. 3. L-C-U.
       IJP 7:99-102 (Win. 1965); JASPR 59:252-54 (July 1965);
JP 29:215 (Sept. 1965); JSPR 43:44 (Mar. 1965).

198 Schmeidler, Gertrude R. ESP in relation to Rorschach
     test evaluation. New York: Parapsychology Founda-
     tion, 1960. 89p (Parapsychological Monographs No. 2)
     $1.75 (pap) (Available only from the Foundation)

In this monograph the author reports research findings based on 1062 college students who were tested for ESP, took the Rorschach test, and indicated whether or not they accepted the possibility of ESP under the experimental conditions. Significant relationships between ESP scoring level, attitude, and personality variables are presented. In the author's words, "General conclusions stated hesitantly about the relation between psychological dynamics and ESP success are: Feelings of constraint, withdrawal or negativism are associated with near-chance ESP scores or with psi-missing; and feelings of free responsiveness are associated with successful ESP scoring" (p. 68). 17-item bibliography. <u>3</u>. L-C-U.

JASPR 55:117-19 (July 1961); JP 25:150-51 (June 1961); JSPR 40:422-24 (Dec. 1960).

REFERENCE BOOKS

Unfortunately, many of the major kinds of reference books, such as bibliographic guides, dictionaries, directories, indexes, etc., have yet to be compiled in the field of parapsychology. In the case of the several bibliographies listed below, some idea of the range of titles relevant to psychical research is presented, but most of the books described are no longer of basic importance except for historical purposes, and in any case are difficult to obtain. Zorab's book is probably the most useful. Other titles belonging in a basic reference collection are the <u>Biographical dictionary of parapsychology</u>, Fodor, and possibly Spence.

<u>Additional books with parapsychology reference material</u>: The combination of <u>Experimental parapsychology</u> (52) and <u>ESP-60</u> (57) provides a fairly comprehensive bibliographic guide and summary of modern quantitative parapsychology beginning with Rhine's work at Duke in the 1930s through 1965. The Rhine-Pratt textbook (58) is useful for reference purposes in that it is a compendium of the facts and methods of modern psi research. Gudas (159) and McConnell (166) are reference guides specifically aimed at students and teachers respectively.

199 Abbot, Ezra. <u>Literature of the doctrine of a future</u>

life: or, A catalogue of works relating to the nature,
origin, and destiny of the soul. In William R. Alger,
The destiny of the soul: A critical history of the doctrine of a future life. 10th ed. Westport, Conn.:
Greenwood, 1968. 2v. $37.50 set (Orig. publ. in
1860 by W. J. Widdleton under title A critical history
of the doctrine of a future life. OP)

Because of its importance for reference, this bibliography is described separately here, though it is a part of
another title listed below (222). The bibliography is comprised of 4977 books in English, German, French, Italian,
Spanish, Dutch, Flemish, Danish, Norwegian, Swedish, He-
brew, and Oriental languages. The titles are briefly annotated and listed chronologically under various subjects.
Those most relevant to psychical research are: Pre-exist-
ence; Death; The intermediate state; The Resurrection; Future life; and Modern "spiritualism or spiritism, ghosts,
etc." Author index; subject index. 3. L-U.
No reviews.

200 Biographical dictionary of parapsychology with directory
     and glossary 1964-1966. (Helene Pleasants, ed.)
     New York: Garrett/Helix, 1964. 371p $9.00
     This volume contains information on living persons
compiled from questionnaire responses, plus searched entries for many historical figures in psychical research. It
is especially valuable because it includes persons famous in
other fields who also had a significant interest in psychical
research, e.g., William James and Henri Bergson. In
such cases it supplements standard reference works where
an interest in psychical research is either not recorded, or
only very briefly. It is also useful in the case of persons
mainly identified with parapsychology for, although their
work is known, there are few sources of biographical information about them. A bibliography for each person is included in his or her entry. There are 467 entries, alphabetically arranged. Although further editions were planned,
this is the only one that has been issued. 44-item glossary.
3. L-C-U.
     IJP 6:363-68 (Sum. 1964); JASPR 59:167-72 (Apr.
1965); JP 29:57-58 (Mar. 1965).
     WilsonLibr.Bull. 39:580 (Mar. 1965).

201 Fodor, Nandor. Encyclopedia of psychic science.
     Foreword to this edition by Leslie Shepard. Preface
     by Sir Oliver Lodge. New Hyde Park, N.Y.: Univer-
     sity Books, 1966. 416p $17.50 (Orig. publ. by

Arthurs Press in 1933. OP)

By a psychoanalyst/psychical researcher, this is a
useful reference work, although limited mainly to historical
material. Alphabetically arranged, it covers terms, publications, people, and events connected with psychical research
and spiritualism. There are survey articles, some broken
down geographically (e.g., spiritualism). Of the scope of
the book Fodor writes: "To the facts of psychical research,
by the exercise of great care, I added, from books and periodicals, many strange accounts which seem to rest on good
authority though, from the experimental viewpoint, wanting in
evidential value. For only by so doing could I hope to illum-
inate the full domain of this coming science. Of occultism,
theosophy and mysticism I steered clear" (p. xxix). Contains
a list of subject headings used. The Foreword to this edition updates some of the information in the book. Bibliographic references given with many entries. 3. A.

JASPR 28:56 (Feb. 1934); JSPR 28:207-08 (Mar. 1934).
Choice 3:1116 (Feb. 1967).

202   Hyre, K. M., and Goodman, Eli. Price guide to the
      occult and related subjects. Los Angeles: Reference
      Guides (11275 Santa Monica Blvd., Los Angeles, Cal.
      90025), 1967. 380p $20.00

This is a list of out-of-print books (arranged alphabetically by author) compiled largely from booksellers' cata-
logs. The compilers say it is "intended to fill a major gap
in the increasingly important field of the occult and meta-
physical--namely, to provide an exhaustive and authoritative
list of the many books in that category. The compilers have
drawn upon numerous and diverse sources--imprints from
both the United States and abroad, and old as well as new
catalogues" (Preface). Useful as a bibliography of psychical
research titles (about half are relevant), as a price guide
for those buying or selling books in this subject area, and
as a buying guide in locating sources of books (the dealers
listing each title and their addresses are given). There are
8,243 citations (author, title, date of publication, bookdealer,
price), but probably a third of these are additional copies.
3.   L-U.

Antiq.Bkmn. 41:12 (Jan. 1, 1968); Extrapolation 9:61-
62 (May 1968).

203   London Spiritualist Alliance. Catalogue of the library
      of the London Spiritualist Alliance. London: The Al-
      liance, 1931. 209p OP (For further information
      apply to: College of Psychic Studies, 10 Queensberry

Place, London SW7 2EB, England)

This catalogue was prepared for the members of the London Spiritualist Alliance (now the College of Psychic Studies). There are two alphabetical listings, by title and by author. Place and date of publication are given a letter signifying the subject under which the book is shelved. The headings used are Spiritualism; Theosophy; Fiction; Works on Swedenborgianism and the New Church; Religious Thought and Mysticism; Psychical Research; Divination, Clairvoyance, Psychometry, Phrenology, Palmistry and Crystal Gazing; Ghosts, Apparitions [and] Hauntings; Dreams, Visions [and] Folklore; Philosophy; Astrology and Astronomy; Psychology, New Thought [and] Therapeutics; Occultism, Magic, Witchcraft [and] Demonology; Biography; Magnetism, Hypnotism [and] Mesmerism; Travel; General Literature not otherwise classified; and Scientific Research. 66-item glossary. 3. U.

No reviews.

204 Naumov, E. K., and Vilenskaya, L. V. Bibliographies on parapsychology (psychoenergetics) and related subjects. Arlington, Va.: Joint Publications Research Service, 1972. 101p $3.00 (Orig. publ. in Moscow in 1971) (Obtainable from National Technical Information Service, Springfield, Va. 22151. Give author, title, date, and JPRS number: 55557)

This bibliography reflects the strong interest in parapsychology in the Soviet Union. It is a listing of "the more important monographs, surveys, and articles on experimental and theoretical studies published in the last 70 years both in special parapsychological journals and in publications from other sources" (p.1). The items are arranged alphabetically by author under several subject areas. In some instances technical literature is listed separately from popular. There are two separate bibliographies, the longest consisting of Russian materials (with English titles) and the other of foreign materials, mainly English, French, Italian, and German. Contains a list of "Principal landmarks in Soviet parapsychology" (20 items). 3. L-C-U.

No reviews.

205 Price, Harry. Short-title catalogue of works on psychical research, spiritualism, magic, psychology, legerdemain and other methods of deception, charlatanism, witchcraft and technical works for the scientific investigation of alleged abnormal phenomena from circa 1450 A.D. to 1929 A.D. London: National

Laboratory of Psychical Research, 1929. (Proceedings of the Laboratory, v. 1, pt. II, April, 1929, 67-
422) OP

Price says "the main purpose of the Library of the
National Laboratory of Psychical Research is to assist the
serious investigator in detecting the psychical imposter, at
the same time enabling him to recognize a genuine phenomenon if and when he sees it" (p. 73). In the introduction Price
describes the collection in general and points out titles of
particular interest. There are over 6000 items in a single
alphabetical order. The most complete information on a
given title is under the author entry (title, place and date
of publication and sometimes a few words describing the
contents if not obvious) or, if the author is not known, under
the title. No entry is given under the title if the author is
known. Subject entries refer the reader to author or title
entries. There is an "Addenda of books relating to Nostra-
damus" (pp. 401-422). Illustrated. 3. U.
No reviews.

206   Price, Harry. Supplement to short-title catalogue of
      works on psychical research, alleged abnormal phe-
      nomena, spiritualism, magic, witchcraft, legerdemain,
      charlatanism and astrology from 1472 A.D. to the
      present day. London: University of London Council
      for Psychical Investigation, 1935. 112p (Bulletin I of
      the Council) OP

This is a supplement to the preceding title (205). It
contains an additional 2500 items acquired since 1929. These
volumes were added to the Research Library of the University of London Council for Psychical Investigation, which was
formed to take over the work of the National Laboratory of
Psychical Research. Included are "verbatim reports of
cases investigated by the University Council or the National
Laboratory" (p. 7), among them Rudi Schneider, the physical
medium; Fred Marion, the stage telepathist; and Jef, the
"Talking mongoose." As in the main catalogue, there is a
single alphabetical order of authors (or titles if the author
is not known) and subjects. Illustrated. 3. U.
No reviews.

207   Society for Psychical Research (London). Proceedings
      and Journal. Combined index to Phantasms of the
      living, v. 1 and 2; Proceedings S.P.R., v. 1-26
      (1882/83-1912/13); Journal S.P.R., v. 1-15 (1884/85-
      1911-12); and Proceedings A.S.P.R., v. 1 (1885/89).
      With a table of contents of Proceedings and classified

list of contents of Proceedings and Journal to June
1932, compiled by Theodore Besterman. Washington,
D.C.: Carrollton Press, 1972. ca.600p $30.00;
$27.50 (pap) (Orig. publ., in three parts, in London
by R. B. Johnson, 1904; in Glasgow by R. Maclehose,
1914; and in Proceedings S.P.R., v. 41, 1932)
This one-volume index is compiled from volumes and
papers already published by the S.P.R. The new format
should facilitate searching. It is a must for those who own
the periodicals indexed. For those who do not, it will be
valuable as a selection aid since many of the issues indexed
are still available from the S.P.R. The recent reprinting
of Phantasms of the living (229) enhances its usefulness because its index entries are much more detailed than those in
Phantasms itself. 3. L-U.
No reviews.

208 Spence, Lewis. An encyclopaedia of occultism: A com-
     pendium of information on the occult sciences, occult
     personalities, psychic science, magic, demonology,
     spiritism, mysticism, and metaphysics. New Hyde
     Park, N.Y.: University Books, 1960. 440p $15.00
     (Orig. publ. by Routledge in 1920. OP)
This alphabetically-arranged encyclopedia contains
2500 entries. It is more detailed than Fodor's (201), but
since there is not much duplication both would be useful.
Fodor covers more psychical research, while Spence concentrates on occultism, drawing heavily on the works of Arthur Edward Waite. There are headings for countries, organizations, and periodicals as well as for persons and
terms. It was compiled "because excursions into the literature of the occult ... led me to the belief that popular mis-
conceptions concerning its several branches were many and
varied. Regarding definitions there did not seem to be any
substantial agreement, and application to ... works of reference ... resulted in disappointment" (p.vii). Illustrated;
"Select bibliography" (68 items); subject headings index. 3.
M-L-C-U.
     JASPR 15:247 (Apr. 1921).

209 Swarthmore College. Library. Catalogue of the John
     William Graham collection of literature of psychic
     science. Swarthmore, Pa.: John William Graham
     Fund for the Study of Psychic Science, 1950. 43p OP
John William Graham, a Quaker and Professor of
Quaker Principles and History at Swarthmore College, was
one of the first of his sect to recognize the spiritual aspects

of psi experience as being related to the voices, visions, healings, and other experiences traditionally associated with mysticism. This catalog of the special collection of 312 books at Swarthmore reflecting his interests consists of author and title listings. Under each author's name are given his titles, their place and date of publication, and a one-sentence annotation followed by at least two numbers, but sometimes as many as 20, indicating the subjects dealt with. There is a key to the 102 subject numbers used and a brief illustrated section on the contributions to psychical research of Robert Hare of the University of Pennsylvania. Illustrated; 143-item glossary; title index. 3. L-C-U.
   No reviews.

210 Techter, David. A bibliography and index of psychic
     research and related topics for the year 1962. Chi-
     cago: Illinois Society for Psychic Research, 1963.
     81p $2.00 (pap) (Available only from the author: P.
     O. Box 362, Highland Park, Ill. 60035)
     This pioneer index was compiled by an archaeologist with access to the Chicago Natural History Museum Library and the John Crehar Library. It was "inspired largely by the example of the annual bibliography of vertebrate paleontology" (p.1). It includes both popular and scientific books, articles, reviews, published correspondence, etc., in English dealing with psychical research in its broadest application which appeared during 1962. Subjects were included even if only tangentially related. There is heavy emphasis on ethnological materials. Primarily an author arrangement, but there is a subject index. (Techter also compiled indexes for 1963 and 1964; they are out of print. 1965 was compiled but never printed because of lack of funds.) 3. U.
     IJP 6:144 (Win. 1964) and IJP 8:152 (Win. 1966).
     Abstr. FolkloreStud. 5:66-67 (Spr. 1967).

211 Zorab, George. Bibliography of parapsychology. New
     York: Garrett/Helix, 1957. 127p $3.75. First sup-
     plement publ. in Les Cahiers de la Tour Saint-Jacques,
     No. 9, 1960 (Available only from La Tour Saint-
     Jacques, 53 Rue Saint-Jacques, Paris V, France)
     This volume compiled by a Dutch parapsychologist is a bibliography of books and periodical articles from earliest times through 1954 arranged by subject. The major headings used are Historical and general, Mental phenomena (ESP), Paranormal phenomena manifesting in sensory and motor automatisms, Physical phenomena, Haunting phenomena, Paraphysiology, Quantitative experiments, Parapsychology

and the sciences and disciplines, Reference books, and Bibliographies. There are finer subject categories within these headings and under each the items are listed by author in chronological order. Several languages are included: Dutch, English, French, German, Italian, and Spanish. The format of the supplement is the same and carries the bibliography through 1959. Author index; subject index. 3. L-C-U.

JP 21:238-39 (Sept. 1957); JSPR 39:198-99 (Mar. 1958).

J. Nerv. &Ment. Dis. 128:566-67 (1959).

RELIGION AND PSI PHENOMENA

Psi phenomena have been related to religion in a number of ways. One approach is typified by Hardy and by Neff, who both suggest that psi is at the base of various religious phenomena, e.g., prayer and healing. Thurston points to the close relationship between the physical phenomena of mediumship and those of sanctity. Crookall represents another approach which stresses similarities between mystical and parapsychic states. Both Ducasse and Smith emphasize the religious implications of survival, while Johnson and Tyrrell are both concerned with the significance for religion of all the varied aspects of psi phenomena.

Additional books with material on religion and psi phenomena: The idea that psi phenomena are the basis of religion is presented by Lang (33) and Smith (179). The relation between mystical states and psi is touched on in James (12), Laski (14), the Bucke Memorial Society volume (32), The Psychic force (87), and LeShan (129). Unorthodox healing, a phenomenon common to both religion and psychical research, is considered by Feilding (101), Weatherhead (280), West (281), and Worrall (282), and from the Catholic viewpoint by Thurston (79), Omez (171), and Haynes (276). The religious significance of psi phenomena is discussed by James (85), Rhine (130), Barrett (151), Tyrrell (182), Vyvyan (184) and in the book edited by Garrett (249). The books in the John William Graham collection (209) stress religion and psychical research.

212 Crookall, Robert. The interpretation of cosmic and

mystical experiences. Foreword by J. D. Pearce-
Higgins. Cambridge: James Clarke, 1969. 175p $4.50,
£3.00; Greenwood, S.C.: Attic Press, 1969. $4.75
  This is a compilation of passages taken from the literature of mysticism and of psychical research illustrating
that the experience of "at-oneness" usually associated with
mysticism is also found in various manifestations of the paranormal: mediumship, clairvoyance, out-of-the-body experiences, experiences under anesthetics and at the time of
death, and experiences supposedly undergone after death as
communicated through mediums. Crookall discusses the various experiences and analyzes the conditions producing them.
There are five appendices which deal primarily with conditions favoring the experiences described in the book, the
longest one entitled "Analogies between mystical and psychical experiences." In what he calls a "glossary" he defines
and differentiates between the terms denoting the various
"bodies," e.g., astral body, the double, etc.   369-item bibliography; index. 2. L-C-U.
  JASPR 66:423-24 (Oct. 1972); PR 3:16-17 (Sept.-Oct.
1972).

213 Ducasse, C. J. A philosophical scrutiny of religion.
    New York: Ronald Press, 1952. 441p OP
  The author writes that this book "considers the various forms religion can take; the essence common to all its
forms; the variety of its manifestations; its vital functions,
both personal and social; and the evils which, historically,
have infested religion. It describes and comments on the
typical religious experiences, including conversion, prayer,
and mystical illumination. And it analyzes ... concepts
such as those of the supernatural, the miraculous, the magi-
cal; divinity, sin, sacredness, worship; soul and spirit;
superstition, belief, faith, knowledge; evil, free will, immortality" (p. v). In addition to a chapter on survival, there
are references to psi throughout the book, particularly in
the chapters on prayer, mysticism, and witchcraft. Bibliographic footnotes; index. 2. L-C-U.
  JASPR 47:119-22 (July 1953).
  Ann. Am. Acad. 288:192 (July 1953); Christ. Cent. 70:
547 (May 6, 1953); U. S. Q. BookRev. 9:172 (June 1953).

214 Hardy, Alister. The divine flame: An essay towards a
    natural history of religion. London: Collins, 1966.
    254p OP
  In this sequel to the Living stream (215), the British
biologist Alister Hardy, in the Gifford Lectures for 1964-65,

urges that religious experience be investigated by science in
the same manner as any other natural phenomenon. He examines the anthropological and psychological roots of religion
and says that neither can "explain" it. He asks whether the
phenomena of mystical experience, inspiration, and faith
healing belong only to man's subconscious mind or whether
they indicate an "extrasensory contact with a Power beyond
the self." In a chapter entitled "The importance of psychical research," he suggests that these basically theological
problems be studied as an aspect of psychical research.
Man's contact with God is seen as extrasensory in nature
and prayer as man's method of lighting the "divine flame"
in his nature. He urges that prayer be put to experimental
test. Bibliographic footnotes; index. 2. M-L-C-U.
        JASPR 62:217-22 (Apr. 1968); JSPR 44:189-95 (Dec.
1967).
        TimesLit. Suppl., p514, June 8, 1967; Zygon 4:105-
06 (Mar. 1969).

215 Hardy, Alister. The living stream: Evolution and man.
        London: Collins, 1965. 292p £1.50; New York: Harper
        & Row, 1967. $6.95
        In the Gifford Lectures of 1963-64 the author outlines
evolutionary theory from its beginning to the present, with
emphasis on the as yet unsolved problems. In the final two
chapters he deals with psychical research. In the first of
these, "Biology and telepathy," he presents a review of the
evidence and indicates why he thinks psychical research is
important. In the last chapter, "Natural theology and the
evolutionary scheme," he suggests the possible role that
telepathy and religion may play in the process of evolution.
He concludes: "If only one per cent of the money spent
upon the physical and biological sciences could be spent upon
investigation of religious experience and upon psychical research, it might not be long before a new age of faith dawned
upon the world" (p.285). Illustrated; bibliographical footnotes;
index. 2. M-L-C-U.
        JASPR 61:365-69 (Oct. 1967); JP 31:300-02 (Dec.
1967).
        Booklist 64:96 (Sept. 15, 1967); Christ. Cent. 84:1161
(Sept. 13, 1967); Choice 4:1231 (Jan. 1968); Geogr. J. 132:
311 (June 1966); Kirkus 35:628 (May 15, 1967); Sci. Books 3:
136 (Sept. 1967); TimesLit. Suppl., p1199, Dec. 23, 1965;
Zygon 4:105-06 (Mar. 1969).

216 Johnson, Raynor C. The imprisoned splendour: An ap-
        proach to reality, based upon the significance of data

drawn from the fields of natural science, psychical
research and mystical experience. Foreword by Leslie D. Weatherhead. London: Hodder, 1953. 424p
£1.75; Wheaton, Ill.: Theosophical Publishing House,
1971. $2.95 (pap)

The first part of this book presents the data of natural
science, in part two the data of psychical research, in part
three those of mysticism, and in part four a summary of the
foregoing and Johnson's views on "the significance of the
whole." The longest section is the one on psychical research;
there are chapters on telepathy and clairvoyance, precognition
and retrocognition, psychometry, apparitions and hauntings,
out-of-the-body experiences, materializations, PK and poltergeists, and the survival problem. In presenting the data the
author's goal was to ask what can be inferred from them
about "our environment, our nature, and our destiny" (p. xi).
Bibliographic footnotes; "books for further reading" (33
items); index. 2. A.

JASPR 49:120-23 (July 1955); JP 18:51-64 (Mar. 1954);
JSPR 37:206 (Nov.-Dec. 1953).

217 Neff, H. Richard. Psychic phenomena and religion:
ESP, prayer, healing, survival. Philadelphia: West-
minster, 1971. 176p $3.50 (pap)

The author, a Presbyterian minister, developed an
interest in psi as an outgrowth of unusual phenomena reported to him during his ministry. This led him to "investigate the area of psychic experience to see whether it is a
part of reality or a psychological aberration" (p. 10). After
a general introductory chapter on the evidence for ESP, he
presents three chapters on those areas where religion and
psi overlap: prayer, healing, and survival. He concludes
with a summary chapter in which he relates religion and psi
under 11 points. He also discusses the religious significance
of four typical reactions to the question whether or not psi
exists. Bibliography by chapter at the end of the book (144
items). 1. A.

Libr.J. 97:884 (Mar. 1, 1972).

218 Smith, Alson J. Immortality: The scientific evidence.
New York: New American Library, 1967. 174p $.75
(pap) (Orig. publ. by Prentice-Hall in 1954. Hardcover ed. OP)

A Methodist minister, the author points out in the introduction that his motive in writing this book was his conviction that "the lost life of the Church can only be restored
through a verification by science through experiment, of the

psychic phenomena on which the church was originally built"
(pp. 12-13). He feels that unorthodox healing and survival
are particularly relevant. He summarizes some of the major
types of evidence for survival and describes various keystone
cases of psychical research, among them the S. P. R. census
of hallucinations, Mrs. Piper, Mrs. Leonard's book tests,
the cross correspondences, Patience Worth, and the experimental work of Rhine and Soal. The last third of the book
deals with the relation of psi phenomena to religion. Bibliographic footnotes; index. 1. M-L-C-U.
> JASPR 49:163-64 (Oct. 1955); JSPR 38:35-36 (Mar.
1955).
> Booklist 50:290 (Apr. 1, 1954); J. PastoralCare 13:
120-21 (1959); Kirkus 21:794 (Dec. 15, 1953); Libr. Jnl. 79:
385 (Feb. 15, 1954); Publ. Wkly 192:70 (Sept. 11, 1957).

219 Thouless, Robert H. An introduction to the psychology
     of religion. 3d ed. Cambridge and New York: Cam-
     bridge University Press, 1971. 152p $7.50; $2.75
     (pap) (Orig. publ. by Macmillan in 1923. OP)
     The first edition of this work by a British psycholo-
gist/parapsychologist would not find a place in this bibliography for it contained no mention of psychical research.
However, in this new edition, which has been so radically
revised as to almost merit a different title, there is a chapter devoted to psychical research and religion. The chapters
on mysticism, meditation, and prayer also contain material
relevant to parapsychology. This book shows how psychical
research, although a field in itself, is also interconnected
with many other disciplines, religion being one of the major
ones. Bibliography at the end of each chapter (153 items,
15 in chapter on psi). index. 2. A.
> JSPR 46:46 (Mar. 1972).
> Cathol. World 118:282 (Nov. 1923); DetroitNews, p23,
Dec. 9, 1923; J. Relig. 3:431 (July 1923); N. Y. TimesBook
Rev., p26, July 29, 1923; Nature 111:805 (June 16, 1923);
Spectator 130:559 (Mar. 31, 1923); SpringfieldRepub., p12,
Apr. 10, 1923; TimesLit. Suppl., p491, July 19, 1923; Wis.
Libr. Bull. 19:405 (July 1923).

220 Thurston, Herbert. The physical phenomena of mysti-
     cism. (J. H. Crehan, ed.). London: Burns and
     Oates, 1952. 419p OP
     A Catholic priest, Thurston had a lifelong interest in
psi phenomena and in what the Roman Catholic Church deemed
to be miraculous. He was particularly concerned with the
need to distinguish the manifestations of genuine sanctity from

the purely psychic. This book is a collection of Thurston's
previously published and unpublished papers, mostly on physical phenomena, which were put together after his death. He
discusses levitation, telekinesis, paranormal lights, clairvoyance, and miraculous phenomena such as stigmata, the absence of cadaveric rigidity, living without eating, and the
multiplication of food. Bibliographic footnotes; index. 2.
M-L-C-U.
        JASPR 47:122-25 (July 1953); JSPR 36:718-23 (Nov.-
Dec. 1952).
        ChurchQ. Rev. 153:525-27 (Oct.-Dec. 1952).

221   Tyrrell, G. N. M.   The nature of human personality.
       Foreword by H. H. Price. London: Allen and Unwin,
       1954. 122p OP
       This is Tyrrell's final book and it was viewed by him
as a sequel to his The personality of man (182). He points
out in the preface that whereas the latter presents the facts
of psychical research, the principal object of this one is to
consider the significance of this evidence and "to probe as
deeply as possible into its meaning" (p. vii). In the foreword
H. H. Price points out that it can also be seen as a sequel
to another of Tyrrell's books, Homo Faber (1951; published
in the U.S. under the title Man the maker), in which he analyzed the reasons why the facts about psi are psychologically
unacceptable. The present book is the final thought of a
man who was a brilliant synthesizer of the myriad data of
psychical research. Bibliographic footnotes; index. 2. M-
L-C-U.
        JP 19:64-68 (Mar. 1955); JSPR 38:30-31 (Mar. 1955).

SPIRITUALISM

       This group of books is about the spiritualistic move-
ment out of which psychical research was born. Although
primarily of only historical interest to parapsychology today,
it was a fascinating period in its own right. Podmore's book
is the classic history of spiritualism. Fornell's survey of
the highlights of the movement is probably the best introduction, while Nelson provides a different approach from the
viewpoint of sociology.

       Additional books with material on spiritualism: A

substantial amount of material on the history of spiritualism
is presented in two additional books by Podmore, Studies in
psychical research (173) and From Mesmer to Christian Science (278).   A biographical approach is provided by Wright
(42) and a critical review of some of the principal figures
of the movement is given by Hall (45).   A sensitive and informed presentation of a positive position toward spiritualism
today can be found in the book by Beard (243).

222   Alger, William R.   The destiny of the soul: A critical
        history of the doctrine of a future life.   10th ed.
        Westport, Conn.: Greenwood, 1968. 2v. $37.50 set
        (Orig. publ. by W. J. Widdleton in 1860 under title
        A critical history of the doctrine of a future life. OP)
        With the advent of psychical research, systematic at-
tempts were initiated to investigate the possibility of life after death.   Prior to that it was a matter of faith, revelation,
and acceptance of theological doctrines on immortality.   One
of the most thorough examinations of the latter throughout
the world and from the beginnings of recorded history to the
middle of the 19th century is this massive work of scholarship compiled by William Rounsville Alger, a Unitarian
clergyman and literary scholar.   Much of his life went into
writing and revising its 10 editions.   Appended to this work
is an extensive bibliography by Ezra Abbot which is described
above (199).   Bibliographic references incorporated in the
text; index.   3.   L-U.
        No reviews.

223   Brown, Slater.   The heyday of spiritualism.   New York:
        Hawthorn, 1970. 264p $7.95;   New York: Pocket Books,
        1972. $1.25 (pap)
        This book provides good popular coverage of the his-
tory of spiritualism in America from its beginnings until
1870.   There are two chapters on animal magnetism and
single chapters on traveling clairvoyance, the Shakers, the
Stratford poltergeist, trance rhetoric (spirit teachings), and
spirit manifestations in general.   There are also chapters
devoted to individual mediums: Swedenborg, Andrew Jackson
Davis, the Fox family, John Murray Spear, the Koons family,
the Davenport brothers, Charles H. Foster, and D. D. Home.
Illustrated; bibliography by chapter at the end of the book (84
items); index.   1.   M-L-C-U.
        JSPR 46:68-69 (Mar. 1971).

224   Fornell, Earl W.   The unhappy medium: Spiritualism

and the life of Margaret Fox.   Ann Arbor, Mich.:
University Microfilms, xerocopy, OP No. 200, 0824.
204p $11.00 (Orig. publ. by University of Texas
Press in 1964. OP)
     The author says he has tried "to illuminate what ap-
pear to be representative episodes, as illustrations of what
must have been the larger story of spiritualism in America"
(p. viii).   He presents much useful information on the Fox
family (Margaret Fox in particular) and the rise of spiritualism in the 1850's not otherwise readily accessible.   The social and political impact of spiritualism is stressed.   There
are chapters on unusual topics such as "Congress and spiritualism, " "Lincoln and the spirits, " and "Spirits in the
courts. "   The heavy emphasis on newspaper accounts supplements the material found in traditional psychical research
sources.   Illustrated; bibliographic footnotes; 137-item bibliography; index.   2.   A.
     JASPR 60:295-96 (July 1966); JSPR 43:321-22 (June
1966).
     Am. Hist. Rev. 71:695 (Jan. 1966); Choice 2:176 (May
1965); J. Am. Hist. 52:393 (Sept. 1965); Libr. J. 90:112 (Jan.
1, 1965).

225 Gutteridge, Joseph.   Autobiography.   In Valerie E.
     Chancellor (ed.), Master and artisan in Victorian
     England: The diary of William Andrews and the auto-
     biography of Joseph Gutteridge.   London: Evelyn,
     Adams and Mackay, 1969. 160 of 237p £2.50; Clifton,
     N. J.: Kelley, 1971. $11.00
     Although histories of spiritualism--good and bad--
abound, we have too few firsthand accounts of the period
when it flourished.   For an "inside view, " the autobiography
of Joseph Gutteridge has recently been published.   In simple
language Gutteridge, a ribbon weaver, tells how he was attracted to spiritualism and how it answered his doubts and
questionings.   He believed it to be "the only means of con-
verting dogged, hard-headed Materialists to a belief in Immortality, or a continued existence for the spirit of man
after the cessation of the physical life" (p. 171).   This is an
interesting human document of the mid-19th century inter-
woven with the life of the times.   2.   L-C-U.
     JASPR 64:229-30 (Apr. 1970).

226 Hardinge, Emma.   Modern American spiritualism: A
     twenty years' record of the communion between earth
     and the world of spirits.   New introduction by Eric J.
     Dingwall.   New Hyde Park, N. Y.: University Books,

1970. 560p $12.50 (Orig. publ. by the author in
1870. OP)
This book, long out of print, is of great historic interest, telling the story of spiritualism when it was at its
peak. The author was a medium, inspirational speaker, and
champion of spiritualism. This book is a kind of travelogue,
being geographically arranged, and is an account of her
visits to various centers of spiritualistic activity all over
the United States and of the phenomena she observed. In
the new introduction Dingwall says: "This book was the
most detailed account of the birth, development, and progress
of Spiritualism in America ever to appear up to the date of
its publication. Full of detail regarding the lives and activities of the early mediums, it reprints numerous passages
from the contemporary press and, as the author herself puts
it, it fills 'an orderly place in the compendious history of
the whole movement' " (p. xiv). Illustrated; bibliographic
references incorporated in the text. 3. L-U.
No reviews.

227 Nelson, Geoffrey K. Spiritualism and society. New
York: Schocken, 1969. 307p $7.50
This is an examination by a British sociologist of the
religious and social factors at work in the rise of modern
spiritualism. He deals with its rapid growth in the United
States in the mid-19th century, as contrasted with the slower
spread in Britain. He writes: "My initial interest in Spiritualism took the form of a study of psychic phenomena, and
out of this developed an interest in the origins of Spiritualism
as a religious movement" (p. ix). He provides the first history of the development of organization within the spiritualistic movement and the growth and development of the movement
per se. The last half of the book is on spiritualism in the
20th century, a topic seldom treated in book form. He also
analyzes the spiritualist movement in terms of sociological
theory. Detailed statistics of British spiritualism are presented in an appendix. This book is based on Nelson's master's and doctoral theses accepted by the University of London. 14-page bibliography by broad topic; index. 2. M-L-
C-U.
JASPR 64:227-30 (Apr. 1970); PR 1:16 (Sept.-Oct.
1970).
Christ. Cent. 86:1044 (Aug. 6, 1969); ChurchHist. 39:
269-70 (June 1970); J. Sci. Stud. Relig. 9:76-77 (Spr. 1970);
Libr. J. 94:3070 (Sept. 15, 1969); TimesLit. Suppl., p707,
June 26, 1969.

228   Podmore, Frank.   Mediums of the 19th century.   Intro-
         duction by Eric J. Dingwall.   New Hyde Park, N.Y.:
         University Books, 1963.   2v. $20.00   (Orig. publ. by
         Methuen in 1902 under title Modern spiritualism.   2v.
         OP)
         Podmore was a member of the early group of S. P. R.
psychical researchers and his work has always been highly
regarded because of his objectivity and thoroughness.   In the
new introduction to this edition Eric J. Dingwall says, "this
work is not only Podmore's most important contribution to
the subject of psychical research: it is the most important
general history of the subject ever written and for the period
with which it deals is not likely to be surpassed" (p. xvii).
In four books, the first describes spiritualistic phenomena
which occurred before the rise of spiritualism as a movement, e. g., poltergeists, clairvoyance, mesmerism.   Book
II is on early American spiritualism, the third on spiritualism in England, and the last is entitled "Problems of mediumship"; it includes chapters on D. D. Home, Stainton
Moses, and Mrs. Piper.   Bibliographic footnotes; index.   2.
M-L-C-U.
         JSPR 44:201-06 (Dec. 1967); PSPR 17:389-403, Pt.45,
(1903).
         Athenaeum 2:761 (Dec. 6, 1902); Dial 34:79-82 (Feb.
1, 1903); Nation 76:158 (Feb. 19, 1903); Quar.Rev. 198:211-
29 (July 1903).

                        SPONTANEOUS PSI PHENOMENA

         Some books in this section contain examples of many
different types of spontaneous psi experiences, while others
deal only with one specific type.   Several of the titles are
classics that are still relevant today, e. g., Phantasms of
the living and the works of Prince, Sidgwick, and Tyrrell.
Collections containing some recent cases are those by
MacKenzie, L. E. Rhine, and Stevenson.   Two contrasting
views on the best methods for studying spontaneous psi experiences are represented by the latter two books.

         Additional books with material on spontaneous psi
phenomena: Descriptions of cases are found in Lang (33),
Bennett (71), MacKenzie (76), Salter (78), Barrett (152),
Knight (164), Murphy (168), Myers (169,170), Tyrrell (183),

Baird (242), and Richmond (263). Specific types of spontaneous psi phenomena are illustrated with examples in the following: experiences of Australian aborigines (35), veridical
dreams (133), precognition (134, 136, 137, 138), retrocognition
(135), in the psychoanalytic situation (140), experiences of
children in the family situation (150), psychokinesis (188),
and deathbed experiences (258). Discussions of spontaneous
cases are included in two Parapsychology Foundation Proceedings (91, 92) and in books by Broad (154), Dingwall and
Hall (74), Heywood (161), and West (185).

229   Gurney, Edmund, Myers, Frederic W. H., and Pod-
      more, Frank. Phantasms of the living. Introduction
      by Leonard R. N. Ashley. Gainesville, Fla.:
      Scholars' Facsimiles and Reprints, 1970. 2v. $47.50
      (Orig. publ. by Trübner for the Society for Psychical
      Research in 1886. OP)
      This is one of the major classics of psychical re-
search. Although, as the title indicates, it deals with apparitions, it does so within the context of telepathy, which is
the main subject of the book. The authors claim "to show
1) that experimental telepathy exists, and 2) that apparitions
at death are a result of something beyond chance; whence it
follows 3) that these experimental and these spontaneous
cases of the action of mind on mind are in some way allied"
(p. xii). It is primarily a massive compilation of evidence
rather than theory. The authors deal exhaustively with the
canons of evidence and the counterhypotheses to telepathy.
It is still one of the major sources of instances of spontaneous psi (702 cases) as well as one of the most complete records of early ESP experiments. Contains a theoretical paper by Myers on "A suggested mode of psychical interaction."
Table of cases; bibliographic footnotes; index. 3. L-C-U.
      JASPR 15:492-93 (Oct. 1921).
      Repr. Bull. 16:8 (Mar.-Apr. 1971); Self-culture, p511-
15, Mar. 1898.

230   Jaffé, Aniela. Apparitions and precognition: A study
      from the point of view of C. G. Jung's analytical
      psychology. Foreword by C. G. Jung. New Hyde
      Park, N.Y.: 1963. 214p $7.50
      In this study the author, Jung's personal secretary
during the last six years of his life, presents a collection
of more than 1200 spontaneous cases reported by readers
of a Swiss popular magazine and sent to Jung. Jaffé made
no attempt to ascertain whether or not the experiences were

veridical, nor does she analyze them from the point of view
of the light they might shed on the nature of psi.   Rather,
they are treated, as the author says, as "wonder tales."
She points out that "they are, from the psychological stand-
point, archetypal, i. e., they recur always and everywhere
and are part of the general experience of mankind.   They
appear to correspond to the basic structure of the psyche"
(p. 13).   The experiences are presented according to the
various archetypes they illustrate.   Bibliographic footnotes;
index.   2.   L-C-U.

IJP 6:227-40 (Spr. 1964); JASPR 58:230-33 (July 1964);
JSPR 42:303-06 (June 1964).

Can. J. Theol.   10:144-46 (Apr. 1964).

231   Jung, C. G.   Memories, dreams, reflections.   Re-
      corded and ed. by Aniela Jaffé.   Trans. by Richard
      and Clara Winston.   New York: Pantheon, 1963.   398p
      $10.00;   New York: Random, n. d. $2.95 (pap)   (Orig.
      publ. in German under title Erinnerungen, Traϋme,
      Gedanken)

In this autobiographical work Jung describes his en-
counters with the paranormal: personal experiences of telepathy, precognition, PK, apparitions, haunts, and poltergeists.   One of the most dramatic occurred in the presence
of Freud and apparently was an outgrowth of Jung's relationship with him.   He describes the séances he engaged in with
his family for nearly two years.   Of them he writes, "This
was the one great experience which wiped out all my earlier
philosophy and made it possible for me to achieve a psychological point of view.   I had discovered some objective facts
about the human psyche" (p. 107).   His observations on the
results of these mediumistic experiments were the subject
of his doctoral thesis.   Jung also touches on his theories
concerning psi phenomena and survival of death.   Illustrated;
26-item glossary of Jungian terms; bibliography of his works.
1.   A.

IJP 5:427-52 (Aut. 1963); JASPR 58:221-27 (July 1964);
JSPR 42:163-80 (Dec. 1963).

Am. Imago 21:187 (1964); Am. J. Psychiat.   120:616
(1963/64); Am. J. Psychother.   19:153 (1965); Arch. Gen. Psychiat.   9:189-90 (1963); Atl. Mon.   211:130 (June 1963); Br. J.
Psychol.   55:233 (1964); Can. Psychiat. Assoc. J.   9:272 (1964);
Christ. Cent.   80:619 (May 8, 1963); Contemp. Psychol.   9:262-
63 (June 1964); Economist 208:268 (July 20, 1963); Int. J.
Psychoanal.   45:450-55 (1964); J. Anal. Psychol.   8:173-75 (1963);
J. Relig. & Health 3:289-90 (1963/64); Libr. J.   88:2506 (June
15, 1963); Listener 70:85 (July 18, 1963); Lit. & Psychol.   15:

57-64 (1965); Ment. Health 23:108-09 (1964); Midstream 9:99
(Dec. 1963); N.Y. Her. Trib. Books, p1, May 12, 1963; N.Y.
TimesBookRev., p3, May 19, 1963; NewStatesman 66:48
(July 12, 1963); NewYorker 40:155 (May 23, 1964); Pastoral
Psychol. 14:61-62 (1963/64); Psychoanal. Q. 33:561-66 and
567-74 (1964); Sat. Rev. 46:23 (June 1, 1963); Sci. Am. 209:
283 (Sept. 1963); Tablet, p841, Aug. 3, 1963; Time 81:100
(May 10, 1963); TimesLit. Suppl., p592, Aug. 2, 1963; Va. Q.
Rev. 39:cxxxix (Aut. 1963); YoungReadersRev. 1:9 (June 1965).

232   Lang, Andrew.   The book of dreams and ghosts.   New
      York: AMS, 1970. 301p $10.00;   Hollywood, Cal.:
      Newcastle [dist. by Herder and Herder], 1972. $2.95
      (pap) (Orig. publ. by Longmans, Green in 1897. OP)
      This volume consists of narratives of various psychic
experiences (veridical dreams and visions, ghosts, and
hauntings), beginning with types that are quite familiar to
those which are strikingly unusual.   Lang says, "This book
does not pretend to be a convincing, but merely an illustrative collection of evidence" (p. vii).   He treats the accounts
as examples of folklore.   He includes many legendary stories
"because the old legends ... show how the fancy of periods
less critical than ours dealt with such facts as are now reported in a dull undramatic manner" (p. viii).   A critical
discussion of the historical sources of these cases is provided.   Bibliographic footnotes.   2.   L-C-U.
      JASPR 65:355 (July 1971); PSPR 13:616-18, Pt. 33
(1898).
      Athenaeum 110:322 (Sept. 4, 1897); Bookman 7:67-68
(Mar. 1898); Bookman[Lond.] 13:20 (Oct. 1897); Critic 32
[n. s. 29]:40 (Jan. 15, 1898).

233   MacKenzie, Andrew.   Apparitions and ghosts: A
      modern study.   Foreword by G. W. Lambert.   Lon-
      don: Barker, 1971. 180p £1.75;   New York: Popular
      Library, 1972. $.75 (pap)
      In the introduction MacKenzie speaks of the desira-
bility of publishing spontaneous cases frequently, a maxim
he himself is following, for this is the third book of this
type he has published (see 76 and 234).   This collection, as
that of G. N. M. Tyrrell (241), is confined to spontaneous
cases of the apparition type.   The accounts were sent to
the author in response to a request he made on BBC television and in the popular press.   He received 97 cases in
all, of which 50 are reported in this book.   Where possible
he investigated the cases, either in person or by mail.   An
interesting feature is that after describing each experience,

he gives references to similar cases in the older literature.
In the concluding chapter he describes the patterns charac-
terizing the cases he has presented.   Bibliographic references
incorporated in the text; index.   1.   H-S-M-L.
          JASPR 66:419-23 (Oct. 1972); JSPR 46:127-36 (June
1971).
          TimesLit. Suppl., p277, Mar. 5, 1971.

234   MacKenzie, Andrew.   Frontiers of the unknown: The in-
        sights of psychical research.   Introduction by C. D.
        Broad.   London: Barker, 1968. 208p £1.50; New
        York: Popular Library, 1970. $.75 (pap)
          This is a collection of spontaneous psi experiences of
many types: poltergeists, precognition, telepathy, clairvoyance, and apparitions.   Many are well-authenticated--some
old and some recent.   Where possible the author adds further
details of his own to the previously published cases.   Mac-
Kenzie believes that the study of spontaneous psi phenomena
"has not had the attention it deserves.   It is in an effort to
restore the balance that I have concentrated in the last few
years on the study of cases in which there is strong evidence
that things do happen in a way for which it is hard to supply
a natural explanation" (p. 25).   Illustrated; bibliographic references incorporated in the text; index.   1.   S-M-L.
          JSPR 44:410-12 (Dec. 1968).

235   Prince, Walter Franklin.   Noted witnesses for psychic
        occurrences.   Introduction by Gardner Murphy.   New
        Hyde Park, N.Y.: University Books, 1963. 336p
        $10.00; New York: Olympia, 1972, under title They
        saw beyond. $1.45 (pap) (Orig. publ. by the Boston
        Society for Psychic Research in 1928. OP)
          This book by a noted American psychical researcher
is a collection of spontaneous psi experiences occurring to
170 prominent men and women.   Prince deliberately collected
the experiences of well-known persons not because they are
necessarily more reliable than the average person, but because "the reader is ... generally in a better position to
judge for himself whether the narrator is a romancer or
not, if that narrator is a person of prominence" (p. 5).
Prince also felt that such persons "are less likely uncon-
sciously to exaggerate and elaborate their experiences, and
they are more protected from the temptation to invent" (p. 6).
Frontispiece; bibliographic footnotes; name index; index of
phenomena.   1.   M-L-C-U.
          JSPR 42:78-81 (June 1963).

236   Rhine, Louisa E.   ESP in life and lab: Tracing hidden
      channels. New York: Macmillan, 1967. 275p $6.95;
      $1.50 (pap)
      In this book the author draws extensively on the huge
collection of spontaneous cases she has gathered as well as
on observations from many experiments conducted at the
Duke Parapsychology Laboratory.   She also deals with the
modus operandi of the psi process; the sense of conviction;
the forms ESP experiences take; the range of targets in experimental psi compared with topics in spontaneous psi; PK;
and the ways in which ESP becomes conscious both in real
life and in the experimental situation.   The implications of
psi are examined in the last two chapters.   Bibliographic
footnotes; index.   2.   A.
      IJP 10:213-16 (Sum. 1968); JASPR 62:94-96 (Jan.
1968); JP 31:302-06 (Dec. 1967); JSPR 45:305-08 (June 1970).
      Am. J. Psychiat. 124:117-18 (1967/68); Bull. Menninger
Clin. 32:60-61 (1968); Choice 4:1054 (Nov. 1967); Kirkus 35:
96 (Jan. 15, 1967); Libr. J. 92:1169 (Mar. 15, 1967); Ment.
Hyg. 52:149-50 (1968); Pub. Wkly 190:92 (Dec. 26, 1966);
Times Lit. Suppl., p938, Sept. 5, 1968.

237   Rhine, Louisa E.   Hidden channels of the mind.   New
      York: Sloane, 1961. 292p OP
      In this volume the author describes spontaneous ex-
periences of telepathy, clairvoyance, and precognition, and
discusses how the information obtained by psi becomes conscious (e.g., in dreams, visions, hunches, etc.).   She is
concerned with the characteristics of people who have psi
experiences, and with what they indicate about human nature.
There is a chapter on puzzling physical effects (attributed
to the agency of the living, the dying, and the dead) and one
entitled "Communications from beyond?"   Also of interest is
a chapter on intervention called "Can a precognized danger
be avoided?"   This book is of special interest to persons
who have had psi experiences and wish to compare them with
those of others.   12-item "Suggested readings."   1.   A.
      IJP 4:97-116 (Spr. 1962); JASPR 57:111-13 (Apr.
1963); JP 25:271-76 (Dec. 1961); JSPR 41:254-57 (Mar. 1962).
      Booklist 58:212 (Dec. 1, 1961); Hibbert J. 60:336
(July 1962); Kirkus 29:662 (July 15, 1961); Libr. J. 86:3792
(Nov. 1, 1961); N. Y. Times Book Rev., p22, Oct. 22, 1961;
Publ. Wkly 189:98 (Feb. 28, 1966); Sat. Rev. 44:37 (Oct. 21,
1961); Times Lit. Suppl., p643, Aug. 24, 1962.

238   Salter, Helen.   Evidence for telepathy: The response
      to a broadcast request for cases.   London: Sidgwick

and Jackson, 1934. 87p OP
This is a presentation of accounts of spontaneous psi
experiences received by the author as the result of a BBC
radio broadcast. Of the 400 letters received, 58 (the cream
of the crop) are analyzed here, although not all are given in
full. She had two objectives in writing the book: to set
forth the kind of evidence still needed, stressing the importance of prompt and complete recording of apparent telepathic experiences, and to show "the great variety we find
both in the form and circumstances of these experiences,
and ... to indicate certain recurring factors which afford
what little knowledge we at present possess concerning the
nature of telepathy" (p. 2). Although dealing specifically with
telepathy, this book provides an excellent introduction to the
study of all types of spontaneous cases. 2. M-L-C-U.
JASPR 28:322-23 (Dec. 1934); JSPR 28:311 (Nov.
1934).

239 Sidgwick, Eleanor Mildred. Phantasms of the living:
     Cases of telepathy printed in the Journal of the Society
     for Psychical Research during thirty-five years.
     Bound with Phantasms of the living (Gurney, Myers,
     and Podmore, 1886), abr. and ed. by Mrs. Sidgwick.
     Introduction by Gardner Murphy. New Hyde Park,
     N.Y.: University Books, 1962. 1041p OP
This volume contains two of Mrs. Sidgwick's previously published papers on telepathy. The first is a collection
of cases arranged in four parts: Experimental and semi-ex-
perimental cases; spontaneous cases in which the percipient's
impression was not externalized; spontaneous cases in which
the percipient's impression was externalized; and collective
and reciprocal cases without evidence of any agency external
to the percipient. The second paper is "On hindrances and
complications in telepathic communication." Bound with
these is her abridgment of Phantasms of the living. The
original book (229) was cut nearly in half by omitting many
of the cases, although the authors' text was retained almost
entirely. This is one of the largest and best collections of
spontaneous cases in existence. Bibliographic footnotes; index of cases. 3. A.
IJP 4:75-81 (Aut. 1962); JP 27:55-58 (Mar. 1963).

240 Stevenson, Ian. Telepathic impressions: A review and
     report of thirty-five new cases. Charlottesville:
     University Press of Virginia, 1970. 198p $6.00
     (Orig. publ. as Proceedings A.S.P.R., v.29, 1970.
     OP)

This monograph consists of a review of the literature from 1882 to the present on a certain type of spontaneous psi experience, termed "impression case" by the author. There is no visual imagery in such cases, but rather a strong feeling or "hunch" that something is happening to another person at a distance from the percipient. In addition to the review of 160 previously published impression cases, Stevenson presents 35 new ones which he investigated himself. Several of these cases involve the communication of pain and indicate that sometimes otherwise inexplicable physical symptoms may be due to ESP impressions. The processes of communication are analysed and the evidence for ESP afforded by cases of the impression type is assessed. 83-item bibliography; index. 2. L-C-U.
JP 35:69-72 (Mar. 1971); JSPR 46:136-38 (June 1971); PR 2:13-14 (May-June 1971).
Am. J. Psychiat. 127:144 (June, 1971); Contemp. Psychol. 16:332 (May 1971); Psychol. Today 5:12 (Feb. 1972).

241 Tyrrell, G. N. M. Apparitions. Introduction by H.
H. Price. London: Duckworth, 1953. 172p £1.50;
New York: Macmillan, 1962. 192p $.95 (pap) (Orig.
publ. by Duckworth for the S. P. R. in 1942. OP)
This is a classic study of apparitions and hallucinations. In his introduction H. H. Price says that "it is probably the best of all Tyrrell's writings" (p. 7). Tyrrell reviews in detail 61 of the best-authenticated apparition cases. In Part I he describes one of the first S. P. R. projects, the "Census of hallucinations." Part II presents the characteristics of apparitions, including a description of "the perfect apparition." In Part III Tyrrell offers his ingenious theory of the production of apparitions. Part IV is on reciprocal apparitions, traveling clairvoyance, pure clairvoyance, and contains a summary of the types of sensory automatism. Part V is entitled "Agency of apparitions" and in the final part he offers his speculations on the nature and significance of apparitions. An appendix contains a list of principal cases and their sources. Bibliographic footnotes; index. 2. A.
JASPR 37:156-61 (July 1943); JP 8:64-83 (Mar. 1944) and 18:199-203 (Sept. 1954).

SURVIVAL

Each of the books under this heading deals in one
way or another with the question whether or not any aspects
of human personality exist after death and, if so, in what
form. The basic titles for the general reader are Hart,
Hyslop, Salter, and the anthology edited by Garrett. Beard's
book is valuable for its informed treatment of the view taken
by spiritualists. Specialized aspects are thoughtfully treated
by Osis, Saltmarsh, Stevenson, and Thomas. High-level
discussions of the problems involved are offered by Ducasse,
who stresses the philosophical issues, and Murphy, who
deals with the empirical and experimental problems entailed
in investigating the survival hypothesis. Negative views on
survival are summarized by Hart and Lamont.

Additional books with material on survival: Two
books stressing concepts of immortality rather than empirical survival research are Flew (127) and Alger (222). The
following books either present new evidence for survival or
review studies bearing on the question: Flammarion (75),
Lodge (84), Cummins (98), Crookall (116), Langdon-Davies
(128), Smythies (131), Barrett (151), Broad (154), Dingwall
and Langdon-Davies (156), Heywood (160), Johnson (163),
Knight (164), Murphy (168), Myers (169, 170), Pratt (174),
Tyrrell (182, 183), Brown (190), Ducasse (213), Johnson (216),
Neff (217), and Smith (218).

242 Baird, Alexander T. One hundred cases for survival
     after death. New York: Bernard Ackerman, 1944.
     224p OP
This collection of cases was compiled to inform the
general public of "the strength of the case for survival of
human personality after bodily death" (p. 7). It could also
serve as a representative sampling of the various phenomena
of psychical research. The cases are arranged under the
following headings: Dreams, haunted houses, apparitions,
deathbed visions, automatic writing, trance phenomena,
cross correspondences, book-tests, proxy sittings, direct
voice, and materializations. Baird provides a commentary
on each section and on each selection. Bibliographic footnotes for each case; 55-item bibliography; case index. 1.
A.
     JASPR 39:62 (Jan. 1945); JSPR 33:40 (Nov.-Dec.
1943).

BookWeek, p22, Nov. 26, 1944; SpringfieldRepub.,
p6, Oct. 30, 1944.

243 Beard, Paul. Survival of death: For and against.
     Foreword by Leslie D. Weatherhead. London: Hodder
     and Stoughton, 1966. 177p OP
     This book approaches the survival problem from a
different angle than most of the other titles in this section.
In Part I Beard presents the many factors involved in asking
whether there is survival. One way of approaching this is
from the evidence provided by psychical research. This he
outlines in Part II, illustrating the pros and cons and concluding that psychical research has not yet established that
survival is a fact. His main contribution is in Part III,
where he describes a second approach which is "mainly
based upon private and personal experience. Many people
... have come to accept, as a result of their investigations,
that abundant and at times convincing evidence of survival
has reached them, and that other people, if they wish, are
likely to be able to obtain similar direct personal evidence
for themselves" (pp. 3-4). He details what mediumistic
communicators have said about survival, and analyzes the
process of communication, the psychology of sitters, and
the role of communicators and controls. Bibliographic footnotes; "Books for further reading" (40 items); index. 2.
M-L-C-U.
     IJP 9:134-35 (Sum. 1967); JASPR 61:173-78 (Apr.
1967); JSPR 43:374-75 (Sept. 1966).
     TimesLit. Suppl., p225, Mar. 17, 1966.

244 Broad, C. D. Personal identity and survival. London:
     Society for Psychical Research, 1968. 32p £.25 (pap)
     (Available only from the Society)
     This pamphlet consists of the paper which Broad, a
prominent Cambridge philosopher, delivered to the S. P. R.
as its Thirteenth Frederic W. H. Myers Memorial Lecture.
It presents in capsule form Broad's thinking about the survival problem. After a discussion of personal identity and
the meaning of human personality, he outlines the difficulties
involved in determining what in human personality can be
said to survive and the many obstacles involved in establishing that it does. Bibliographic references incorporated in
the text. 3. U.
     JASPR 53:28-30 (Jan. 1959).

245 Carington, Whately (W. Whately Smith). The founda-
     tions of spiritualism. New York: Dutton, 1920. 123p OP

Whately Carington, a gifted experimenter and original
theorist, began his psychical research investigations with
mediumship and ended them with studies of telepathy.
Throughout his career he was intensely interested in survival and in this, his first book, he indicates the kind of evidence needed to establish it experimentally. He analyzes
the different types of evidence thus far obtained and discusses the theories, other than survival, which might account for them. The last quarter of the book is an analysis
of the process of mediumistic communication, with particular attention to the often unintelligible, capricious, and di-
dactic qualities of the communications thus received.
Throughout the book he deprecates the approach of spiritualists and stresses the need for psychical researchers to deal
with the survival problem. Most of his statements are but-
tressed by liberal references to the literature so that the
book reads in places almost like a running bibliography.
Bibliographic references incorporated in the text. 2. M-L-C-U.
        JASPR 16:397 (July 1922); JSPR 20:25 (Jan. 1921).
        Athenaeum, p108, July 23, 1920; Cathol.World 113:
544 (July 1921); N.Y. TimesBookRev., p22, July 31, 1921.

246 Ducasse, C. J.   A critical examination of the belief in
      a life after death.   Springfield, Ill.: Thomas, 1961.
      318p $8.75
      This book provides an exhaustive discussion of the
problem of survival of death from a philosophical and logical
point of view. Ducasse says it "attempts ... a philosophical
scrutiny of the idea of a life after death ... to set forth the
various questions which arise on the subject; to purge them
both of ambiguity and of vagueness; ... to examine without
prejudice the merits of the considerations--theological or
scientific, empirical or theoretical--which have been alleged
variously to make certain, or probable, or possible, or im-
possible, that the human personality survives bodily death;
to state what kind of evidence would ... conclusively prove
that a human personality ... has survived after death; and
to consider the variety of forms which a life after death, if
any, could ... be conceived to take" (p.vi). Contains a
chapter in which Ducasse answers all the objections to survival raised by Lamont in The illusion of immortality (255).
Bibliographic footnotes; index. 3. S-M-L-C-U.
        JASPR 56:52-56 (Jan. 1962); JP 25:223-26 (Sept. 1961).

247 Ducasse, C. J.   Nature, mind, and death.   La Salle,
      Ill.: Open Court, 1951. 514p $7.50

This book is based on the Paul Carus lectures, eighth
series. In it the author discusses the nature of mind and
body. In the last part of the book, entitled "The mind-body
relation and the possibility of a life after death, " he presents
the case against the possibility of survival and the case for
the possibility of survival. In the final chapter he describes
six possible forms of survival not inconsistent with the mind-
body relation set forth in the first part of the book and consistent with all the empirical facts. However, Ducasse
points out that there is insufficient evidence to establish any
one of these forms as fact. Frontispiece; bibliographic footnotes; index. 3. L-U.

JASPR 46:73-79 (Apr. 1952); JP 16:130-46 (June 1952);
JSPR 37:96-101 (May-June 1953).

HibbertJ. 51:83 (Oct. 1952); J. Philos. 49:239 (Mar. 27,
1952); Philos. Rev. 61:551-56 (Oct. 1952); U. S. Q. BookRev. 8:
40 (Mar. 1952).

248 Ducasse, C. J. Paranormal phenomena, science, and
     life after death. Introduction by J. M. O. Wheatley.
     New York: Parapsychology Foundation, 1969. 63p
     (Parapsychological Monographs No. 8) $1. 75 (pap)
     (Available only from the Foundation)
     In 1962 the author gave a lecture at Vassar entitled
"Paranormal phenomena, science, and life after death, " re-
peating it at five other colleges or universities. Each lecture was attended by large audiences and because of this interest it was decided to publish the lecture. The monograph
also contains two previously published papers on survival by
Ducasse, "What would constitute conclusive evidence of survival after death?" (Journal S. P. R. , December 1962) and
"How good is the evidence for survival after death?" (Journal
A. S. P. R. , July 1959). It is valuable to have these essays
in book form because they were written with a more general
audience in mind than his other books dealing with survival
(246, 247). Bibliographic footnotes. 2. L-C-U.

JP 33:164-66 (June 1969).

249 Garrett, Eileen J. (ed.) Does man survive death?: A
     symposium. Introduction by Eileen J. Garrett. New
     York: Garrett/Helix, 1957. 204p OP
     This is an anthology of articles on various approaches
to the survival problem by psychical researchers, philosophers, physicists, and religious thinkers. In five parts, the
first four deal with the problem of survival as defined by
the philosophers; what parapsychological research can do;
the limitations set by the pure sciences; and the position
taken by the various religions. The fifth part consists of

seven previous published case histories having a bearing on
survival. Bibliographic references incorporated in the text.
2.   M-L-U.
        JASPR 52:156 (Oct. 1958); JSPR 39:244-45 (June 1958).
      Bull. MenningerClin. 23:34 (1959).

250 Guirdham, Arthur. The Cathars and reincarnation.
      London: Neville Spearman, 1960. 208p £1.75
      The author, a British psychiatrist, recounts the ex-
periences of a patient with a minor disorder who in the
course of therapy told him how she had recorded, years before when in her teens, detailed dreams and memories of a
previous life in the 13th century among the persecuted here-
tics, the Cathars. Guirdham personally investigated her
story and found much of it accurate. Some details in her
"recollections" were unknown to scholars at the time she
recorded them, but were later found to be correct. The
final chapter resulted after a scholar asked if she could re-
call any 13th-century poetry. She had, in fact, written poetry when young, and when Guirdham compared it with the
poetry of the troubadors of the 13th century, many striking
resemblances were found. Bibliographic footnotes; 94-item
bibliography; index. 1. M-L-C-U.
        JASPR 66:113-18 (Jan. 1972); JSPR 45:422-24 (Dec.
1970).
      TimesLit. Suppl., p683, June 11, 1971.

251 Hart, Hornell. The enigma of survival: The case for
      and against an after life. Springfield, Ill.: Thomas,
      1959. 286p OP
      This survey of the evidence bearing upon the question
of survival after death is characterized by the fact that the
author has tried to cover all sides of each aspect presented.
The format is that of a debate in which pros and cons are
provided and then an attempt is made to resolve the conflicting opinions expressed. There are five "books." The
first presents the debate about ESP. The second is on evidence for survival provided by mediums. Book Three is on
conflicting interpretations of mediumistic phenomena. The
fourth is on the relevance of apparitions to survival, pro
and con. In the final book an attempt is made to reconcile
the conflicting issues by means of a theory proposed by
Hart--the "persona" theory. 259-item bibliography; index.
2.   M-L-C-U.
        JASPR 55:3-23 (Jan. 1961); JP 25:136-46 (June 1961);
JSPR 40:265-66 (Mar. 1960).

252   Head, Joseph, and Cranston, S. L. (eds.) Reincarna-
      tion: An East-West anthology. Wheaton, Ill.: Theo-
      sophical Publishing House, 1968. 341p $2.25 (pap)
      (Orig. publ. by Julian in 1961. Hardcover ed. OP)
         This anthology, consisting largely of writings by over
400 Western thinkers, was compiled to offset the idea that
reincarnation is primarily an Eastern concept. The arrangement is mainly by country. Part one is on reincarnation in
the world's religions; the second part consists of the works
of Western thinkers on the subject; and parts three and four
present what scientists and psychologists say on reincarnation and on immortality. The compilers feel that the import
of their book is to suggest "that an idea that has occupied
so many exceptional minds cannot be lightly dismissed, but
is worthy of questioning, study, and investigation" (p. vii).
Bibliographic footnotes; index. 1. M-L-C-U.
         JASPR 57:113-16 (Apr. 1963).

253   Head, Joseph, and Cranston, S. L. (eds.) Reincarna-
      tion in world thought: A living study of reincarnation
      in all ages; including selections from the world's re-
      ligions, philosophies, and sciences, and great think-
      ers of the past and present. New York: Julian, 1967.
      461p $8.50
         This book is in effect both a revision of and a supple-
ment to the title above (252). Most of the material is new,
but some of the old is retained. Arranged chronologically,
it deals with reincarnation in myth and symbol; in the world's
religions; in theosophy and masonry; among primitive peoples;
views of Western thinkers; and what psychologists, philosophers, and scientists say. Pro and con views are represented. The editors point out that "while it is true that a
surprising number of distinguished thinkers of every era
have considered the problem in terms of repeated existence
upon earth--as this work serves to demonstrate--such testimony hardly establishes reincarnation as a fact. But it does
suggest that the doctrine merits investigation" (p. v). Bibliographic footnotes; index. 1. M-L-C-U.
         Christ. Cent. 84:945 (July 19, 1967); Libr. J. 92:2416
(June 15, 1967).

254   Hyslop, James H. Contact with the other world: The
      latest evidence as to communication with the dead.
      Ann Arbor, Mich.: Finch Press, 1972. 493p price
      not set (Orig. publ. by Century in 1919. OP)
         The author, a philosopher and psychologist, was
greatly interested in uniting the data of psychology and psy-

chical research. In this book, his final one, he summarizes
the evidence for survival. Although personally believing that
it is conclusive, he "endeavored in this work to canvass the
subject as though survival still had to be proved" (Preface).
Part I provides an historical survey; Part II concerns "pre-
liminary problems" such as canons of evidence, telepathy,
the nature of human personality, and the process of communication. The third part deals with specific examples offering evidence for survival. The fourth and final section is
on miscellaneous aspects of psychical research. Illustrated;
bibliographic references incorporated in the text; index. 2.
L-U.

  A. L. A. Booklist 16:5 (Oct. 1919); Dial 67:220 (Sept. 6,
1919); N. Y. TimesSat. Rev. 25:30 (Jan. 18, 1920); Nation 109:
762 (Dec. 13, 1919); Outlook 123:145 (Sept. 24, 1919); Publ.
Wkly 96:484 (Aug. 16, 1919); SpringfieldRepub., p15, Aug.
24, 1919 and p17, Sept. 21, 1919.

255 Lamont, Corliss. The illusion of immortality. Intro-
     duction by John Dewey. 4th ed. New York: Ungar,
     1965. 303p $5.00, $1.75 (pap); New York: Citadel,
     n. d. $1.65 (pap) (Orig. publ. by Putnam in 1935.
     OP)
  A well-known humanist philosopher, the author presents arguments against the survival hypothesis. He deals
with the importance of the problem and describes the funda-
mental issues involved. He presents what he calls "the
verdict of science" and its implications for immortality. In
a section entitled "the environment of heaven" he discusses
the difficulties in providing "the personality with ... a proper
environment in the hereafter" (p. 127). The various arguments in favor of immortality are described and he offers
refutations of them. (Lamont's arguments, in turn, are de-
bated by C. J. Ducasse in A critical examination of the belief in a life after death, 246.) He deals with the desire
for immortality and in a final chapter presents his philosophy
of a "life without immortality." Bibliography by chapter at
the end of the book (306 items); index. 2. M-L-C-U.
  JASPR 44:127-28 (July 1950); JSPR 36:375-76 (Jan. -
Feb. 1951).
  Am. J. Sociol. 41:380 (Nov. 1935); Booklist 31:328
(June 1935); Cathol. World 141:370 (June 1935); Int. J. Ethics
45:492 (July 1935); J. Philos. 32:277 (May 9, 1935); J. Relig.
15:323 (July 1935); N. Y. Her. Trib. Books, p11, Apr. 21,
1935; N. Y. TimesBookRev., p10, Apr. 14, 1935; NewRepub.
82:318 (Apr. 24, 1935); Sat. Rev. 11:653 (Apr. 27, 1935);
Sci. &Soc. 30:508 (Fall 1966); Surv. Gr. 24:314 (June 1935).

256 Marchant, James (ed.). Survival. London and New
         York: Putnam, 1924. 199p OP
         This is a collection of essays on different aspects of
the survival question by persons associated with psychical
research. Because of the eclectic nature of the selections
and the large number of contributors, the best method of
describing the book is to list the contents in full: "The ra-
tionality of survival in terms of physical science," by Oliver
Lodge; "Supernormal faculties in their relation to survival,"
by Stanley de Brath; "Metapsychics and human survival," by
Lady Grey of Fallodon; "Spirit communications," by Camille
Flammarion; "Experiences with automatic writing," by Edward Marshall-Hall; "Psychic experiences," by Arthur Conan
Doyle; "Ectoplasm as associated with survival," by Felicia
R. Scatcherd; "The philosophy of survival," by David Gow;
"Religion and survival," by C. Drayton Thomas; "Psychical
evidence for survival," by J. Arthur Hill; "Metapsychic
science and survival," by Charles Richet; and "On behaviour
to the dying," by Edith Lyttelton. Bibliographic footnotes.
2. M-L-C-U.
         Booklist 22:6 (Oct. 1925); N.Y.Trib., p12, May 24,
1925; N.Y.TimesBookRev., p15, May 17, 1925; NewRepub.
42:322 (May 13, 1925); Sat.Rev. 2:468 (Jan. 2, 1926);
Spectator 134:536 (Apr. 4, 1925); SpringfieldRepub., p79,
Apr. 26, 1925.

257 Murphy, Gardner. Three papers on the survival prob-
         lem. New York: American Society for Psychical Re-
         search, 1945. 90p $3.00 (pap) (Orig. publ. in
         Journal A.S.P.R. in 1945) (Available only from the
         Society)
         In the first paper, "An outline of survival evidence,"
the author defines the various types of survival evidence
and arranges them in the chronological order in which they
originally appeared within the general history of psychical
research. In the second, "Difficulties confronting the survival hypothesis," he presents the obstacles involved in obtaining final proof of survival and points out that "if progress
is to be made, it will be through squarely confronting the
difficulties, not by seeking to escape them" (p.35). In the
final paper, "Field theory and survival," he suggests other
ways of formulating the survival problem and indicates the
most cogent types of evidence for survival. Bibliographic
footnotes. 3. M-L-C-U.
         JSPR 33:256-63 (Oct.-Nov. 1946).

258 Osis, Karlis. Deathbed observations by physicians

and nurses.   New York: Parapsychology Foundation,
1961. 113p (Parapsychological Monographs No. 3)
$1.75 (pap) (Available only from the Foundation)
     The author used modern research methods to learn
if there is a factual basis for the conclusion reached by some
psychical researchers at the beginning of the century "that
the large collection of observations concerning hallucinations
or visions of dying patients gave some evidence pointing to
post-mortem existence" (p.9).   The monograph reports on
observations by 285 doctors and 355 nurses of persons approaching death.   The data were obtained by means of questionnaires filled out by the doctors and nurses.   Detailed
analyses are given of the dying patients' moods (from panic
to exaltation), hallucinatory experiences, and visions.
Samples of the five questionnaires used in the study are
provided in an appendix.   53-item bibliography.   3.   L-C-U.
     JASPR 57:233-39 (Oct. 1963); JSPR 41:377-79 (Sept.
1962).

259 Penelhum, Terence.   Survival and disembodied exis-
     tence.   New York: Humanities, 1970. 114p $3.00
     In this book philosopher Terence Penelhum examines
the conceptual difficulties raised by belief in survival after
death.   He sees such belief as twofold: the belief in disembodied survival and the belief in resurrection of the body.
For each he asks whether we can intelligently discuss what
form such a survivor would take and whether it can be
claimed that such a surviving being is identical with ourselves.   Theories of disembodied existence and perception,
reincarnation, and spirit agency are dealt with, and recent
philosophical discussions of problems connected with personal
identity are summarized.   Bibliographic footnotes; 32-item
bibliography; index.   3.   L-C-U.
     JASPR 66:321-28 (July 1972); JSPR 45:413-15 (Dec.
1970).
     ChurchQ.Rev. 3:167-68 (Oct. 1970); Contemp.Psychol.
16:411 (June 1971); HeythropJ. 12:312-15 (July 1971); Mod.
Sch. 48:395-98 (May 1971); Philos.Q. 20:404-05 (Oct. 1970);
Philos.Rev. 80:528-30 (Oct. 1971); Philosophy 46:176-78
(Apr. 1971).

260 Pike, James A. (with Diane Kennedy).   The other side:
     An account of my experiences with psychic phenomena.
     Garden City, N.Y.: Doubleday, 1968. 398p OP
     The well-known iconoclastic Episcopal bishop presents
evidence for survival based on his experiences in connection
with the death of his son, and his sittings with Arthur Ford

and other mediums. He points out that the book's title has
a double meaning: It refers not only to the "other side" of
death, but also to his intention to set forth his side of the
events he experienced as opposed to the credulity and naiveté
with which they were headlined by the news media. Contains
a list of nine organizations where further information on
psychical research can be obtained. 120-item bibliography
arranged by broad subject. 1. A.
     JASPR 63:388-95 (Oct. 1969).
     BookWorld, p6, Dec. 29, 1968; Christ. Cent. 86:713
(May 21, 1969); Kirkus 36:1097 (Sept. 15, 1968); Libr. J.
93:4571 (Dec. 1, 1968) and Libr. J. 94:320 (Jan. 15, 1969);
NewStatesman 78:465 (Oct. 3, 1969); Newsweek 72:112 (Nov.
11, 1968); PastoralPsychol. 20:65-67 (Oct. 1969); Publ. Wkly
194:60 (Sept. 9, 1968); TimesLit. Suppl., p723, July 3, 1969.

261 Podmore, Frank. The newer spiritualism. New York:
     Holt, 1911. 320p OP
     This book, written in the year that Podmore died,
presents his final views on mediumship and the question of
survival. When he first became interested in psychical research in the 1880s, he was an ardent spiritualist, but the
exposure as fraudulent of several well-known mediums of
his day and the growth of knowledge concerning unconscious
manifestations such as automatism and cryptomnesia converted him to skepticism as regards the veracity of "spirit
communications." However, the theories expressed in
Myers' Human personality (169) gave him new hope. In
this book he describes the encouraging results obtained in
the years following Myers' death, especially the trance communications of Mrs. Piper and the cross correspondences.
Bibliographic footnotes; index. 2. M-L-C-U.
     JASPR 6:1-34 (June 1912); PSPR 25:70-89, Pt. 62
(1911).
     Bookman[Lond.] 39:160 (Dec. 1910).

262 Richmond, Kenneth. Evidence of identity. London: G.
     Bell, 1939. 111p OP
     The purpose of this volume is to select from the
literature of psychical research cases that illustrate evidence
of identity; that is, that deceased persons purportedly com-
municating with the living through mediums are in fact the
persons they claim to be. After an introductory chapter on
human identity, Richmond goes on to discuss the various
types of evidence of identity. The remainder of the book
consists of illustrative examples from the literature of psychical research: The "Oscar Wilde" scripts; "Le livre de

revenants, " the "buried medal" case, and the "Lethe" case.
This book provides a good introduction to one of the classical problem areas of psychical research, and one that is
directly relevant to the question of survival.   32-item glossary; bibliographic footnotes.   2.   L-U.
        JASPR 33:284-86 (Sept. 1939); JSPR 31:96-97 (July
1939).

263 Richmond, Zoe. Evidence of purpose. London: G.
        Bell, 1938. 112p £.25
        This book is a collection and discussion of cases in
which the deceased give evidence of intention in their communications.   In three sections, the first consists of cases
of spontaneous apparitions which showed apparent intention
or purpose, e.g., urging that a debt be paid.   The second
presents cases of compulsive impressions which subsequently
were shown to be purposive, e.g., a daughter's impression
of her dead father which disclosed money which had been
thrown away with his old clothes.   The final section describes
purposive messages communicated through mediums, e.g.,
the well-known medium, Mrs. Osborne Leonard, was warned
by her control not to sit in a room in which the ceiling subsequently fell.   31-item glossary; bibliographic references
incorporated in the text.   2.   M-L-C-U.
        JASPR 33:156-58 (May 1939); JSPR 30:239-40 (June
1938).

264 Salter, W. H. Zoar; or, The evidence of psychical
        research concerning survival. London: Sidgwick and
        Jackson, 1961. 238p OP
        This is the final distillation of the thoughts on survi-
val of a man intimately associated with research on the
question throughout most of his long life.   In his capacity as
honorary secretary of the S.P.R., he was often consulted
by bereaved persons who "wished for enlightenment on the
question whether man survives the death of the body" (p.9).
This book is primarily for such persons and in it the author
demonstrates why a definite yes or no answer cannot be
given.   He surveys all the types of evidence for survival:
apparitions and hauntings, poltergeists, ecstasy and inspiration, dissociation, mediumistic communications, and (especially) the cross correspondences.   Evidence not previously published is also presented, particularly in regard to the
cross correspondences, with which Salter and his family
were intimately involved.   Bibliographic references incorporated in the text; index.   2.   M-L-C-U.
        IJP 4:88-93 (Sum. 1962); JASPR 51:146-49 (July 1962);

JP 26:232 (Sept. 1962); JSPR 41:203-10 (Dec. 1961).

265 Saltmarsh, H. F. Evidence of personal survival from
    cross correspondences. London: G. Bell, 1939. 159p
    OP
    This is an introduction to and summary of the phe-
nomena of joint mediumship termed "cross correspondences, "
which are thought by many parapsychologists to provide
strong evidence for survival. There is an introductory
chapter on psychical research in general, with emphasis on
mediumship. Saltmarsh next outlines the plan of the cross
correspondences and the important personalities involved,
living and dead. Then he turns to specific cases, dealing
first with simple cross correspondences and then with complex ones. He provides detailed summaries of the Statius
and the Ear of Dionysius cases. The concluding chapter is
a discussion of the arguments for and against the cross correspondences as evidence for survival. 32-item glossary;
52-item bibliography. 2. M-L-C-U.
    JSPR 30:227-28 (May 1938).

266 Stevenson, Ian. Twenty cases suggestive of reincarna-
    tion. Foreword by C. J. Ducasse. New York:
    American Society for Psychical Research, 1966. 362p
    OP (Proceedings A. S. P. R., v. 26, 1966)
    Although there are many books on the doctrine of re-
incarnation, empirical studies are extremely rare. This
book is a detailed presentation of 20 cases suggestive of reincarnation personally studied by the author on field trips
to India, Ceylon, Brazil, Alaska, and Lebanon. In each
case he specifies the number of items purportedly indicating
knowledge of a previous life and presents the verification
available for each statement. He also discusses theories
competing with reincarnation to explain the data of these
cases, e. g., fraud, cryptomnesia, personation, possession,
etc., and compares them with the more familiar types of
cases in the psychical research literature. He concludes
that "the chief contribution of the present cases may lie in
their illustration of the kinds of cases which, if we could
obtain them more abundantly and study them more thoroughly,
would ... provide compelling evidence of survival" (p. 354).
Bibliographic footnotes; index. 2. M-L-C-U.
    JP 30:263-72 (Dec. 1966); JSPR 44:88-94 (June 1967).
    Am. J. Psychiat. 124:128 (1967/68); Br. J. Med. Psychol.
42:84-86 (1969); Br. J. Psychiat. 113:698-99 (1967); Bull. MenningerClin. 31:253 (1967); J. Nerv. &Ment. Dis. 144:330-32
(1967); MD 11:256 (June 1967); Psychiat. Dig. 28:51 (Nov. 1967).

267   Thomas, C. Drayton.   Some new evidence for human
      survival.   Introduction by Sir William F. Barrett.
      London: Collins, 1922. 261p OP
         Thomas, a Methodist clergyman, was a regular sitter
with Mrs. Osborne Leonard and in working with her took
part in the development of the "book tests" and "newspaper
tests." Part I is on book tests, giving detailed examples
and a discussion of the evidence thus obtained and its implications. Part II discusses the newspaper tests, some of
which were precognitive in nature. In the introduction Barrett says, "the great merit of the present volume lies in the
fact that the author conclusively shows that any explanation
based on telepathy or clairvoyance on the part of the medium,
or [any] other person on earth, or any subliminal knowledge
possessed by the medium or sitter, fails to account for all
the facts he has recorded with such patient care and examined
with critical acumen" (p. xi). Bibliographic footnotes. 2.
L-C-U.
         JASPR 18:150-51 (Feb. 1924).
         BostonEve. Trans., p5, Oct. 1, 1924; Lit. Rev., p12,
Oct. 25, 1924.

268   Toynbee, Arnold, and others.   Man's concern with
      death.   New York: McGraw-Hill, 1968. 280p $7.95
         This anthology on death is by experts in a variety of
fields. There are three parts: Death and dying, Attitudes
toward death, and Frontiers of speculation. The subject of
psychical research forms a significant part of the final section. It contains "Attitudes to death in the light of dreams
and other out-of-the-body experience" by the sensitive and
psychical researcher, Rosalind Heywood, as well as her
"Death and psychical research." Also included is an important paper by the British philosopher H. H. Price entitled "What kind of next world?" in which he discusses
what a life after death might be like. Bibliographic footnotes; index. 2. M-L-C-U.
         JSPR 45:88-90 (June 1969).
         Br. J. Psychiat. 116:450 (1970); Can. J. Theol. 15:274-
75 (July-Oct. 1969); Christ. Cent. 86:996 (July 23, 1969);
ChurchQ. Rev. 1:349 (Apr. 1969); Contemp. Psychol. 15:733-
36 (Dec. 1970); Dialogue 10:206-07 (Mar. 1971); Downside
Rev. 88:202-10 (Apr. 1970); Frontier 12:65-67 (Feb. 1969);
Libr. J. 94:1506 (Apr. 1969); Life-Threaten. Behav. 1:67-74
(1971); N. Y. TimesBookRev., p22, Sept. 21, 1969; Natl. Rev.
21:1074 (Oct. 21, 1969); NewStatesman 76:789 (Dec. 6, 1968);
Omega 1:85-86 (1970); PastoralPsychol. 21:62-64 (1970);
Theol. Today 27:88-93 (Apr. 1970); TimesLit. Suppl., p43,

Jan. 9, 1969.

269 Walker, Nea. The bridge: A case for survival. With
       a prologue and epilogue by Sir Oliver Lodge. London:
       Cassell, 1927. 314p OP
       Nea Walker was Oliver Lodge's secretary for psychi-
cal research matters. The materials which she has recorded
in this book concern the efforts of a Mrs. White to contact
her deceased husband through mediumistic sittings arranged
by the author. These sittings differed from the usual type
in that "the object was to get as much evidence as possible
of the personality and identity of Mr. White through mediums
who had never seen or heard of either Mr. or Mrs. White,
working with sitters who had also seen neither and who knew
nothing of them..." (p. 9). The author was one of the principal sitters. By using these "proxy" sitters, it was hoped to
exclude the telepathic transmission of information from the
sitter to the medium. The bulk of the book consists of verbatim transcripts of the communications purportedly received
from Mr. White, and also from Mrs. White after her death.
Illustrated. 2. L-U.
       PSPR 38:10-16, Pt. 105 (1928).

270 Walker, Nea. Through a stranger's hands: New evi-
       dence for survival. Foreword by Sir Oliver Lodge.
       Edited, with a critical introduction, by Kenneth Rich-
       mond. London: Hutchinson, 1935. 432p OP
       This is a record of an attempted repetition of the
work reported in The bridge (269), but under improved and
tightened conditions. In the case reported in that volume,
there gradually grew a bond of sympathy and common interest between Mrs. White and the proxy sitter (Nea Walker),
while in the present case the author served as proxy sitter
for a series of bereaved persons and did not develop personal contacts with any of them. Mrs. Osborne Leonard was
the only medium involved. The communications received are
recorded in detail and would appear to offer even better evidence for survival than those reported in The bridge. Illustrated; index. 2. L-U.
       PSPR 44:13-15, Pt. 144 (1936).

TESTS FOR PSI

Except for Pratt's monograph, which deals exclusively with sophisticated methods for evaluating free verbal material, there is considerable overlap in content in the guides for carrying out psi experiments listed in this section. Ebon's book is probably the most useful for the beginner since it is the least technical and covers a broad range of experimental situations. The volumes by Humphrey and by West are the most detailed and are primarily addressed to researchers in the field.

Additional books with material on tests for psi: The textbook by Rhine and Pratt (58) and McConnell's ESP curriculum guide (166) both contain valuable material on how to conduct and evaluate parapsychological experiments. Thouless' From anecdote to experiment in psychical research (64) is also geared to the design of parapsychological experiments and is an excellent guide to the interpretation of results. Some of the more sophisticated statistical tests used in experimental parapsychology are spelled out in ESP-60 (57).

271 Ebon, Martin (ed.). Test your ESP. New York: New
       American Library, 1971. 143p $.75 (pap); Hollywood,
       Cal.: Wilshire, 1971. $2.00 (pap) (Orig. publ. by
       World in 1970. Hardcover ed. OP)
       The editor points out in the Foreword that in ESP
testing "it isn't the equipment that counts. What matters
are the controls exercised during a test, and just how the
results are evaluated. You can arrange perfectly tight and
scientifically acceptable experiments in your own living
room" (p.v). This handbook was compiled in collaboration
with the staff of the Institute for Parapsychology of FRNM
and it presents in non-technical language various methods of
ESP and PK tests. The first three chapters are on ESP
testing in general. Other chapters cover such topics as
testing children, the use of photographs and drawings as
targets, testing animals, psi-missing, "party games," and
PK tests. There is also a chapter on investigating haunted
houses. 32-item glossary; "Suggested reading" (11 items).
1. A.
       JP 35:300-01 (Dec. 1971); JSPR 45:420 (Dec. 1970).
       Libr. J. 95:2270 (June 15, 1970).

272   Humphrey, Betty M.   Handbook of tests in parapsychol-
        ogy.   Foreword by J. B. Rhine.   Durham, N.C.:
        Parapsychology Laboratory, 1948. 152p OP
        This was the first handbook of methods of psi testing
written primarily for research workers, although it can also
be used by the intelligent layman.   It provides a detailed
record of the testing techniques developed at the Duke Parapsychology Laboratory, starting in the 1930s.   The author
was one of the main participants in the Duke research when
these methods were evolved.   Part I of the handbook contains
nine chapters on tests of ESP, including several matching
techniques, group tests, and tests with drawings, as well as
card tests.   Part II is on PK tests.   Both these sections contain useful summaries of precautions to be taken and chapters on the evaluation of results.   Part III is on the design
of original ESP and PK experiments and some problem areas
are discussed.   Further methodological details are given in
appendices.   Illustrated; "Suggested readings" (67 items); index.   2.   H-M-L-C-U.
        JP 11:310-12 (Dec. 1947); JSPR 35:20-22 (Jan.-Feb.
1949).

273   Pratt, J. G.   On the evaluation of verbal material in
        parapsychology.   New York: Parapsychology Founda-
        tion, 1969. 78p (Parapsychological Monographs No.
        10) $2.00 (pap) (Available only from the Foundation)
        This is a valuable tool for persons wishing to engage
in psi research using materials for which chance probabili-
ties are not readily obtainable, e.g., mediumistic statements,
verbal descriptions of photographs, art prints, etc.   The
author is one of the pioneers in this area of psi testing.   In
1934 he published a study of Eileen Garrett's mediumship
entitled "Towards a method of evaluating mediumistic material" in which he developed a quantitative method for
assessing mediumistic statements.   In 1948 a similar but
more refined method was published by Pratt and Birge.   An
abridged version of the former and the major part of the
latter are reprinted in the present monograph.   In the final
section Pratt reviews innovations in assessing free materials
developed since the earlier papers were published.   Bibliographic footnotes.   3.   L-C-U.
        JSPR 46:79-89 (June 1972).

274   Rhine, Louisa E.   Manual for introductory experiments
        in parapsychology.   Durham, N.C.: Parapsychology
        Press, 1966. 25p (multilithed) $1.00 (pap)
        In this booklet the author describes some basic ESP

and PK testing procedures.   Under ESP testing she discusses various card-calling and card-matching tests.   There
is a section on generating targets for precognition experiments.   Under PK testing she describes dice throwing for
face and for placement.   General precautions are indicated
and elementary methods of evaluating results are given.
Some problems for testing are suggested.   4-item bibliography.   2.   A.
No reviews.

275   West, Donald J.   Tests for extrasensory perception:
        An introductory guide.   Rev. ed.   London: Society
        for Psychical Research, 1954. 27p £.25 (pap) (Orig.
        publ. by the Society in 1953. OP) (Available only
        from the Society)
        This useful handbook describes the basic quantitative
tests in parapsychology.   In the introduction the author says,
"Research into ESP is in its infancy, and the findings so
far reported raise more problems than they solve.   It is
the purpose of this pamphlet to outline a few of the simple
experimental techniques, so that anyone who is willing to
take the necessary pains can make a useful contribution to
research" (p.4).   Not only does West describe ESP card
tests, but also the use of free material such as drawings,
and the British innovation, "clock card" tests.   He discusses
specific tests for telepathy, clairvoyance, precognition, and
psychokinesis.   There are sections on conditions favoring
success and on "secondary effects."   Methods for the statistical evaluation of results are described.   17-item glossary;
"Suggestions for further reading" after each topic (30 items).
2.   M-L-C-U.
        JP 18:64-65 (Mar. 1954).

UNORTHODOX HEALING

        Books in this group deal with cures that cannot be
accounted for by normal physical or psychological explanations.   Podmore and Weatherhead give the most complete
and scholarly coverage.   West's book, although dealing with
only one aspect of unorthodox healing--the cures at Lourdes--
is an excellent introduction to the problems involved in establishing the reality of claims of paranormal healing.

Additional books with material on unorthodox healing:
Summaries of papers given at a conference on unorthodox
healing (held in 1954) are given in a Proceedings of the Parapsychology Foundation (91).   Parapsychology and medicine is
dealt with in Angoff (87), the Ciba Foundation Symposium (88),
and Rhine (130).   There are large sections on unorthodox
healing in the books by Holms (162) and Neff (217).   A critical view of unorthodox healing is expressed by Rawcliffe (49).

276 Haynes, Renée.   Philosopher king: The humanist pope
     Benedict XIV.   London: Weidenfeld and Nicolson,
     1970. 246p £3.00
     This biography of Pope Benedict XIV (Prospero Lam-
bertini) is by a converted Catholic and psychical researcher.
It has been included because of the groundwork provided by
Lambertini in the matter of judging miraculous claims (including unorthodox healing).   His job, like that of the parapsychologist, was to seek normal explanations such as
trickery, etc., before considering that the miraculous (paranormal) had occurred.   The chapters of most relevance to
psychical research are three in which the author summarizes
the substance of Lambertini's great work, De canonizatione
(as yet not translated into English).   These chapters are
subtitled "The holy and the paranormal," "When is a miracle
not a miracle?" and "Psyche and body."   Illustrated; bibliography by chapter at the end of the book (99 items); 78-
item bibliography; index.   2.   L-C-U.
     JP 35:154-55 (June 1971); JSPR 46:71-74 (Mar. 1971).
     DownsideRev. 89:104-05 (Jan. 1971).

277 Hutton, J. Bernard.   Healing hands.   Introduction by
     Edward T. Bailey.   London: W. H. Allen, 1966.
     201p £1.50; New York: McKay, 1967. $3.95; New
     York: Paperback Library, 1968. 224p $.75 (pap)
     This book gives an account of the author's healing by
a personality which purported to be a deceased surgeon,
William Lang, through the British medium, George Chapman.
Hutton describes the details of Lang's career, how Chapman
discovered that he was Lang's medium, and how, by means
of tape-recorded sessions with Lang speaking through Chapman, the operations were performed on the "spirit bodies"
of many patients.   Several case histories of psychic surgery
and healing are described.   Hutton says that although he was
a skeptic when he first visited Chapman, he became "convinced that ... daily cures of a miraculous nature are
brought about" (p.217).   Bibliographic references incorporated

in the text.   1.   M-L.
        JSPR 43:375-76 (Sept. 1966).
        BookWeek, p5, Apr. 23, 1967; Libr.J. 92:1501 (Apr.
1, 1967); TimesLit.Suppl., p637, July 21, 1966.

278 Podmore, Frank.   From Mesmer to Christian Science:
        A short history of mental healing.   Introduction by
        Eric J. Dingwall.   New Hyde Park, N.Y.: University
        Books, 1965. 306p $10.00   (Orig. publ. by Methuen
        in 1908 under the title Mesmerism and Christian
        Science)
        This is a scholarly historical survey of unorthodox
healing, beginning with Mesmerism and ending with Quimby
and Christian Science.   Podmore was interested in the interpretations offered to explain the effective healing agent; he
shows how initially it was thought to be entirely physical,
but gradually changed until with Christian Science it was considered wholly spiritual.   There are several substantial
chapters on other matters of relevance to psychical research:
clairvoyance, spiritualism in France and Germany, the pro-
phecies of Andrew Jackson Davis, and the inspired teachings
of Thomas Lake Harris.   Bibliographic footnotes; index.   2.
M-L-C-U.
        JSPR 44:202-06 (Dec. 1967); PSPR 24:687-97, Pt. 61
(1910).
        Bookman[Lond.] 37:100 (Nov. 1909).

279 Rose, Louis.   Faith healing.   (Bryan Morgan, ed.)
        Foreword by Donald J. West.   Baltimore: Penguin,
        1971. 191p $1.50 (pap)   (Orig. publ. by Gollancz in
        1968. Hardcover ed. OP)
        The author, a British psychiatrist, says in the intro-
duction that he believes faith healing "to be a phenomenon
important and common enough to call for serious study.   If
it takes place (and there is evidence that something benefi-
cial happens to some sufferers) then it should be brought into
line with the main body of medical knowledge" (p.14).   This
book is an attempt toward this goal.   In Part 1 Rose provides an historical survey of the subject and in Part 2 gives
an account of his own investigations of the claims of some
faith healers.   He sets up criteria for the study of faith
healing claims and indicates the kinds of evidence required
to validate them.   84-item bibliography; index.   2.   L-C-U.
        JSPR 45:85-87 (June 1969).
        NewStatesman 75:706 (June 7, 1968); TimesLit.Suppl.,
p399, Apr. 18, 1968.

280 Weatherhead, Leslie D. Psychology, religion and heal-
     ing. London: Hodder and Stoughton, 1951. 543p
     £1.75;   rev. ed., New York: Abingdon, 1954. $2.25
     (pap)
     The title page of this book by a British Methodist
minister states that it is "a critical study of all the non-
physical methods of healing, with an examination of the principles underlying them and the techniques employed to express them, together with some conclusions regarding further
investigation and action in this field." There are seven main
sections: 1/Earlier methods of healing through religion,
2/Earlier methods of healing through psychology, 3/Modern
methods of healing through religion; 4/Modern methods of
healing through psychology; 5/Do modern psychological
methods of healing need religion? 6/Do modern religious
methods of healing need psychology? and 7/The modern
search for healing through psychology and religion. 195-
item bibliography arranged by subject; name index; subject
index. 2. A.
     JASPR 65:358-59 (July 1971).
     Booklist 48:224 (Mar. 15, 1952); Christ. Cent. 69:901
(Aug. 6, 1952); Interpretation 7:1045 (Jan. 1953); Kirkus 20:
118 (Feb. 15, 1952); Manch. Guard., p5, Oct. 29, 1951;
Scott. J. Theol. 7:428-32 (Dec. 1954); TimesLit. Suppl., p681,
Oct. 26, 1951.

281 West, Donald J. Eleven Lourdes miracles. New York:
     Garrett/Helix, 1957. 134p OP
     The author, a British psychiatrist/psychical research-
er, examined in detail the records of 11 cases of cures at
Lourdes judged by the Catholic Church as "miraculous."
Although aware from previous experience how difficult it is
to obtain sufficient medical information to be able to draw
any conclusions from cases of faith healing, West felt that
the situation at Lourdes would be different because "the files
at the Lourdes Medical Bureau contain an accumulation of
medical data on faith cures that has no parallel elsewhere"
(p. viii). Nevertheless, although the cases he reviews are
among the best documented on record, he shows that even
in these crucial information is missing. As an objective
presentation of the difficulties involved in assessing the effi-
cacy of faith healing, this book should be read by everyone
with an interest in the subject. It contains an appendix of
cures accepted by the Lourdes Medical Bureau in the period
1925-1950. 112-item glossary of medical terms; 49-item
bibliography. 2. M-L-C-U.
     IJP 2:91-97 (Spr. 1960); JASPR 52:73-76 (Apr. 1958);

JP 21:312-13 (Dec. 1957); JSPR 39:90-91 (June 1957).

282   Worrall, Ambrose A. (with Olga N. Worrall).   The
      gift of healing: A personal story of spiritual healing.
      New York: Harper & Row, 1965. 220p $4.95;   New
      York: New American Library, 1968, under title
      Miracle healers. 190p $.75 (pap)
      Both members of this husband-and-wife team were
faith healers.   Ambrose Worrall was an industrial consultant
and his wife is Director of the Healing Clinic at the Mt.
Washington Methodist Church in Baltimore.   The book is in
three sections.   The first, entitled "Search, " tells how they
discovered their healing abilities.   The second, "Ministry, "
describes how their healing activities became organized, culminating in the work at the clinic.   In the final chapter,
"Meanings, " they present their theories about healing, describe the procedures used in their healing practice, and
offer suggestions for efficacious prayer.   1.   S-M-L.
      IJP 8:492-94 (Sum. 1966); JASPR 60:390-93 (Oct.
1966).
      Booklist 62:743 (Apr. 1, 1966); Kirkus 33:1089 (Oct.
15, 1965); Libr.J. 90:5285 (Dec. 1, 1965).

II. PARAPSYCHOLOGY IN ENCYCLOPEDIAS

Since every library and most homes contain encyclopedias, it was decided to describe and evaluate the information on parapsychology in a number of these reference tools.
Both general and specialized encyclopedias were examined.

No special effort was made to consult the latest editions of the general encyclopedias examined (the search was
confined mainly to the holdings of the East Meadow, Long
Island, Public Library) as it seemed unlikely that these editions would contain more or significantly improved information
than the earlier ones. To substantiate this, however, a
check was made of more than one edition of some of the encyclopedias. It was found that for Collier's Encyclopedia no
change was made between the 1962 and 1970 editions. Only
minor revisions were made in Encyclopedia Americana between 1957 and 1969. In the case of the Encyclopedia Britannica, however, between 1961 and 1971 the entire article
on parapsychology was rewritten and the bibliography more
than doubled. For Encyclopedia International no change was
made between 1963 and 1970. In the case of the Lincoln
Library of Essential Information there was minimal coverage
in the 1957 edition and none at all in 1965. In Our Wonderful World between 1969 and 1971 the basic articles remained
unchanged, but a new one was added on telepathic dreams.
Finally, the coverage in the 1972 World Book was considerably improved over the 1962 edition.

From the foregoing it can be seen that in most cases
later editions contain essentially the same information as
earlier ones. Thus the "continuous revision" policy supposedly in use by today's major encyclopedias is obviously not
being applied to parapsychological subjects. When revisions
are made, they rarely amount to more than the addition of
a few sentences or paragraphs to the existing text and new
items to the bibliography, if any. The Encyclopedia Britannica and World Book, however, are outstanding exceptions.

Another way in which the major encyclopedias attempt
to keep up to date is by publishing yearbooks. However, an
examination of the Encyclopedia Americana Annual from 1964
to 1971, Britannica Book of the Year from 1957 to 1971, and
Collier's Yearbook from 1965 to 1971 revealed no information on parapsychology.

In order to check the information on parapsychology
in both the general and the specialized encyclopedias, 11
basic psychical research "key terms" were looked for in
each case: Apparition(s), Clairvoyance, Extrasensory perception, Medium(s), Parapsychology, Poltergeist(s), Precognition, Psychical research, Psychokinesis, Spiritualism, and
Telepathy. The use of these key terms helped in assessing
the degree of coverage given to psychical research within
each encyclopedia and also in making comparisons between
encyclopedias.

In the encyclopedia descriptions to follow the thoroughness of the coverage is assessed on the basis of the number
of key terms appearing in the indexes and its overall quality
in the light of authoritativeness, recency, adequacy of indexing, bibliographic citations, and accuracy. The author's
name is given in the case of articles which are signed. Illustrations are noted and are also included in the "Index to
Illustrations in Books and Encyclopedias" (see Appendix 2).
Finally, at the end of this section on encyclopedias an overview is provided in which they are compared, any unusual
features pointed out, and the most useful for various needs
indicated.

GENERAL ENCYCLOPEDIAS

An attempt was made to examine as many encyclopedias as possible listed as "recommended" in the latest edition of Walsh, General Encyclopedias in Print: A Compara-
tive Analysis, New York: R. R. Bowker, 1971. Of a total
of 26 titles, the following 18 (items 283-301) were checked:

283   American Peoples Encyclopedia. New York: Grolier,
        Inc., 1968. 20v.
        This encyclopedia is of intermediate size. It is
aimed at students at the junior high school level through college, and is also suitable for adult use. Of the 11 basic
psychical research key terms, the index volume has all ex-

cept Medium and Poltergeist.   Several of the index entries
refer to three main articles.   One is under Extrasensory
perception and is by Michael Scriven.   It is a half page long
and is the main entry for parapsychology.   It describes not
only ESP, as the heading would indicate, but PK as well.
J. B. Rhine wrote two entries, three paragraphs under
Clairvoyance and one paragraph under Parapsychology.   None
of these entries contain any bibliographic citations.   There
is a four-paragraph article under Spiritualism, by W. G.
Garrison, which stresses the religious aspects of the subject
and has a nine-item bibliography.   There are two paragraphs
under Ghosts, emphasizing literature, by Michael Fixer.
This entry has three bibliographic citations.

     Although the indexing in this encyclopedia is fairly
complete, the treatment in the entries themselves is uneven
and non-parapsychological aspects are often emphasized.
Moreover, although the encyclopedia includes bibliographic
citations, the primary parapsychological entries do not.   For
these reasons this encyclopedia is not recommended as a
source of information on psychical research.

284   Britannica Junior Encyclopedia for Boys and Girls.
       Chicago: Encyclopaedia Britannica, Inc., 1971. 15v.
       This encyclopedia is aimed specifically at elementary
and junior high school students.   As is true of many encyclopedias for children and young people, it provides definitions of terms in the index volume.   When this is the case,
often there are no references to further information in the
encyclopedia itself.   The index contains only four of the 11
key terms.   Of the four, Extrasensory perception, Mediums,
and Telepathy are only given brief definitions in the index.
The only article of relevance to psychical research is under
Spiritualism.   It is defined in the index and receives two
paragraphs in the text, which concludes with a mere mention
of parapsychology.   There are no bibliographic citations.
       Definitely not recommended.

285   Catholic Encyclopedia for School and Home.   New York:
       McGraw-Hill Book Company, 1965. 12v.
       Although this encyclopedia is written from the Catholic
point of view, it contains much information of a general nature and can be used by 10-year-olds as well as adults.   All
11 key terms were found in the index volume.   The main
treatment is under Parapsychology, Psychic phenomena,
Spiritism, and Spiritualist churches.   The first is a three

and a quarter page illustrated introduction to the subject, by
Allan B. Wolter, in which quantitative methods and evidence
for psi are stressed. Psychic phenomena is treated in a
three-page article by John B. Murray, who provides a rather
eclectic overview, somewhat repetitive, but informative none-
theless. The article for Spiritism, two pages long, is by
Myles Nolan, who deals with the history of the survival problem, beginning with the Bible through modern psychical research. Bibliographic citations are incorporated in the text.
Leslie Rumble wrote the entry for Spiritualist churches. It
is a page and a half long and is historically oriented, beginning with the Fox sisters and Andrew Jackson Davis. As
would be expected, religious aspects are emphasized. It
has bibliographic citations incorporated in the text.
        This encyclopedia is updated by means of supplements.
The only one published thus far does not have any information on parapsychology.
        The indexing in this encyclopedia is superb as re-
gards psychical research topics in the index proper and also
as regards cross references, which are given not only at the
end of articles but often within them. The coverage of parapsychological subjects is both objective and detailed. The
Catholic point of view, when expressed, is pinpointed, and
so may be used or not, as the reader prefers.
        This encyclopedia is recommended as providing a
very good introduction to all aspects of psychical research.

286 Chambers's Encyclopedia. London: International Learn-
        ing Systems Corporation, 1967. 15v.
        This encyclopedia is the largest produced in Great
Britain. It is comprehensive in scope and is for use by advanced high school students, graduate students, and specialist
adults. All 11 key terms are included in the index; they usually refer not only to separate articles on each subject, but
also to mention of each in connection with many other articles. For example, under Clairvoyance the reader is referred to a one-page article on the subject by J. B. Rhine,
which includes two bibliographic citations, and also to references under Psychical research, Survival, Telepathy, and
Witchcraft. (Although this feature is present in most encyclopedias, it is carried out in much more detail in Chambers's.)
Under Apparitions there is an outstanding three and a half
page article by Whately Carington and R. H. Thouless.
They give a history of the subject, delineate the types and
characteristics of apparitions, and present the theories that
have been offered to account for them. There is a 10-item

bibliography. These same authors also wrote the two-page
entry under Psychical research, stressing the types of phenomena studied and the different kinds of evidence, with a
six-item bibliography, and a two and a half page article on
Precognition, which is easily the best treatment of this subject in any of the encyclopedias under review. It has a six-
item bibliography. J. B. Rhine provides a two and a half
page article under Telepathy, with two bibliographic citations.
He stresses the spontaneous and experimental work which
was carried out at the Duke University Parapsychology Laboratory. Carington and Thouless team up once more with
the article under Poltergeists, which has a five-item bibliography. Again, this is the best on the topic in the encyclopedias checked. Carington and Rhine wrote a page on
Spiritualism, which deals with mediumship and psychical research and has a five-item bibliography. Finally, Carington
and Thouless provide a five-page article on Survival which
once more takes top honors. It is an excellent discussion
of the evidence and has an eight-item bibliography. In many
cases the bibliographies are supplemented by bibliographic
citations incorporated in the text.

    Chambers's is highly recommended for information on
all aspects of psychical research. Not only is the indexing
the most complete and detailed and the bibliographic citations
the most extensive, but the coverage of each subject is by
far the most authoritative, scholarly, and detailed of any of
the encyclopedias examined.

287 Collier's Encyclopedia. New York: Crowell-Collier Edu-
     cational Corporation, 1970. 24v.
    This is a large encyclopedia geared to students from
the upper elementary grades through college; it also serves
the needs of adults. All 11 key terms can be found in the
index volume. There is a one and a quarter page entry
under Apparitions by Alfred Hall-Quest and a brief item under Clairvoyance by J. B. Rhine. The remaining index entries all refer to a six-page article by Gardner Murphy and
Laura A. Dale under Parapsychology or psychical research.
It contains sections on telepathy (spontaneous and experimental), extrasensory perception (including precognition), mediumship (including survival), and physical phenomena (including
poltergeists, physical mediums, and psychokinesis). It is a
very well-rounded article with bibliographic citations incorporated in the text. Charts and diagrams are included.
The bibliography volume contains only one reference for
further reading under Parapsychology, but this is offset by

the citations in the main article itself.

This encyclopedia is recommended as providing an excellent, intensive introduction to all aspects of psychical research.

288   Columbia Encyclopedia.   New York: Columbia University Press, 1963. 1v.

This encyclopedia was conceived as a ready-reference source of brief factual background information for use by high school and college students as well as by adults.   Two of the 11 key terms are not included: Precognition and Psychokinesis.   There is a long paragraph under Parapsychology and another under Spiritism or spiritualism.   The former is an historical survey, stressing the S. P. R. and Duke work and outlining methodology.   The latter emphasizes studies of survival and mediumship rather than spiritualism as a religion.   Each article occupies a third of a column and has a bibliography of four items.   The reader is referred from Spiritism or spiritualism to Parapsychology, but not vice versa.   There are brief definitions under Apparitions, Clairvoyance, Telepathy, and Poltergeists.   All but the last refer the reader to Parapsychology, Spiritism or Spiritualism, or both.

Although it can be used for definitions, this encyclopedia cannot be recommended because its coverage is too brief to provide an adequate introduction to psychical research, even at a superficial level.

289   Compton's Encyclopedia and Fact Index.   Chicago: F. E. Compton Company, 1972. 22v.

Compton's is specifically aimed at upper elementary grade and high school students, but to some extent it may also be useful to adults.   Each volume has its own index. Some index entries refer the user to the encyclopedia proper; sometimes the definition or description of a term is given in the index alone.   Only four of the 11 key terms are included and of these, three are defined only in the index: Extrasensory perception, Parapsychology, and Telepathy.   There is a four-paragraph entry under Spiritualism.   No bibliographic citations are given.

Not recommended because the coverage is much too spotty and the entries too brief.

290   Encyclopedia Americana.   New York: The Americana

Corporation, 1969. 30v.

This large and comprehensive encyclopedia is for general and advanced use by high school pupils, college students, and specialist adults. Of the 11 key terms, only one, Apparition, is missing. Some idea of the range of topics included can be obtained from the additional headings listed under Psychical research in the index: American Society for Psychical Research; Clairvoyance; Divination; Hypnosis; Immortality; James, William; Lodge, Oliver; Occultism; Omen; Palladino, Eusapia; Psychopathology; Society for Psychical Research; Spiritualism; Telepathy; Trance; and Tranquillizing drugs. The main article, Psychical research, is by J. B. Rhine, as are most of the other entries. It is three pages long and broken down into "extrasensory perception," "psychokinesis," and "other problem areas." It is primarily concerned with the investigations carried out under Rhine's direction at Duke University and their implications as he views them. There is an 11-item bibliography under Psychical research and bibliographic citations are given after several of the shorter entries. Another important article is under Spiritualism and is also by Rhine. It is primarily a discussion of mediumship and survival. The subheadings are "practice," "organization," and "psychical research." There is a 10-item bibliography entitled "spirit survival." Under Clairvoyance is a half-page article by Gertrude R. Schmeidler in which the experimental work is stressed. Finally, there is a three-quarter page unsigned article under Telepathy which emphasizes the work at Duke, but also provides an historical summary.

Although the main article under Psychical research is somewhat restricted in its approach, it is balanced by the information provided under Spiritualism.

Recommended as an introductory survey of parapsychology: its history, phenomena, methods, and implications.

291   Encyclopaedia Britannica. Chicago: Encyclopaedia Britannica, Inc., 1971. 24v.

The largest encyclopedia in the English language, the Britannica is for advanced use, but can also be of assistance to junior and senior high school students. All 11 key terms can be found in the index volume, either referring the user to four actual entries (Clairvoyance, Parapsychology, Psychical research, and Spiritualism) or to articles in which these subjects are dealt with. The entry under Clairvoyance is simply a definition with a cross reference to Parapsychology. The articles under Parapsychology, Psychical research, and Spiritualism, taken together, provide a well-rounded intro-

duction to the full range of psychical research, historical
and modern. Spiritualism should be read first. It is a one
and a half page article by R. H. Thouless and is mainly on
mediumship, including mental phenomena, physical phenomena, spirit photography, and spirit healing. It has a six-
item bibliography. The two-page article under Psychical research should be read next. It is also by Thouless. He
covers survival, precognition, physical phenomena, spontaneous phenomena, and concludes with an eight-item bibliography.
The article on Parapsychology is by Paul Meehl and Edward
Girden. They cover the experimental literature from 1934
on, beginning with Rhine's work at Duke. The question of
evidence and the scientific status of parapsychology is
stressed and the bibliography is sizeable (26 items).

The indexing, both in the index volume and in specific
articles, is such that the user is led to the pertinent information from whatever point he may choose to start. Recommended as an excellent survey of the field, strong not only
for historical material but for modern parapsychology as
well.

292 Encyclopedia International. New York: Grolier, Inc.,
      1970. 20v.
This encyclopedia is for general family use not only
for school purposes but also as a source of cultural and
practical information. All 11 key terms are in the index.
There are brief definitions under Clairvoyance and Poltergeists. The main treatment, to which the other headings
refer, is under Parapsychology, a three-page article by
Gardner Murphy. He covers spontaneous and experimental
telepathy, precognition, survival, and the organization of
parapsychology. There are two illustrations and the article
concludes with a nine-item bibliography. There is also a
half-page article under Spiritualism by Charles S. Braden,
who stresses the religious aspect of spiritualism and provides a three-item bibliography.

Recommended as an excellent introduction which emphasizes the historical continuity of psychical research and
touches on all the major facets of the field.

293 Grolier Universal Encyclopedia. New York: Grolier,
      Inc., 1968. 20v.
This is an intermediate encyclopedia aimed at the
entire family. It does not have an index. In checking the
text alphabetically, nine of the key terms were located, the

two missing ones being Apparition and Precognition. The entries under Clairvoyance and Poltergeist consist of two-sen-
tence definitions with a cross reference from the former to
Parapsychology. The remaining terms simply refer the
reader to Parapsychology, Spiritualism, or both. The major
treatment is under Parapsychology, which consists of an unsigned article a page and a half long, with two illustrations.
There are also two paragraphs under Spiritualism. No bibliographic citations are given.

In comparison with the other full-size encyclopedias,
the Grolier Universal Encyclopedia is not recommended as a
source of information on parapsychology.

294   Lincoln Library of Essential Information. Columbus,
       Ohio: The Frontier Press, 1965. 1v.
       This encyclopedia is conceived as a ready reference
source and aid to individual study. It is aimed at high school
students and the general adult. In the earlier editions
checked it had the same unsigned paragraph under Parapsychology, a sub-heading under Psychology which in turn is
subsumed under Science. The item is skeptical in tone, but
represents fairly the attitude of most psychologists toward
parapsychology. There are no bibliographic citations. In
the latest edition checked (1965) no reference at all is made
to parapsychology.
       Not recommended.

295   Merit Students Encyclopedia. New York: Crowell-Col-
       lier Educational Corporation, 1969. 20v.
       Merit is a recent encyclopedia based on an analysis
of curriculum materials. It is aimed at students in the upper grades through high school, but can also be generally
used by adults. Of the 11 key terms, four are missing:
Apparition, Poltergeist, Precognition, and Psychokinesis.
Most of the other entries refer the user to a half-page article under Extrasensory perception by Samuel Ball who outlines the history of the subject, beginning with the study of
mediumship and going on to mention of Rhine's work at Duke.
He gives two bibliographic citations for further study. Ball
also wrote the article under Spiritualism, three-quarters of
a page long, and paragraph-length entries under Rhine, Telepathy, and Psychic phenomena. Strangely enough, although
the latter refers to the article on Telepathy, there is no
cross reference to this heading from the others so, although
it is definitely relevant, the reader is left to discover it by

chance.

The information in this encyclopedia is not well organized and the coverage is incomplete.

Not recommended.

296   New Book of Knowledge.   New York: Grolier, Inc.,
      1968. 21v.

The New Book of Knowledge was compiled specifically for use by elementary school children.   The index has only four of the key terms.   Of these, two (Telepathy and Spiritualism) are simply defined in the index, but are not included in the text.   Parapsychology refers to Extrasensory perception, the main source of information.   It is the equivalent of two pages long and includes a photograph.   The article describes what ESP involves, the types of evidence for it, the major criticisms, and offers the conclusion that it has neither been proven nor disproven.   Rhine's work is stressed. No bibliographic citations are provided.

Although very limited in scope, this encyclopedia is recommended for children as an introduction to ESP because of the simple and clear-cut description.

297   New Catholic Encyclopedia.   New York: McGraw-Hill
      Book Company, by arrangement with the Catholic Uni-
      versity of America, 1967. 15v.

This is a scholarly encyclopedia which includes much material on Catholicism, but which is also useful as a source of general information for advanced students and specialist adults.   All the 11 key terms are listed in the index volume. The article to which the reader is led from Apparitions, however, is religious rather than parapsychological.   The main treatment is under the headings of Parapsychology and Spiritism, with briefer entries under Extrasensory perception, Poltergeists, Psychokinesis, and Telepathy.   The writer of all the articles on psychical research (except Spiritism) is Cyril P. Svoboda.   The article under Parapsychology, two and a half pages long, is an excellent overview, dealing not only with historical material but also with modern quantitative methods and attitudes toward them.   The Catholic slant is indicated and a four-item bibliography included.   The article under Spiritism is a page and a half long and is by Michael D. Griffin, S. T. B.   It deals with the history of the subject, the interpretation of the phenomena, and the Catholic viewpoint on the subject.   There is a seven-item bibliography.   There is a page and a half under Poltergeists, with

a four-item bibliography; a half page under Extrasensory
perception, also with a four-item bibliography; three paragraphs under Telepathy, with three bibliographic citations;
and a half page under Psychokinesis, with a three-item bibliography. Although it would appear from this description
that the number of bibliographic citations is unusually liberal
in this encyclopedia, unfortunately the same four or five
references are constantly cited.

     This encyclopedia is recommended for its excellent
coverage of parapsychology, which compares favorably with
the other major multi-volume sets. The Catholic point of
view is not objectionable as it is spelled out and may be dis-
regarded if desired.

298 The New Caxton Encyclopedia. London: Caxton Publish-
     ing Company, Ltd., 1969. 20v.
     This is a general encyclopedia for use by junior and
senior high school students. It is noted for the number and
quality of its illustrations. All of the 11 key terms are in
the index. There are articles under Clairvoyance (a half
page), Psychical research (one page), and Telepathy (one-
third page). The remainder of the key terms in the index
refer the user to one or more of these articles. The page
on Psychical research offers a succinct summary, providing
descriptions of the various types of mental and physical
phenomena (with an illustration of D. D. Home levitating),
apparitions, and poltergeists. The various opinions on the
evidence for psi are pointed out and capsule summaries of
historical psychical research and modern quantitative work
are provided, including Russian work. The index refers the
reader to a "classified list of articles" under Clairvoyance,
Spiritualism, and Telepathy, but this could not be checked
as the bibliography volume was still in preparation when this
section of the present book was written.
     Recommended as a good introduction to psychical re-
search. However, the complexity combined with the compara-
tive brevity of the treatment necessitates searching elsewhere
for additional information. The material included is sophisticated enough to make this encyclopedia useful to older students and adults as well as junior high school pupils.

299 The New Outline of Modern Knowledge. London: Victor
     Gollancz, 1956. 1v.
     Although not included in General Encyclopedias in
Print 1971-72, this encyclopedic compendium has been listed

here because of the coverage it gives to parapsychology. It
is noteworthy that one of the 26 branches of modern knowledge with which it deals is parapsychology. The average
number of pages per subject area, or chapter, is 26; the article under Psychology, for example, is 25 pages long. The
one under Parapsychology is 19 pages, thus indicating that
the treatment is extensive in itself and also on a par with
that of the other subject areas. Of the 11 key terms, Clairvoyance, Extrasensory perception, Parapsychology, Precognition, Psychokinesis, and Telepathy are in the index. They
all refer, directly or indirectly, to the article under Parapsychology. It was written by J. B. Rhine and the only limi-
tation in coverage appears to have been self-imposed by the
author. It is devoted entirely to modern parapsychological
experiments either carried out by Rhine and his co-workers
at Duke, or as offshoots from their work. There are a few
bibliographic citations in the text and a six-item "Books suggested for further reading" at the end. Although this compendium will probably not be published in later editions, the
age of the parapsychological material compares favorably
with articles in general encyclopedias having a policy of continuous revision.

Recommended as one of the best expositions of experimental parapsychology in a general encyclopedic work.

300 Our Wonderful World. New York: Grolier, Inc., 1971.
       18v.

Our Wonderful World is an outline of general knowledge presented in a manner geared to the needs and interests
of young people from ages 9-17. It is arranged by 372 broad
subject areas of general knowledge. The information related
to psychical research is in the area entitled "Strange beliefs
of yesterday and today." The index guides the reader to
this area under eight of the key terms, those missing being
Apparition, Poltergeist, and Psychical research. The main
articles are a one-page one entitled "The mind reaches out:
ESP and psi" (which includes an illustration) and another one-
page article on "The spirit world." The former is an open-
minded survey of the different types of psi phenomena, with
a brief historical background and a summary of opinions on
the existence of psi. The latter summarizes pro and con
views on survival, mediumship, poltergeists, and spirit photography, ending with a verdict of "not proven." Each major
section has a list of "other books to read," but only one citation is directly relevant to parapsychology. In the index under
Telepathy the reader is referred not only to the article on

ESP summarized above, but also to one entitled "Dreams
and extrasensory perception," which is in the section on
Sleep, this in turn being subsumed under "The world and our
senses." Two pages long, it summarizes the evidence for
paranormal dreams and describes some of the experiments
conducted in the Dream Laboratory at Maimonides Medical
Center in Brooklyn. It is exciting and refreshing to find a
timely article such as this in an encyclopedia, and one designed for young people at that!

Our Wonderful World is recommended as one of the
best introductions to psychical research suitable for young
students and of value to older readers as well.

301 World Book Encyclopedia. Chicago: Field Enterprises
     Educational Corporation, 1972. 22v.

This well-known and popular home and school encyclopedia is geared to answer the general information needs of
the entire family. The coverage of parapsychology in the
latest edition is greatly improved in comparison with earlier
editions. For one thing, this edition is the first to have an
index. (Earlier editions, however, have cross references to
related articles at the end of individual articles. For example, under Extrasensory perception the reader is referred to
Clairvoyance, Mind-reading, Parapsychology, Psychical research, and Telepathy. This feature is retained in the 1972
edition.) All 11 key terms are in the index except for Apparition. The present edition contains most of the information on parapsychology under Extrasensory perception (which
also includes information on psychokinesis). It is a one-page
article by William M. Smith, who emphasizes the evolution
of the experimental evidence for psi rather than reviewing
the entire field. He also wrote paragraph-length entries
under Clairvoyance, Mind-reading, Parapsychology, Psychical Research, and Telepathy. Although each is critical in
tone, the case is left open. No bibliographic citations are
given. There is also an unsigned article under Spiritualism
which is mainly on the religious aspects of the subject, but
the work of psychical researchers is summarized in the historical section.

Recommended as an introduction to experimental parapsychology especially useful for young readers.

SPECIALIZED ENCYCLOPEDIAS

In addition to the general encyclopedias, a number of
specialized encyclopedias in the social and behavioral sciences,
general science, philosophy, and religion were checked for information on psychical research. As a rule these encyclopedias differ from the general ones in several respects:
their subject matter is more specific, the treatment within
a given subject area is more detailed and intensive, and new
editions, if any, are published infrequently. With the exception of the general science encyclopedias, they are usually
written by experts for experts, although suitable as well for
college and some high school students.

302   Book of Popular Science.   New York: Grolier, Inc.,
      1972. 10v.
      This is a non-technical science encyclopedia for young
people. Only four of the key terms are in the index: Clairvoyance, Extrasensory perception, Parapsychology, and Telepathy. All but Parapsychology refer to a one-paragraph entry under "The study of the human mind" in the 20th century.
Parapsychology has its own paragraph under "Special fields"
in a section entitled "Introduction to psychology."
      Not recommended as a source of information on para-
psychology.

303   Dictionary of Philosophy and Psychology.   Edited by
      James Mark Baldwin, with the cooperation and assist-
      ance of an international board of consulting editors.
      New edition, with corrections, 1925.   Reprinted in
      New York: Peter Smith, 1960. 2v. of 4.
      Some of the consulting editors for this dictionary were
well-known psychical researchers: for English, William
James and Henry Sidgwick; for French, Théodore Flournoy.
Among the contributors are Josiah Royce for Philosophy and
Eleanor M. Sidgwick for Psychology.
      Of the 11 key terms, five are missing in the index:
Extrasensory perception, Parapsychology, Poltergeist, Precognition, and Psychokinesis. (With the exception of Poltergeist, these terms were not in use when this work was compiled and thus Baldwin cannot be faulted for not having included them.) Joseph Jastrow wrote three paragraphs under
Clairvoyance, concluding that there is no evidence for its
existence. He also wrote three critical paragraphs under

Mediums. There are nearly four pages under Psychical research, with an 11-item bibliography, by Mrs. Sidgwick,
who also wrote a five-page article under Telepathy, with an
11-item bibliography. These are both valuable contributions
on the early findings and views of psychical researchers,
particularly from the British point of view. In addition to
the bibliographies, many bibliographic citations are incorporated in the text of both articles. Jastrow wrote a two
and a half page article under Spirit (and Spiritualism). It is
an objective review of the phenomena of spiritualism with
negative conclusions as to any paranormal or spiritistic interpretation of the phenomena. There is a 10-item bibliography.

   Recommended as a source of information on psychical
research as it existed before modern quantitative methods
were introduced. Mrs. Sidgwick's articles, in particular,
not only provide basic information, but are rich in bibliographic citations.

304 Encyclopedia of Philosophy. Editor-in-Chief, Paul Ed-
     wards. New York: Macmillan and the Free Press,
     1967. 8v.
   Nine of the 11 key terms (all but Apparition and
Poltergeist) are included in the index. All the headings refer to one or more of three main articles relevant to psychical research. The primary one is under ESP phenomena,
philosophical implications of, by C. W. K. Mundle. It examines the various types of psi phenomena, the evidence for
them, and their philosophical implications. Bibliographic
citations are incorporated in the text, and there is also a
50-item bibliography. Antony Flew contributed a five and a
half page article under Precognition that provides an excellent survey of the evidence, the proposed explanations, and
the implications of precognition. It has a 17-item bibliography. Flew also wrote a 12-page article under Immortality.
Although it deals primarily with philosophical conceptions of
immortality, there is a subsection entitled "Personal identity
and parapsychology" in which the evidence of psychical research is summarized in a half page. There is a 40-item
bibliography, nearly a third of which is relevant to parapsychology.
   Highly recommended as an up-to-date survey of the
evidence for psi and the implications of the phenomena. Also useful as a guide to further reading.
   Reviewed in JP 31:306-10 (Dec. 1967).

305   Encyclopedia of Psychology. Edited by H. J. Eysenck.
      New York: Herder and Herder, 1972. 3v.
      This new British-oriented encyclopedia is still being
published. The first two of the three projected volumes
have appeared. John Beloff is the editor for parapsychological topics. Only the first five of the 11 key terms could be
checked because volume 2 ends with PH. However, these
five are all included, and there are paragraph-length definitions of them (by Beloff) under Apparitions, Clairvoyance,
Extrasensory perception, and Medium. H. H. J. Keil added
a supplement to Beloff's entry under Extrasensory perception
which consists of a half-page criticism of the use of the term
from a scientific point of view. There is a two-page article
by Beloff under Parapsychology. In the first part he discusses the current status of the subject and in the last half
its history. In the latter section he covers the pre-1930
period which was dominated by studies of the survival question and the period from 1930 to the present which has
stressed experimental studies of ESP and PK. There is a
20-item bibliography.
      Recommended as the most recent and one of the most
authoritative sources of succinct information on parapsychology.

306   The Encyclopedia of Psychology. Edited by Philip L.
      Harriman. New York: Philosophical Library, 1946.
      1v.
      This encyclopedia does not have a true index but
rather a list of topics covered. Only one of the 11 key terms
appears in the list: Parapsychology. This refers to a 20-
page article under that heading by Gardner Murphy. He presents the history, problems, methods, and basic findings of
psychical research. There is an 80-item bibliography.
      Highly recommended for serious students as an inten-
sive introduction with an exceptionally fine bibliography.
      Reviewed in JP 11:147-49 (June 1947).

307   Encyclopedia of Religion and Ethics. Edited by James
      Hastings. New York: Scribner's, 1956. (Reprint of
      1908-1926 ed.) 13v.
      The only key terms included in the index are Clair-
voyance, Psychical research, and Telepathy. Because of
the original date of publication, one would not expect to find
such terms as Extrasensory perception, Parapsychology, Precognition, or Psychokinesis, but it is surprising that Appari-

tion, Medium, Poltergeist, and Spiritualism were not included. Under Psychical research there is a three-page article by James Leuba that provides a good introduction to
the early history of the subject and includes a discussion of
automatisms, the survival problem, mediumship, and telepathy. There is a 9-item bibliography. Under Telepathy
there is a one-page article by F. C. S. Schiller, who gives
a detailed critical review of the evidence. There is a six-
item bibliography.
       Recommended for information on the early history of
psychical research.

308   Encyclopedia Science Supplement for 1966. New York:
          Grolier, Inc., 1966. 1v.
       This science yearbook is a supplement to the Grolier
Universal Encyclopedia (293). Although it is published annually, only the 1966 volume has any information on parapsychology. It contains a seven-page article under ESP by
Daniel Cohen, originally published in Science Digest, Novem-
ber 1965. It is a fairly up-to-date summary of experimental
parapsychology based primarily on J. B. Rhine's work and
views. It is illustrated and has a sample ESP test.
       Recommended as an introduction to modern experiment-
al parapsychology.

309   Harper's Encyclopedia of Science. 2d ed. New York:
          Harper & Row, 1967. 1v.
       Although this is a good general science encyclopedia
stressing ideas and concepts, there is nothing in it related to
parapsychology. Not one of the 11 key terms appears in
the index!

310   International Encyclopedia of the Social Sciences. Edi-
          ted by David R. Sills. New York: Macmillan and the
          Free Press, 1968. 17v.
       The index volume does not contain the key terms Ap-
parition, Medium, Psychical research, and Spiritualism.
The other seven terms are included and all refer to an article under the heading of Parapsychology by Gertrude R.
Schmeidler. This 14-page article provides an excellent general introduction to all aspects of the subject, although
modern quantitative experiments are stressed, particularly
those dealing with the psychology of the psi process. There
is a 52-item bibliography. Under Parapsychology the index

also refers to entries under James, William and Significance,
tests of.
     Highly recommended for psychology students interested
in psi research as well as for anyone wanting an intensive
overview of the field.
     Reviewed in JP 33:84-86 (Mar. 1969).

311   McGraw-Hill Encyclopedia of Science and Technology.
     New York: McGraw-Hill Book Company, 1971. 15v.
     The index volume does not include the key terms Ap-
parition, Medium, Poltergeist, Psychical research, and
Spiritualism. The other six terms all refer to an article
by Fred D. Sheffield under the heading Extrasensory perception (ESP). A page and a half long, it is a good summary
of modern laboratory experiments. Sheffield discusses telepathy, clairvoyance, and precognition, and also has a section
on psychokinesis. He points to the elusiveness of psi phenomena and summarizes the criticisms of ESP and PK research. There are no bibliographic citations.
     Recommended as a brief introduction to quantitative
experimental parapsychology.

312   New Shaff-Herzog Encyclopedia of Religious Knowledge.
     Edited by Samuel Macauley Jackson. Grand Rapids:
     Baker Book House, 1949. (Reprint of 1908-1912 edi-
     tion.) 13v.
     Only three of the 11 key terms appear in the index:
Medium, Psychical research, and Spiritualism. Because of
the early date of original publication, one would not expect
to find such terms as Extrasensory perception, Parapsychology, Precognition, or Psychokinesis. But there seems to
be no excuse for the omission of Apparition, Clairvoyance,
Poltergeist, and Telepathy--unless these were not considered
to be matters of "religious interest." There is a one and a
half page article by Hereward Carrington under Psychical research and the future life. The material is pre-1910, but
the coverage of this limited area is better than in most of
the more recent encyclopedias. There is an 18-item bibliography. There is also a two-page article under Spiritualism,
spiritualists by W. H. Larrabee, who considers the question
of survival as well as spiritualism as a religious movement, .
and provides a 52-item bibliography.
     Recommended as a good introduction to the older psy-
chical research materials.

313 Young People's Science Encyclopedia. Chicago: Chil-
       dren's Press, 1970. 20v.
       Only two of the 11 key terms are listed in the index:
Extrasensory perception and Precognition (which is a see
reference to the ESP article). The entry under Extrasensory
perception, by Jean C. Kraft, is a half-page long and consists of definitions of ESP, precognition, and telepathy. It
concludes, "Many scientists believe that there is not enough
evidence to prove the existence of ESP and that the methods
used in obtaining the evidence are not accurate." There are
no bibliographic citations.
       Not recommended.

SCIENCE YEARBOOKS

       There are a number of excellent science yearbooks,
several of which were checked under the key terms of Parapsychology, Psychical research, and Extrasensory perception.
The titles and volumes examined were Science Year (1965-
66, 1968-69, 1972), World Book Science Annual (1965-66,
1968-69), Britannica Yearbook of Science and the Future
(1969), McGraw-Hill Yearbook of Science and Technology
(1963-72), and Encyclopedia of Science Supplement (1965-71).
Only the 1966 volume of the latter [see 307] has any information on parapsychology.

SUMMARY

       There are a number of good to excellent articles on
parapsychology in both the general and the specialized encyclopedias described above. By far the best treatment from
every point of view--authority, accuracy, detail of indexing,
completeness of coverage, and number of bibliographic cita-
tions--is provided by Chambers's (286) in the articles by W.
Carington, Rhine, and Thouless. The only possible short-
coming the material could be considered to have is that it is
too detailed and technical for use below the senior high
school level.

       Of the remaining general encyclopedias, leaving out
of consideration those aimed primarily at children, Murphy
and Dale's article in Collier's (287), Murphy's in Encyclopedia International (292) and Rhine's in New Outline of Modern
Knowledge (299) are highly recommended. The first two

have the virtue of surveying the entire field of psychical research, while Rhine covers modern experimental parapsychology in considerable detail. The Catholic Encyclopedia for
School and Home (285), Encyclopedia Americana (290), Encyclopaedia Britannica (291), New Catholic Encyclopedia (297),
and New Caxton Encyclopedia (298) also provide good introductions, although in each case two or more articles must
be read to gain a full picture.

As for general encyclopedias aimed at children, the
New Book of Knowledge (296) and Our Wonderful World (300)
stand out above the rest. Both deal almost entirely with
modern experimental parapsychology, however, and so must
be supplemented from other sources to provide information
on early psychical research.

Of the specialized encyclopedias, the articles by
Murphy in the Encyclopedia of Psychology (305) and Schmeidler in the International Encyclopedia of the Social Sciences
(310) are outstanding introductions, the latter being more recent and more heavily concentrated on experimental parapsychology. For a review of the evidence for and the philosophical implications of psi phenomena, the Encyclopedia of
Philosophy (304) is unparalleled. Cohen's article in the Encyclopedia Science Supplement 1966 (308) provides a good introduction to modern experimental parapsychology suitable
for both adults and young people.

Since most of the current encyclopedias--with the exception of Chambers's (286), Collier's (287), Americana (290),
Britannica (291), and International (292)--do not stress studies
of spontaneous psi or mediumship, some of the older works
should be consulted for this aspect of psychical research.
Especially valuable are Mrs. Sidgwick's articles in Baldwin
(303), H. Carrington's article on psychical research in New
Shaff-Herzog (312), and Leuba's on the same topic in Hast-
ings (307).

For articles that are critical or stress criticisms of
parapsychology, see Jastrow's entries in Baldwin (303),
Sheffield's article in McGraw-Hill Encyclopedia of Science
and Technology (311), the article on parapsychology in Britannica (291), the one on extrasensory perception in World
Book (301) and Cohen's article in the Science yearbook (308).

For brief definitions of parapsychological terms, the
Encyclopedia of Psychology (305) and Columbia Encyclopedia
(288) are most useful, in that order.

In conclusion, although one might not ordinarily think of consulting an encyclopedia for information on parapsychology, the best of the articles reviewed above are very good indeed. When more specialized works are not available, a thorough grounding in the major findings, methods, criticisms, implications, and scientific status of the subject can be gained from consulting encyclopedias alone. If readers who want to go further are fortunate enough to have access to Chambers's (286) and the two Macmillan/Free Press specialized encyclopedias (304, 310), they will have at hand the necessary basic bibliography from which to start. In the absence of a good general dictionary of parapsychological terms, the new work edited by Eysenck (305) will be a helpful substitute.

III. PARAPSYCHOLOGICAL ORGANIZATIONS

No attempt is made here to list all the parapsychological organizations currently in existence. An "International Directory of Organizations" published in the Parapsychology Review (1:5-9, Mar. -Apr. 1970) lists 150. However, most of these are either peripheral groups more interested in fringe subjects than in hard-core parapsychology, student organizations or clubs mainly concerned with sharing ideas and enthusiasms, or reading and study groups. Such groups almost always have a short life span. The primary criterion for the inclusion of organizations in this section is that their main purpose must be serious research, either directly, as in the case of the A. S. P. R., or indirectly, as in the case of the Parapsychology Foundation. Secondly, the past, present, and projected research of the organizations must be of high enough quality to merit publication in the better-known scholarly parapsychological journals.

An effort has been made to provide a brief history of each organization and to describe its purpose, functions, and current status. The organizations are listed alphabetically by title.

314 AMERICAN SOCIETY FOR PSYCHICAL RESEARCH (ASPR)
      5 West 73rd St.
      New York, N. Y. 10023

President: Montague Ullman

Under the leadership of William James, the A. S. P. R. was organized in 1885 with Simon Newcomb, the astronomer, as its first president. Later it became a branch of the Society for Psychical Research (London), with Richard Hodgson, working out of Boston, directing its research. Hodgson died in 1905, at which time an independent A. S. P. R. was organized in New York with James H. Hyslop as its secretary-

treasurer. He initiated the Society's publications program
in 1907.

The purpose of the A. S. P. R. , a non-profit institution,
"is to advance the understanding of phenomena alleged to be
paranormal: telepathy, clairvoyance, precognition, psychokinesis, and related occurrences that are not at present
thought to be explicable in terms of physical, psychological,
and biological theories. " The Society maintains an active
Research Department under the direction of Karlis Osis. In
addition it publishes a quarterly Journal (330), a Proceedings
(332), and a Newsletter (335). It also disseminates information by lectures, forums, seminars, and workshops, and by
providing counsel to research workers, writers, and educa-
tors. Students and others are supplied with information and
materials upon request. The Society maintains a library.
Anyone may use the library, but only members may borrow
books.

There are no membership requirements. The basic
dues are $5. 00 (Students); $15. 00 (Regular). Higher classes
of membership will be described upon request to the A. S. P. R.
in care of the executive secretary. Members in all
classes receive the publications of the Society. In 1972 the
membership stood at 2300.

315 DEPARTMENT OF PSYCHOLOGY AND PARAPSYCHOLOGY
     Andhra University
     Waltair
     Visakhapatam 3, India

     Director: K. Ramakrishna Rao

The Department was established in 1967 by the University Grants Commission. In addition to Rao there were
two research scholars on the staff. Regular students for
graduate study were first admitted in the fall of 1968. It
was reported in 1970 that "the Department restricts admis-
sions to eight students every year.... The minimum eligibility requirement for admission to Ph. D. in Parapsychology
is a Master's degree in arts or science with satisfactory
evidence of competence to carry on research in parapsychology. The minimum required residence at the University is
two years. The Ph. D. degree is awarded entirely on the
basis of the thesis. Ph. D. students have no required
course work.

"The M. A. Degree in Psychology in a two-year course of study. Minimum eligibility for admission is a bachelor's degree in arts or science. Parapsychology is offered as a subject for the final year students. Also the student may select to write a dissertation on a parapsychological topic."

Currently there are seven staff members. In 1972 there were four Ph. D. candidates doing work in parapsychology.

A Psi Newsletter is published for private circulation by the Convener of the Parapsychological Society of India, the headquarters of which is in the Department of Psychology and Parapsychology. It is sent free of charge to all persons known to have a scientific interest in the field. Although no subscription is required, contributions are accepted. The first issue, published in May 1970, consisted of eight pages, with several photographs.

316   DIVISION OF PARAPSYCHOLOGY
      Department of Psychiatry
      University of Virginia Medical Center
      Charlottesville, Va. 22901

Director: Ian Stevenson

Established in 1968, "the policy of the Division aims at the development of a broad program of investigation covering a variety of aspects of the field of parapsychology with an effort to concentrate and develop excellence in certain topics of special interest to the individual members of the staff." Part of the Department of Psychiatry, the Division "is partly supported by a parapsychology research endowment fund. This fund supports a Research Professorship in Psychiatry with the provision that the incumbent will devote at least fifty per cent of his time to research into the question of the survival of human personality after death." Presently there are four members of the research staff in addition to Stevenson. The Division hopes to have a regular training program which will allow for one or two summer fellowships and one or two year-long fellowships annually. As far as known, this is the first division of parapsychology completely integrated into a department in an American university.

317 DREAM LABORATORY
     Department of Psychiatry
     Maimonides Medical Center
     4802 Tenth Ave.
     Brooklyn, N. Y. 11219

     Director: Stanley Krippner

        Established in 1962 as part of the Department of Psy-
chiatric Services by the chairman of the department, Montague Ullman, the purpose of the Dream Laboratory is to "ex-
plore the problem of telepathy and dreams by means of the
newly discovered Rapid Eye Movement monitoring technique."
A number of experiments on psi occurring in sleep and in
other altered states of consciousness have been conducted,
many of them published in the professional psychiatric, psychological, and parapsychological journals.

        The main function of the Laboratory is research, but
it also serves as an informal meeting place for scholars in
parapsychology. It provides an educational service by means
of the wide interdisciplinary dissemination of its experimental reports and by lectures to outside groups by staff members. Training is provided for summer volunteers.

318 FOUNDATION FOR RESEARCH ON THE NATURE OF
     MAN (FRNM)
     Box 6847
     College Station
     Durham, N. C. 27708

     Executive Director: J. B. Rhine

        Established in 1962, the founding Board of Directors
of FRNM was drawn primarily from the Duke University
Parapsychology Laboratory. Its aim was to make the tran-
sition over a period of time from the Duke Laboratory to an
international world center for the advancement of parapsychology and its integration with other scientific studies of
the nature of man.

        The Foundation's stated purpose is to "explore fully
and carefully all the unusual types of experiences known to
man that suggest underlying capacities or principles as yet
unrecognized." In addition to research, FRNM serves as a
clearinghouse for information on parapsychology and as a

training base for persons interested in pursuing empirical studies of psi.

The Institute of Parapsychology is a division of FRNM and is described separately below.

FRNM owns the Parapsychology Press, which publishes the quarterly Journal of Parapsychology. The Press also publishes a limited number of books, especially collections of papers originally appearing in the Journal of Parapsychology (329) which have been rewritten in less technical language (see 55 and 57).

319 INSTITUT FUR GRENZGEBIETE DER PSYCHOLOGIE
     (Institute for Border Areas of Psychology)
     78 Freiburg im Breisgau
     Eichhalde 12, West Germany

Director: Hans Bender

Two institutions are subsumed under the general title given above: Institut für Grenzgebiete der Psychologie und Psychohygiene (Institute for Border Areas of Psychology and Mental Hygiene) and Abteilung für Grenzgebiete der Psychologie des Psychologischen Instituts der Universität Freiburg (Department for Border Areas of Psychology of the Psychological Institute of Freiburg University). The first is a foundation which was responsible for erecting the building which houses the Institute, for installing the library, and for part of the equipment. It was founded in 1950 by Bender. In 1954 the Institute became affiliated with the Chair for Border Areas of Psychology at Freiburg University, held by Bender.

The Department for Border Areas of Psychology is part of the Psychological Institute at the University. It was established in 1966 when the chair held by Bender was extended to psychology in addition to the border areas of that subject, indicating that at Freiburg parapsychology is now viewed as an integral part of psychology. Freiburg students can take courses in parapsychology at the Institute and the University offers graduate degrees in psychology for work in parapsychology. The instruction offered and the research undertaken at the Institute cover a wide range of parapsychological topics. The psychology and psychopathology of psi is stressed, and scientific research is actively promulgated as a combatant to superstition.

Since 1957 the Institute has published a scholarly
journal, the <u>Zeitschrift für Parapsychologie und Grenzgebiete</u>
<u>der Psychologie</u>, which contains English summaries of most
articles.   It also publishes monographs.

320   INSTITUTE FOR PARAPSYCHOLOGY
      Box 6847
      College Station
      Durham, N. C. 27708

      Acting Director: Walter J. Levy, Jr.

The designated successor to the Duke University Parapsychology Laboratory is the division of FRNM known as the
Institute for Parapsychology.   Among several research units
envisaged as part of the larger body, it was the first to be
created because "as a branch of inquiry already far advanced
in methods, and with a body of confirmed knowledge well
tested by decades of controversy, parapsychology is the subject of study qualified to lead the advance further into the
territory of what identifies man."   The Institute houses the
Duke collection of more than 10,000 accounts of spontaneous
psi experiences.   The founders state that "the increasing re-
sponsibilities of the center have come to require an independent, self-governing and self-sustaining institution, inter-
university in character, and international in scope."

The Institute conducts research, serves as an international forum, and holds review meetings several times a
year to which research workers from other centers are invited.   The resulting papers, as well as reports of the Institute's own research, are published primarily in the <u>Journal</u>
<u>of Parapsychology</u> (329) and also in book form (see 55 and
57).

321   INSTITUTE OF PSYCHOPHYSICAL RESEARCH
      118 Banbury Road
      Oxford, OX2 6JU England

      Director: Celia E. Green

This group was organized in 1962 by some members
of the Society for Psychical Research, all graduates of Oxford, who felt the need for a professional organization which
would stress the psychophysiological aspects of psi phenomena

in its investigations.   Although an independent group, it was
established in a university community in order to take advantage of contact with experts in related sciences.   In 1972
there were three full-time staff members and three assis-
tants.

The main aim of the Institute is research and the results are published in parapsychological periodicals and in
the Institute's own Proceedings (see 11, 118, and 167), issued
irregularly.

322   PARAPHYSICAL LABORATORY
        Downton
        Wiltshire, England

        Director: Benson Herbert
        Research Officer: Manfred Cassirer

This unit was organized by a group of members of
the Society for Psychical Research who wished to specialize
in studying the physical aspects of psi phenomena.   In addition to conducting research, the Paraphysical Laboratory
publishes the bimonthly Journal of Paraphysics.

323   PARAPSYCHOLOGICAL ASSOCIATION (P. A.)
        No permanent address.   Address inquiries to A. S. P. R.

        President: elected yearly

International in scope, this is the professional society
of parapsychology.   Formed in 1957, its Constitution states
that the aim of the Association is "to advance parapsychology
as a science, to disseminate knowledge of the field, and to
integrate the findings with those of other branches of science." It aims further to enlarge the number of active research workers by improving working conditions in the field
and by fostering communication both inside parapsychology
and with the scientific community as a whole.   One of its
major activities is to hold an annual convention, the results
of which are published in its Proceedings (333).   In 1969 the
Association was granted affiliation with the American Association for the Advancement of Science.

The Council for 1973 consists of Rex G. Stanford
(President), and John Beloff, Charles Honorton, J. G. Pratt,

Helmut Schmidt, Montague Ullman, and Robert Van de Castle.
In 1972 there was a total of 208 members, of which 96 were
full members, 108 associate members, and 4 honorary members.

    Announcements of the Parapsychological Association
are carried in its affiliated journals: Journal of Parapsychology and Journal A. S. P. R.

324   PARAPSYCHOLOGICAL DIVISION OF THE PSYCHOLOGI-
      CAL LABORATORY
      Varkenmarkt 2
      Utrecht, The Netherlands

      Research-Leader: Martin Johnson

    Originally known as the Parapsychology Institute of
the State University of Utrecht, this organization was founded
by W. H. C. Tenhaeff, who became "privaat docent" in parapsychology at the University upon receipt of his doctorate in
1933. When he was appointed a full professor in 1953, he
was also made director of the Institute. The Institute (now
Division) is supported by funds provided by the state. During Tenhaeff's directorship he and his co-workers conducted
parapsychological research and published their results in
books, parapsychological periodicals, and occasionally in reports put out by the Institute itself, some in English. Tenhaeff also taught parapsychology and supervised graduate students working on parapsychological topics.

    When Tenhaeff retired, the directorship of the Insti-
tute was placed on an annual basis. The present (1972) incumbent is Martin Johnson, formerly of the Department of
Psychology, University of Lund. The Parapsychological Division functions primarily as a research laboratory, but it
also maintains a parapsychology library. The results of
Johnson's research are published in the professional parapsychological journals and in the Research Letter (published
irregularly) of the Division.

325   PARAPSYCHOLOGY FOUNDATION (P. F.)
      29 West 57th St.
      New York, N. Y. 10019

      President: Mrs. Eileen Coly

Founded in 1951 as a "non-profit educational organization to support impartial scientific inquiry into the total nature and working of the mind and to make available the results of such inquiry," the Foundation's first president was Mrs. Eileen J. Garrett, who played an active role until her death in 1970. The Foundation's concern is not only with parapsychology as such, but also with its relation to other fields as they touch on the nature of mind such as psychology, psychiatry, physics, religion, philosophy, medicine, and psychopharmacology.

Although at one time the Foundation maintained an active research department on its premises, this was discontinued. One of its major functions is to provide financial support for research and education in the form of grants to individuals. Grants are also made to institutions for parapsychologically-oriented teaching facilities, libraries, or research equipment. It maintains an active publications program which includes a series of parapsychological monographs, occasional hardcover books on subjects of general interest to psychical research, and the bimonthly Parapsychology Review (336). The Foundation also holds a number of international and interdisciplinary conferences, many of which are published in book form and all of which are summarized in Parapsychology Review. Finally, the Foundation maintains "The Eileen J. Garrett Library of the Parapsychology Foundation," a reference library which is open to students and researchers to facilitate studies in psychical research and related subjects.

326 PSYCHICAL RESEARCH FOUNDATION (P. R. F.)
     Duke Station
     Durham, N. C. 27706

     Project Director: W. G. Roll

The Psychical Research Foundation was established in 1960 by Charles E. Ozanne for the investigation of phenomena bearing on the view that some aspects of human personality survive bodily death. The Foundation's premises consist of two adjacent five-room houses rented from Duke University. One contains a parapsychology laboratory and the other a library-seminar room available to students and others interested in the field. It has been used for the undergraduate tutorials in parapsychology directed by Robert L. Morris, research associate of the Foundation and post-

doctoral fellow in psychiatry at Duke University.   The Foundation's research program stresses studies of special sensitives,
haunting and poltergeist phenomena, and out-of-the-body experiences.   News of the Foundation and of survival research
in general is published in its quarterly bulletin, Theta (337).

In 1972 the Foundation announced that it had created
a position for "visiting research assistantships" which can be
sponsored on a yearly basis by interested individuals or organizations.   These assistantships would be available either
for summer work or for longer periods, depending on the
sponsor's contribution.

327   RELIGIOUS EXPERIENCE RESEARCH UNIT
Manchester College
Oxford OX2 6JU England

Director: Alister Hardy

Founded in 1969, the purpose of the Religious Experience Research Unit is "to provide a center where ordinary people, religious or not, who have had experiences of
feeling themselves upheld or given new strength 'by some
kind of power which seems to come from beyond themselves'
will contribute their information.   These reports will be
studied, using social anthropology and psychology techniques,
followed when necessary by interviews in depth."   The Research Unit will also include work on telepathy and allied
phenomena in its program.

328   SOCIETY FOR PSYCHICAL RESEARCH (S. P. R.)
1, Adam & Eve Mews
London W8 6UQ England

President: C. W. K. Mundle (1971-72)

The S. P. R. was organized in 1882 by a group of distinguished scholars and scientists, with Henry Sidgwick of
Cambridge University as its first president.   The object of
the Society was stated initially as being to investigate "that
large group of debatable phenomena designated by such terms
as mesmeric, psychical and spiritualistic."   Its purpose is
stated today as being "to examine without prejudice or pre-
possession and in a scientific spirit those faculties of man,
real or supposed, which appear to be inexplicable on any

generally recognized hypothesis." Since its inception a number of brilliant thinkers have occupied the presidential chair,
among them Oliver Lodge, William F. Barrett, Charles Richet, Eleanor Mildred Sidgwick, Andrew Lang, Henri Bergson, Gilbert Murray, William McDougall, Hans Driesch,
Camille Flammarion, C. D. Broad, and the Americans William James, Walter Franklin Prince, and Gardner Murphy.
The presidential addresses of these and many others provide
a valuable contribution to psychical research.   (They are
published in the Society's Proceedings.)

   In addition to conducting research, mainly by six research-oriented committees of members (Research advisory,
Experimental ESP, Hypnosis, Mental mediumship, Physical
phenomena, and Spontaneous cases), the S. P. R. maintains
a library and valuable archives.   It has published its Proceedings (334) since 1882 and the Journal (331) since 1884.
The Myers Memorial Lectures and a number of pamphlets
on various aspects of psychical research have also been published by the Society.   It sponsors lectures and provides
speakers upon request from groups and organizations.   Recently the S. P. R. set up a studentship trust fund to support
graduate work in parapsychology in British universities.

   Membership in the S. P. R. entitles one to receive
free all its publications, to attend its meetings, and to use
its library.   Applicants for membership must be sponsored
by two members of the Society.   Dues are £4. 00 per year.
College and university students or persons between the ages
of 18 and 25 may become Student Associates at £2. 00 per
year.   In 1971 there were 1180 members, the highest in the
Society's history.   This included 1047 full members and 106
student associates.

IV. PARAPSYCHOLOGICAL PERIODICALS

Since virtually all of the most significant material on parapsychology is published, at least initially, in the professional periodicals and because the newsletter-type publications are of value as sources of current information in the field, the major English-language periodicals are described below in four categories. For each periodical information for obtaining copies is given along with a description of its purpose, contents, style, indexing, availability of back issues, and the names of major libraries owning complete runs.

The first category deals with the six major professional periodicals. Those fortunate enough to own complete sets of these have almost everything of importance ever published on psychical research. Three of these publications (329, 330, 331) are also the best sources for reviews of books in the field.

The second category describes the newsletters of three parapsychological organizations: The American Society for Psychical Research, the Parapsychology Foundation, and the Psychical Research Foundation. These publications provide news items about the organizations which publish them and about the field in general.

The third category concerns popular magazines. At present there is only one in this group--Psychic, which is the "Psychology Today" of parapsychology.

The final group describes periodicals which, though no longer published, still serve as valuable sources of information on major events of parapsychology during the last 20 years.

Although each of the titles listed below contributes (or has contributed), in one way or another, to the growing

literature of psychical research, a general collection does
not need all of them.   The basic scholarly journals are the
Journal of Parapsychology and Journal A. S. P. R.   They both
emphasize experimental papers, but the latter is more well-
rounded in that it also contains many theoretical papers and
case reports.   By means of its abstracts the Proceedings of
the Parapsychological Association presents the most complete
record of current, on-going research in parapsychology.
Psychic provides popular treatment of a wide range of topics.
For those wishing to keep up with what is happening in parapsychology as regards personnel, courses, lectures, and
other current news items, Parapsychology Review is useful.

MAJOR PROFESSIONAL PERIODICALS

329   Journal of Parapsychology (JP)
      V. 1, 1937 to date
      Published quarterly in March, June, Sept., and Dec.

Editors: Louisa E. Rhine,   Publisher:
        Dorothy H. Pope   Parapsychology Press
Pages: average 88/issue   Box 6847
Size: 22. 8cm   College Station
Circulation: 1350   Durham, N. C. 27708
Price: $8/year; $2/issue

Purpose: "Devoted primarily to the original publication of experimental results and other research findings in
extrasensory perception and psychokinesis.   In addition, articles presenting reviews of literature relevant to parapsychology, criticisms of published work, theoretical and philosophical discussions, and new methods of mathematical analysis
will be published as Journal space allows. "

Style: Scholarly.   Abstracts are provided at the beginning of most articles and a glossary is included in each
issue for lay readers.   Tables, charts, diagrams.

Contents: Each issue contains an average of four papers averaging 13 pages in length and two book reviews
averaging three pages.   As an affiliated organ of the Parapsychological Association, it carries announcements of that
organization and, from 1958 through 1971, abstracts of its
convention.   Other features are "News and Comments, " ex-
panded in 1972 to replace the Parapsychology Bulletin (342),

correspondence, and "Books Received." Most issues contain
a valuable section "Parapsychological Abstracts," initiated in
1958. This section presents abstracts (averaging half a page
in length) of relevant articles published in other journals,
both parapsychological and non-parapsychological, some in
foreign languages, and of unpublished reports on file at the
Institute for Parapsychology of FRNM. Xerox copies of the
original versions of the unpublished reports may be obtained
from the Journal at 10 cents per page.

Indexes and abstracts: Each volume has a table of
contents and a name and subject index. The table of contents for v.1, 1947, through v.16, 1952, was published in
the Sept. 1953, issue. The Journal is abstracted in Psychological Abstracts and indexed in Mental Health Book Review
Index.

Back issues: For information about vols. 1-12, 1937-
1948, write to Walter J. Johnson, Inc., 111 Fifth Ave., New
York, N. Y. 10003. Also available from University Microfilms, Ann Arbor, Mich. 48106. Back issues from v.13,
1949 to date may be obtained from the Journal at $2.25 per
issue or $9.00 per volume.

Libraries: The following libraries are listed in the
Union List of Serials as having the Journal of Parapsychology
from v.1 to date: Academy Medicine (Brooklyn); U Arkansas;
U California (Berkeley); U California (Los Angeles); Case
Western Reserve U; U Chicago; City Coll of City U of N Y;
Clark U; Cleveland P L; Colgate U; Coll Physicians of Phila;
Columbia U; Dartmouth Coll; Denver U; Detroit P L; Duke
U; U Florida; Free L Phila; Harvard U; Honnold L (Clare-
mont, Cal); U Illinois; Indiana U; U Iowa; Iowa St U; Los
Angeles P L; U Michigan; Milwaukee P L; U Minnesota; U
Mississippi; U Missouri; U Nebraska; N Y Academy Medi-
cine; N Y P L; N Y U School of Commerce L; Ohio St L;
Ohio St U; U Oregon; U Pennsylvania; U Rochester; Stanford
U; Swarthmore Coll; Syracuse U; U Texas; Vanderbilt U; U
Washington; Wesleyan U; Williams Coll.

330 Journal of the American Society for Psychical Research
     (JASPR)
     V.1, 1907 to date
     Published quarterly in Jan., Apr., July, and Oct.

Editor: Laura A. Dale   Publisher:
Pages: average 108/issue   American Society for
Size: 22.8cm   Psychical Research
Circulation: 2500   5 West 73rd St.
Price: free to members; $3/issue   New York, N. Y. 10023

Purpose: To further the advance of parapsychology
by publishing reports of experimental work carried out at
the ASPR and at other major research centers, case reports and discussions, theoretical and statistical papers, articles dealing with relevant trends in other disciplines, and
reviews of current books and periodicals in the field.

Style: Scholarly. Abstracts are provided for all experimental articles. Illustrated. Tables, charts, diagrams.

Contents: Each issue contains an average of five papers averaging 15 pages in length, plus three book reviews
averaging five pages. Also contains correspondence and
"Books Received." As an affiliated organ, it carries announcements of the Parapsychological Association.

Selections: Three papers on the survival problem by
Gardner Murphy, originally published in the Journal, are
available in book form (257).

Indexes and abstracts: The Journal provides a name
and subject index for each volume as well as a table of contents. A cumulative card index is maintained at the ASPR's
headquarters. It is abstracted in Psychological Abstracts
and indexed in Mental Health Book Review Index and in Social Science Citation Index. The table of contents of each
issue is reproduced in Selected List of Tables of Contents
of Psychiatric Periodicals.

Back issues: Pre-1941 and post-1960: some issues
available from the ASPR at $3.00 each. Vols. 35-54, 1941-
1960, available from Walter J. Johnson, Inc. (111 Fifth Ave.,
New York, N. Y. 10003): Paperbound set, $230; per paper-
bound volume, $11.50. Also available from University Mi-
crofilms: (Ann Arbor, Mich. 48106): Vols. 1-4, 1907-1948,
for $143.00; v.43, 1949, to date for $4.00 per volume.

Libraries: Listed in the Union List of Serials as
owning the Journal from v.1 to date are the following libraries: Buffalo & Erie Co P L; Carnegie L Pittsburgh;

Cleveland P L; U Colorado; Columbia U; Dartmouth Coll; De-
troit P L; P L of District of Columbia; Duke U; Free L
Phila; Harvard U; Haverford Coll; Houston P L; U Iowa;
Los Angeles P L; L of Congress; U Michigan; Michigan St
L; U Nebraska; N Y P L; Ohio St U; U Pennsylvania; Spo-
kane P L; Stanford Coll Libraries; Williams Coll; Yale U.

331   Journal of the Society for Psychical Research (JSPR)
        V.1, 1884 to date
        Published quarterly in March, June, Sept., and Dec.

Editor: Renée Haynes   Publisher:
Pages: average 52/issue   Society for Psychical Research
Size: 21.3cm   1 Adam & Eve Mews
Circulation: unknown   London, England W8 6UQ

Price: free to members (v.1-34, 1884-1948, restricted to
        members only. From Sept. 1949 to date available to
        others at £2/year and £.50/issue).

Purpose: From 1884 to 1948, when the circulation of
the Journal was limited to members, it was used as the main
vehicle for publishing spontaneous cases. Since 1949 it has
also published experimental reports and various other kinds
of material which serve to inform readers about what is happening in parapsychology.

Style: Scholarly. Tables, charts, diagrams.

Contents: Average of three articles per issue,
averaging 12 pages in length, dealing with quantitative studies,
mediumistic and spontaneous case reports, theoretical papers
and criticisms. Also included are correspondence, notices,
additions to library, and approximately six book reviews per
issue averaging two pages in length. Periodicals are also
reviewed.

Indexes and abstracts: A name and subject index and
a table of contents are provided for each volume. The Society has issued a list of the principal contents of the Journal
from v.35, 1949 to v.45, 1969. The Journal is included in
the index to the Society's publications (reproduced in part in
207) for v.1-33, 1884-1946. It is abstracted in Psychological Abstracts.

Back issues: Some bound volumes from v.35 on, as

well as individual copies, are available from the S. P. R. or,
in the U. S. A. , from the F. W. Faxon Co. (155 S. W. Park,
Westwood, Mass. 02090). AMS (56 E. 13th St. , New York,
N. Y. 10003) is reprinting v. 1-43, 1884-1966; $200. 00.

Libraries: The Union List of Serials lists the following libraries as having the Journal from v. 1 to date: Bowdoin Coll; Buffalo & Erie Co P L; Case Western Reserve U;
Colgate-Rochester Divinity School; Columbia U; Duke U;
Enoch Pratt L; Free L Phila; Harvard U; James Jerome
Hill Reference L (St. Paul, Minn.); L of Congress; U Minnesota; New Hampshire St L; N Y P L; U Pennsylvania.

332   Proceedings of the American Society for Psychical Re-
        search (PASPR)
        V. 1, 1885-1889; new series, v. 1, 1907 to date
        Published irregularly

Editor: Laura A. Dale   Publisher:
Pages: 32-500   American Society for
Size: 22. 5 or 22. 7cm   Psychical Research
Circulation: 2500   5 West 73rd St.
                                New York, N. Y. 10023

Price: free to members; prices vary according to size of
        issue for non-members.

Purpose: The publication of experimental reports,
theoretical papers, or field studies too long for inclusion in
the Journal.

Style: Scholarly. Illustrated. Tables, charts, diagrams.

Contents: Up to 1926 a varying number of articles
were published per issue, but since then usually only one
monograph-like paper appears in each issue. Experimental
reports, large case collections, and theoretical or methodological articles are included.

Indexes and abstracts: The Society has an unpublished
card index of its Proceedings (1907-1960). The index to S.
P. R. publications (207) includes v. 1 of the old A. S. P. R.
Proceedings. The contents of v. 1 of the old Proceedings
and v. 1 through v. 31 (1907-1927) of the new series is given
in Fodor (201).

Back issues: Some issues are still available from
A. S. P. R. at varying prices.

Libraries: The following libraries are listed in Union
List of Serials as having the Proceedings from the old v.1 to
date or from new series v.1 to date: Boston Athenaeum;
Carnegie L Pittsburgh; Columbia U [n. s. v.1-]; Detroit P L;
Duke U; Free L Phila; Harvard U; Haverford Coll [n. s.
v.1-]; Los Angeles P L; U Michigan; Peabody Institute [n. s.
v.1-]; Toledo P L [n. s. v.1-].

333   Proceedings of the Parapsychological Association
       No. 1, 1966 to date
       Published annually

Editors: W. G. Roll   Publisher:
         R. L. Morris   The Parapsychological Association
         J. D. Morris   c/o Psychical Research Foundation
Pages: average 124/issue   Duke Station
Size: 21.5cm   Durham, N. C. 27706
Circulation: unknown   [To be published by Scarecrow
Price: $3 (pap)   Press after No. 8; see note
                               under Back issues]

Purpose: To provide a published record of the annual
convention of the Parapsychological Association (323), the professional parapsychological society.

Style: Scholarly. Illustrated.

Contents: No. 1 summarized the conventions held
from 1957-1964. Beginning with No. 2, each volume contains shortened versions of the papers delivered, arranged
by subject; the complete text of the presidential address;
and the complete text of the invited dinner address, usually
given by an outstanding scholar from another field.
Reviewed in JASPR 64:449-54 (Oct. 1970); and JP
35:226-29 (1971)--No. 5 only.

Indexes and abstracts: Each number has a combined
subject index and glossary, and a name index.

Back issues: All numbers (1-8) are still available
(from the Psychical Research Foundation only). Nos. 1-5
are $3.50 each and $1.95 each (paperbound). From No. 6
on, each is $3.00 (paper only). Special price for first four

numbers is $12.00; $6.00 (paper). (The hardcover edition
of No. 5 and paperbound edition of No. 1 are no longer in
print.) Information on issues after No. 8, to be published
by the Scarecrow Press, may be obtained from Scarecrow;
this new series, beginning with virtually "No. 9" of the old
series, will be called Research in Parapsychology 19(72) and
will be an annual, hardcover only; exact continuity of the
proceedings will not be lost.

Libraries: The following libraries are listed in New
Serial Titles as having the Proceedings of the Parapsycho-
logical Association from No. 1 to date: Boston P L; Brook-
lyn Coll; U California (Los Angeles); U Colorado; Columbia
U; Cornell U; Georgia St Coll; Indiana U; L of Congress;
Linda Hall L (Kansas City, Mo.); Los Angeles P L; Michi-
gan St U; Montana St U; N Y P L; N Y St L; Pennsylvania
St U; U Santa Clara; Syracuse U; Temple U.

334 Proceedings of the Society for Psychical Research (PSPR)
     V. 1, 1882 to date
     Published irregularly. Each volume contains unspeci-
     fied number of "parts" (issues)

Editor: Renée Haynes   Publisher:
Pages: 30-600   Society for Psychical Research
Size: 21. 3cm   1 Adam & Eve Mews
Circulation: unknown   London, England W8 6UQ

Price: free to members; prices vary according to size of
     issue for non-members.

Purpose: To publish the "cream" of the Society's
work at whatever length and however often as determined by
the amount of material available. The Proceedings contain
major research reports, the Society's presidential addresses,
and papers of an analytical or theoretical nature.

Style: Scholarly. Tables, charts, diagrams.

Contents: From 1882 through the 1920s each issue
contained four to 10 articles, but from 1930 on there is usually only one article per part. Included are experimental,
theoretical, critical, and review papers on psychical research topics, as well as collections of spontaneous cases,

presidential and other addresses, and obituaries of prominent persons associated with the field. Until Part 177, 1949, the Proceedings also contained from two to four lengthy reviews of important books, but all reviews (except for an occasional review article) are now published in the Journal.

Indexes and abstracts: Indexed in vols. 3-11 (1920-1949) of the Social Sciences and Humanities Index (then the International Index), in British Humanities Index, and in Psychological Abstracts. The Society has issued an index to its publications, including the Proceedings, in three volumes, covering 1882-1946 (207 includes the first two). It has also issued a list of the principal contents of Proceedings from 1882 to 1969. The contents from 1882 through 1933 are included in Fodor (201).

Back issues: Some bound volumes or separate parts are still available from the Society at varying prices (half price to members). AMS (56 E. 13th St., New York, N. Y. 10003) plans to reprint v.1-53, 1882-1962, at $325.00.

Libraries: The following libraries are listed in Union List of Serials as having the Proceedings from v.1 to date: Amherst Coll; Boston P L; Bowdoin Coll; Brooklyn P L; Bryn Mawr Coll; Buffalo & Erie Co P L; U California (Berkeley); Carnegie L Pittsburgh; Case Western Reserve U; Chicago P L; Cleveland P L; Cincinnati & Hamilton Co P L; Detroit P L; Duke U; Free L Phila; Harvard U; Haverford Coll; James Jerome Hill Reference L (St. Paul, Minn.); U Illinois; Indiana U; L of Congress; Los Angeles P L; U Michigan; Milwaukee P L; U Minnesota; U Nebraska; N Y Academy Medicine; N Y P L; N Y St L; Northwestern U; Ohio St U; U Pennsylvania; Princeton U; U Rochester; St. Louis P L; Seattle P L; Stanford U; Swarthmore Coll; U Tennessee; U Washington; Wellesley Coll; U Wisconsin; Yale U.

ORGANIZATIONAL NEWSLETTERS AND BULLETINS

335 ASPR Newsletter
        No. 1, Nov. 1968 to date
        Published quarterly in Spring, Summer, Autumn, and
        Winter

Editor: Marian L. Nester   Publisher:
Pages: 4-6/issue   American Society for
Size: 28cm   Psychical Research
Circulation: 2500   5 West 73rd St.
                                   New York, N. Y. 10023
Price: free to members; not available to non-members

Purpose: To keep members informed of the activities
and opportunities of the Society. Also, to make research
reports more easily understood by readers lacking the necessary technical vocabulary. To this end, short rewrites of
JASPR articles in layman's language occasionally appear in
the Newsletter.
Style: Non-technical. Illustrated.
Contents: Each issue usually contains a brief lead
article, followed by news of ASPR activities and parapsychological news in general.
Indexes and abstracts: None.
Back issues: None.

336 Parapsychology Review
     V. 1, 1970 to date
     Published bimonthly.

Editor: Betty Shapin   Publisher:
Pages: average 24/issue   Parapsychology Foundation
Size: 27.8cm   29 West 57th St.
Circulation: 2000   New York, N. Y. 10019
Price: $4/year; $.85/issue

Purpose: Took over the functions of the Newsletter
of the Parapsychology Foundation (341) and the International
Journal of Parapsychology (340). It presents directory-type
information such as the latest news coverage on persons and
organizations associated with parapsychology, as well as
items on events, grants, courses, lectures, symposia, degrees, etc. International in scope.
Style: Non-technical. Magazine-type format; illustrated.
Contents: Contains an average of three or four brief
articles on parapsychology in various countries or state-of-
the-art reviews of various aspects of psychical research.
Also profiles of persons associated with parapsychology, book
reviews, conference reports, obituaries, and books received.
Indexes and abstracts: An annual index is published
in the Jan-Feb. issue of the following year.

Back issues: Some are available from the Parapsychology Foundation.

337 Theta
     No. 1, 1963 to date
     Published quarterly in Spring, Summer, Autumn, and
     Winter

Editor: W. G. Roll   Publisher:
Pages: 4-8/issue   Psychical Research Foundation
Size: 22. 8cm   Duke Station
Circulation: 700   Durham, N. C. 27706
Price: $1. 50/year

Purpose: Named after the first letter of the Greek
word thanatos [death] this publication is subtitled "A Bulletin
for Research on the Problem of Survival after Bodily Death. "
Roll writes: "The Foundation and its bulletin represent no
position regarding survival except the belief that scientific
observation and experimentation may lead to a solution. "
Theta was begun "in order that the work of the Foundation,
as well as other research and educational efforts concerned
with the survival problem, might become more widely
known. " Not intended as a substitute for other publications
in the field, one of the bulletin's functions is to "direct
readers to papers and books by abstracts or reviews. "
     Style: Scholarly.
     Contents: Each issue usually contains a lead article
discussing current research and other activities touching on
the survival problem, plus one or two book reviews.
     Indexes and abstracts: None.
     Back issues: A special edition of Theta is available
for issues 1-32 (1963-1971), bound in softcover, at $3. 00.
     Libraries: The following libraries are listed in New
Serial Titles as having Theta from No. 1 to date: Harvard
U; U Illinois; L of Congress; N Y P L; U Washington.

POPULAR MAGAZINES

338 Psychic
     V. 1, 1969 to date
     Published bimonthly

Editor: James G. Bolen   Publisher:
Co-editor: Alan Vaughan   James G. Bolen
Pages: average 48/issue   680 Beach Street
Size: 27.5cm   San Francisco, Calif. 94109
Price: $3/year; $.75/issue

Purpose: Initiated, writes Bolen, because of "the
field's publication gap at the popular level...." The function
of Psychic is to "bring forward interesting and assorted material of every perspective and from every corner, fairly
and forthrightly. The conclusions, if any, will be left to the
venturesome reader."

Style: Popular. Illustrated.

Contents: Regular features include an interview with
a prominent person associated with parapsychology. In addition there are three or four articles; a section entitled "Phenomena" (mostly case reports); "News Ambit" (brief items
of international scope); "Comments" (readers' opinions); book
reviews, and a list of books and articles relevant to the interviews and articles in each issue.

Indexes and abstracts: None.

Back issues: Most issues are still available at $1.00
each.

DISCONTINUED PUBLICATIONS

339 FRNM Bulletin
     No. 1, Summer 1965 through No. 14, Autumn 1969 [No.
     15 continued as Parapsychology Bulletin (342)]; quarter-
     ly

Editor: FRNM Staff   Publisher: Parapsychology Press
Pages: 4   Box 6847, College Station
Size: 28cm   Durham, N. C. 27708

Purpose: Similar to that of the Parapsychology Bulletin, but geared to communicate news of FRNM rather than of
the Duke University Parapsychology Laboratory. More emphasis was given to growing research centers elsewhere.

Style: Non-technical. Illustrated.

Contents: Similar to the Parapsychology Bulletin,
with the addition of an editorial column by J. B. Rhine and
"From Life Situations" by L. E. Rhine, on types of spon-

taneous psi experiences.

Indexes and abstracts: None.

Back issues: Some are available from FRNM. Also,
in 1972 University Microfilms announced that it had received
permission to reproduce the Parapsychology Bulletin from
1965 to 1971, which includes a complete run of the FRNM
Bulletin.

340 International Journal of Parapsychology (IJP)
     V.1, Summer 1959 through v.10, Winter 1968; quar-
     terly

Editor: Martin Ebon   Publisher:
Pages: average 108/issue   Parapsychology Foundation
Size: 22.5 and 28cm   29 West 57th St.
                                 New York, N. Y. 10019

Purpose: Established to act "as a forum for scholarly inquiry, linking parapsychology with psychology, physics,
biochemistry, pharmacology, anthropology, ethnology, and
other scientific disciplines, the International Journal of Parapsychology publishes contributions dealing with the total nature of the mind."

Style: Scholarly. Tables, charts, diagrams.

Contents: An average of six articles per issue, consisting of general and critical review papers, theoretical
contributions, exploratory essays, and some experimental
reports. A résumé of each article is given in French, German, Italian, and Spanish. About six book reviews per issue, averaging three pages.

Selections: The Psychic Force (87) is composed of
articles originally published in the International Journal.

Indexes and abstracts: Separate indexes were published for v.1-3, v.4, v.5, v.6, v.7, and v.8-10.

Back issues: v.1-10 available from University Microfilms (Ann Arbor, Mich. 48106) for $60.00.

Libraries: The following libraries are listed in New
Serial Titles as having the International Journal from v.1:

Bell Telephone Lab (Murray Hill, N. J.); Brooklyn Coll;
Brown U; U California (Berkeley); U Chicago; Columbia U;
Cornell U; Duke U; Harvard U; John Crerar L (Chicago);
L of Congress; Los Angeles P L; Michigan St U; N Y P L;
U Washington; U Wisconsin; Yale U.

341   Newsletter of the Parapsychology Foundation
      V. 1, 1953 through v. 16, 1969 [Continued as Parapsy-
      chology Review (336)]; bimonthly

Editors: Laura Oteri,   Publisher:
         Sylvia Shearer   Parapsychology Foundation
Pages: average 12/issue   29 West 57th St.
Size: 28cm   New York, N. Y. 10019

Purpose: To publish news items concerning the
Foundation's activities as well as those of parapsychologists
and psychical research groups the world over.
      Style: Popular.   Illustrated.
      Contents: One or two articles per issue, often re-
printed from parapsychological periodicals or books.   Notices
of lectures, courses, symposia, and other directory-type information.   Average of two book reviews, paragraph-length
descriptions of five or six other books, and books received.
      Indexes and abstracts: None.
      Back issues: Some available from the Parapsychology
Foundation.
      Libraries: The following libraries are listed in New
Serial Titles as having the Newsletter: Harvard U (from v. 1
on); L of Congress (from v. 2 on).

342   Parapsychology Bulletin (PB)
      No. 1, 1946 through No. 72, 1965 and new series No.
      15, 1970 through No. 20, 1971.   Between 1965 and
      1970 published as FRNM Bulletin (339); quarterly

Editor: Dorothy H. Pope   Publisher: Parapsychology Press
Pages: 4-6   Box 6847, College Station
Size: 22. 8 and 28cm   Durham, N. C. 27708

Purpose: Initiated to bring parapsychological research closer to the general reader and "to help bring together the family of parapsychologists everywhere, many of whom
... know [each other] only through the formal medium of
their scientific publications. " These functions have now been

taken over by a new section in the Journal of Parapsychology
(329) entitled "News and Comments."

    Style: Informal. Illustrated.

    Contents: An average of six articles a paragraph or
two long. Regular features are "Events," "Personnel," and
very brief reviews of books and periodical articles (mostly
in non-parapsychological publications).

    Indexes and abstracts: None.

    Back Issues: Some are available from FRNM. The
first series is available from University Microfilms (Ann
Arbor, Mich. 48106) bound in with the Journal of Parapsychology. In addition, University Microfilms announced in
1972 that it had received permission to reproduce the Parapsychology Bulletin from 1956 to 1971, which includes the
issues that were too large to bind with the Journal of Parapsychology and also the FRNM Bulletin.

    Libraries: Many libraries owning bound copies of
the Journal of Parapsychology will also have the initial series
(size, 22.8cm) of the Parapsychology Bulletin bound in with
it, and may also have the new series since it was sent to
all subscribers to JP.

V. SCIENTIFIC RECOGNITION OF PARAPSYCHOLOGY

What do "experts" in other fields think about psi? Has its investigation received academic sanction and recognition? Actually, the opinions of scientists in other disciplines cover a wide range. The distinguished British psychologist H. J. Eysenck has written: "Unless there is a gigantic conspiracy involving some thirty University departments all over the world, and several hundred highly respected scientists in various fields, many of them originally hostile to the claims of psychical researchers, the only conclusion the unbiased observer can come to must be that there does exist a small number of people who obtain knowledge existing either in other people's minds, or in the outer world, by means yet unknown to science" [Sense and Nonsense in Psychology (192), Harmondsworth: Penguin, 1957; p. 13].

A reverse position, however, was indicated by the University of Minnesota chemist, George R. Price, who wrote: "If, then, parapsychology and modern science are incompatible, why not reject parapsychology? We know that the alternate hypothesis, that some men lie or deceive themselves, fits quite well within the framework of science. The choice is between believing in something 'truly revolutionary' and 'radically contradictory to contemporary thought' and believing in the occurrence of fraud and self-delusion. Which is more reasonable?" ["Science and the Supernatural," Science 122:359-67 (Aug. 26, 1955) p361.] Price opted for the latter hypothesis.

Finally, there is McGill University psychologist Donald O. Hebb's frank admission: "Personally, I do not accept ESP for a moment, because it does not make sense. My external criteria, both of physics and physiology, say that ESP is not a fact despite the behavioral evidence that has been reported. I cannot see what other basis my colleagues have for rejecting it; and if they are using my basis,

they and I are allowing psychological evidence to be passed
on by physical and physiological censors. Rhine may still
turn out to be right, improbable as I think that is, and my
own rejection of his views is--in the literal sense--preju-
dice" ["The Role of Neurological Ideas in Psychology, "
Journal of Personality 20:39-55 (Sept. 1951) p45.]

Thus it appears that at the individual level opinions
about the reality of psi are often based on a gut response
of belief or doubt. Perhaps a better way to approach the
question of scientific and academic acceptance of parapsychology is to consider it not from an individual angle, but from
that of institutions and organizations. This approach will
provide an idea of the number and kinds of footholds that
parapsychology has found or made in the academic and scientific stronghold. The remainder of this section will therefore consist of examples of academic and scientific recognition of parapsychology.

RECOGNITION BY ACADEMIC INSTITUTIONS (CHRONOLOGY)

One way of assessing academic recognition is to note
any evidence that parapsychology has been accepted by colleges and universities. Some significant events indicative of
such acceptance are listed below in chronological order.

1884. University of Pennsylvania. Bequest accepted from
Henry Seybert to establish a Chair of Moral Philosophy in order to investigate modern spiritualism in
particular, as well as related subjects.

1908. Clark University (Worcester, Mass.). Establishment
of the Smith Battles Fund to defray expenses for lectures or experimental research on spiritualism and
psychical research.

1911. Stanford University. Establishment of an endowed
laboratory for psychical research.

1912. Harvard University. Establishment of the Hodgson
Fund for parapsychological research.

1927. Duke University. William McDougall and J. B.
Rhine began research in parapsychology in the Department of Psychology.

1932. University of Leyden (Holland). Paul A. Deitz ap-
       pointed as tutor in parapsychology.

1934. Duke University. Establishment of the Parapsychology
       Laboratory under the direction of J. B. Rhine.

1934. University of Utrecht (Holland). A readership in
       parapsychology was given to W. H. C. Tenhaeff.

1940. Cambridge University. Perrott Studentship in Psychi-
       cal Research was established. (Now the Perrott-
       Warrick Studentship. For details see JSPR 43:105-
       07, June 1965.)

1950. University of Freiburg (West Germany). Institute for
       Border Areas [Grenzgebiete] of Psychology and Mental
       Hygiene was opened under the direction of Hans Bend-
       er.

1951. Swarthmore College. A collection of literature on
       "psychical science" and funds for an annual lecture
       series on psychical research were presented by John
       William Graham. (See 209.)

1953. University of Pittsburgh. A grant was received from
       the A. W. Mellon Educational and Charitable Trust
       for parapsychological research under the direction of
       R. A. McConnell of the Department of Biophysics.

1953. University of Utrecht. An international congress of
       parapsychology was held at the University sponsored
       by the Parapsychology Foundation, the Minister of Ed-
       ucation of the Netherlands, and the University.

1953. University of Utrecht. A professorship of parapsy-
       chology was established under the direction of W. H.
       C. Tenhaeff.

1954. University of Freiburg. The Chair for Border Areas
       [Grenzgebiete] of Psychology was given to Hans Bend-
       er.

1956. St. Joseph's College (Philadelphia). A Parapsychology
       Laboratory was established under the direction of
       Carroll B. Nash.

1956. Wayland College (Plainview, Texas). A Parapsychol-
       ogy Laboratory was established under the direction of
       John A. Freeman.

1957. National Littoral University (Rosario, Argentina). A
       professorship of parapsychology was established.

1960. National Littoral University. Parapsychology was
       made a required course for candidates for the Ph. D.
       degree in psychology.

1960. Utkal University and the Seth Sohan Lal Memorial In-
       stitute of Parapsychology held a joint symposium on
       "religion and parapsychology" in Cuttack, India.

1961. Leningrad State University. A state-supported re-
       search laboratory in parapsychology was established
       under the direction of L. L. Vasiliev.

1961. University of King's College (Halifax). Authorized
       the opening of a Parapsychology Laboratory. (How-
       ever, it was never realized because of a lack of
       qualified personnel.)

1962. Lucknow University (India). The Department of Psy-
       chology and Philosophy hosted a two-day seminar on
       yoga and parapsychology.

1963. Rajasthan University (India). A Department of Para-
       psychology was established.

1964. University of Chile. Brenio Onetto received a pro-
       fessorship of parapsychology in the School of Psychol-
       ogy.

1964. City College of the City University of New York.
       Two fellowships for research in parapsychology were
       established under the direction of Gertrude R. Sch-
       meidler of the Department of Psychology.

1964. Hradec Kralove University (Czechoslovakia). A para-
       psychological research center was established under
       the direction of Ctibor Vesely of the Department of
       Physiology.

1965. University of California (Los Angeles). Held a sym-
       posium entitled "Extrasensory perception: Fact or
       fantasy ?"

1967. Andhra University (India). A Department of Psychol-
       ogy and Parapsychology was established under the di-
       rection of K. Ramakrishna Rao.

1968. University of Virginia. Within the Department of
       Psychiatry, a Division of Parapsychology was estab-
       lished under the direction of Ian Stevenson.

1969. University of California (Los Angeles). Sponsored a
       symposium entitled "A new look at extrasensory per-
       ception."

1969. Kazakh State University (U.S.S.R.). A "scientific
       method" seminar was held on questions of bioenerget-
       ics (which includes parapsychology).

1970. Nowrosjee Wadia College (India). A parapsychology
       research laboratory was established under the direc-
       tion of V. V. Akolkar.

1970. University of Maine. Held a seminar on ESP.

1970. University of California (Berkeley). Held a two-day
       symposium entitled "ESP and psychic phenomena:
       The invisible forces of the mind."

1971. Moscow University. The Department of Geology held
       a seminar on dowsing attended by over a hundred rep-
       resentatives of various scientific organizations.

1972. University of Utrecht. The University and the De-
       partment of Psychology sponsored an international
       symposium on parapsychology.

GRADUATE DEGREES IN PARAPSYCHOLOGY

     The question is often asked: can one get a graduate
degree in parapsychology? Although the first response is
generally no, because there are no parapsychology departments in American colleges and universities, the second response is a cautious yes--for those hardy students who
either persevere in obtaining sponsorship for a parapsychological thesis in another department such as psychology or
philosophy, or who are willing to travel to countries where
a degree in parapsychology may be obtained. To provide a

picture of the number of theses that have been accepted in partial fulfillment of graduate degrees, a listing is given below. Along with the date the degree was conferred and the name of the person receiving it, wherever possible the specific degree, the thesis title, and the name of the sponsoring department or school are given. In addition, any published version or summary of the work is noted. The doctorates are listed first, followed by the master's theses.

DOCTORAL DISSERTATIONS

1893. Albert Coste. Ph. D. University of Montpellier (France). Department unknown. "Les phénomènes psychiques occultes. "

1902. Carl G. Jung. M. D. University of Zurich. School of Medicine. "On the psychology of so-called occult phenomena. " (Published in v. 1 of Jung's Collected Works: Psychiatric studies, Princeton: Princeton University Press, 1957.)

1918. Johan Liljencrants. Ph. D. Catholic University of America. Department unknown. "Spiritism and religion. " (Published in book form under the same title by Devin-Adair in 1918.)

1933. W. H. C. Tenhaeff. Ph. D. University of Utrecht. Department of Psychology. "Paragnosie en 'einfuhlen. ' "

1933. John F. Thomas. Ph. D. Duke University. Department of Psychology. "An evaluative study of the mental content of certain trance phenomena. " (See 115.)

1941. William L. Reuter. Ed. D. Temple University. Department of Education. "An objective study in extrasensory perception. "

1941. Charles E. Stuart. Ph. D. Duke University. Department of Psychology. "An analysis to determine a test predictive of extrachance scoring in card-calling tests. " (Published, with minor alterations, under the same title in JP 5:99-137, June 1941.)

1942. John Björkhem. Ph. D. University of Lund. Department of Psychology. "De hypnotiska hallucinationerna. "

1943. Laurence J. Bendit. M. D. Cambridge University.
Department of Medicine. "Paranormal cognition: Its
place in human psychology." (Published, with slight
emendations, as a book. See 139.)

1944. V. G. Kirk-Duncan. Ph. D. Oxford University. Department unknown. "A study of certain aspects of
prima facie extrasensory cognition."

1946. Betty M. Humphrey. Ph. D. Duke University. Department of Arts and Sciences. "Discrimination between high and low scoring subjects in ESP tests on
the basis of the form quality of their response drawings." (Published in two parts in JP: "Success in
ESP as related to form of response drawings: I.
Clairvoyance experiments," 10:78-106, June 1946,
and "Success in ESP as related to form of response
drawings: II. GESP experiments," 10:181-196, Sept.
1946.)

1948. S. G. Soal. D. Sc. University of London. Department of Psychology. Granted for his work with Basil
Shackleton and Gloria Stewart. (Published in his
book with F. Bateman: Modern experiments in telepathy, see 63.)

1950. Karlis Osis. Ph. D. University of Munich. Department of Psychology. "Hypotheses of extrasensory
perception."

1953. Remi J. Cadoret. M. D. Yale University. School
of Medicine. "The effect of amytal and dexadrine on
ESP performance." (Published under the same title
in JP 17:259-74, Dec. 1953.)

1955. Harmon Bro. Ph. D. University of Chicago. Divinity School. "The charisma of the seer: A study in
the phenomenology of religious leadership."

1956. Michael Scriven. Ph. D. Oxford University. Department of Philosophy. "Explanations of the supernatural."

1957. Sigurd Binski. Ph. D. University of Bonn. Department of Psychology. Title unknown. (A paper based
on his thesis entitled "Report on two exploratory PK
series" was published in JP 21:284-95, Dec. 1957.)

1959.   Maurice Marsh.   Ph. D.   Rhodes University.   Depart-
        ment of Psychology.   "Linkage in extrasensory per-
        ception."   (Mimeographed copies on file at the ASPR,
        FRNM, SPR, and the Parapsychological Division of
        the Psychological Laboratory, University of Utrecht.
        An article summarizing the thesis appears in JSPR
        40:219-39 (Mar. 1960); also see PB, No. 25 (Feb.
        1952) 1-2.)

1961.   Gerhard Sannwald.   Ph. D.   Albert Ludwigs University
        (Freiburg).   Department unknown.   "Beziehungen
        zwischen 'parapsychischen Erlebuissen' und Person-
        lichkeitmarkmalen. "

1962.   Ruby Yaryan.   Ph. D.   University of London.   De-
        partment of Psychology.   "The effect of various forms
        of conditioning upon liminal, subliminal and extra-
        sensory perception. "

1963.   J. H. Robbertse.   M. D.   University of Utrecht.   De-
        partment unknown.   "Die bruikbaarheid van die begrip
        telepatie in die psigiatri. "   (Abstract in JP 28:148,
        June 1964.)

1964.   Gita H. Elguin.   Ph. D. ?   [unidentified graduate de-
        gree].   University of Chile.   Department of Psychol-
        ogy.   "Psicoquinesis en la tumerogenesis experiment-
        al. "   (Abstract in JP 30:220, Sept. 1966.)

1965.   B. H. Bhadra.   Ph. D.   Sri Venkateswara University.
        Department of Psychology.   "The relationship of test
        scores to belief in ESP. "   (Published under the same
        title in JP 30:1-17, Mar. 1966.)

1966.   Thelma S. Moss.   Ph. D.   University of California at
        Los Angeles.   Department of Psychology.   "A study
        of experimenter bias through subliminal perception,
        non-verbal communication, and ESP. "   (Dissertation
        Abstracts, 10-B, 3677-78.)

1969.   B. K. Kanthamani.   Ph. D.   Andhra University.   De-
        partment of Psychology and Parapsychology.   "Per-
        sonality patterns of ESP subjects. "   (Being published,
        with K. R. Rao, over a period of time in JP under
        the title "Personality characteristics of ESP subjects."
        Three parts have thus far appeared: "I. Primary
        personality characteristics and ESP, " 35:189-207,

Sept. 1971; "II. The combined personality measure
(CPM) and ESP, " 36:56-70, Mar. 1972; and "III. Extraversion and ESP, " 36:198-212, Sept. 1972.)

1971. Christofer Wiesinger. Ph.D. University of Freiburg.
Department of Psychology. "Investigations of extrasensory perception in the social field of the classroom. "

1972. Erlendur Haraldsson. Ph.D. University of Freiburg.
Department of Psychology. "Vasomotor reactions as
indicators of extrasensory perception. "

MASTER'S THESES

1937. Fabian L. Rouke. M.S. Fordham University. Department of Psychology. "An experimental investigation of telepathic phenomena in twins. " (JP 1:163-71,
Sept. 1937.)

1938. Ralph Edward Rothera. M.A. State Teachers College at Fitchburg. Department of Education. "A
study in extrasensory perception. " (Described in JP
2:325-26, Dec. 1938.)

1938. James C. Crumbaugh. M.A. Southern Methodist
University. Department of Psychology. "A questionnaire designed to determine the attitudes of psychologists toward the field of extrasensory perception. "
(JP 2:302-07, Dec. 1938.)

1939. Joseph L. Woodruff. M.A. Duke University. Department of Psychology. "Size of stimulus symbols
in extrasensory perception. " (With J. G. Pratt, published in JP 3:121-58, June 1939.)

1950. Leo Eilbert. M.S. City College of the City University of New York. Department of Education. Title
unknown. (With Gertrude R. Schmeidler, published
under the title "A study of certain psychological factors in ESP performance. " JP 14:53-74, Mar. 1950.)

1951. Beatriz Weinstein. M.A. University of Chile. Department of Education. "Parapsicología o percepción
extrasensorial basado en las investigaciones de la
Universidad de Duke. "

1952. F. Claude Palmer. M. A. University of London.
Department of Psychology. Title unknown. (Described in PB, No. 32:1-3, Nov. 1953.)

1952. Robert L. Van de Castle. M. A. University of Missouri. Department of Psychology. Title unknown.
(Published under the title "An exploratory study of
some variables relating to individual ESP performance."
JP 17:61-72, Mar. 1953.)

1955. Sita Ram Gupta. M. A. Benares Hindu University.
Department of Philosophy and Psychology. "Precognitive elements in extrasensory perception."

1955. K. Ramakrishna Rao. M. A. Andhra University. Department of Philosophy. Title unknown. (Revised
version published under the title Psi cognition, Tenali,
India: Tagore Publishing House, 1957; reviewed in JP
22:292-93, Dec. 1958.)

1957. Rebecca Gerber. M. S. City College of the City University of New York. Department of Psychology.
"An investigation of relaxation and of acceptance of
the experimental situation as related to ESP scores
in maternity patients." (With Gertrude R. Schmeidler, published in JP 21:47-57, Mar. 1957.)

1958. Arnon Deguisne. M. S. MacMurray College. Department of Psychology. Title unknown. (Article adapted
from thesis published under the title "Two repetitions
of the Anderson-White investigation of teacher-pupil
attitudes and clairvoyance test results. Part I. High-
school tests." JP 23:196-207, Sept. 1959.)

1958. Gerald Goldstone. M. S. MacMurray College. Department of Psychology. Title unknown. (Article
adapted from thesis published under the title "Two
repetitions of the Anderson-White investigation of
teacher-pupil attitudes and clairvoyance test results.
Part II. Grade-school tests." JP 23:208-13, Sept.
1959.)

1959. Krzysztof Jach. M. S. Academic Polytechnic School
(Warsaw). Department of Electromedical Apparatus
Designing. "An investigation of telepathy based on
the hypothesis of electromagnetic wave transmission."
(Abstract in JP 27:60-61, Mar. 1963.)

1961. John Lanctot. M. S. <u>City College of the City Univer-</u>
<u>sity of New York</u>. Department of Psychology. Title
unknown.

1962. Kenneth R. Davis. M. S. <u>University of Denver</u>. Department of Psychology. "The relationship of suggest-
ibility to ESP scoring level."

1965. Helen Moses. M. A. <u>City College of the City Univer-</u>
<u>sity of New York</u>. Department of Psychology. "A
study of task-orientation and personality factors related to ESP performance." (Abstract in JP 30:219-
20, Sept. 1966.)

1966. Margaret Eastman. M. A. <u>City College of the City</u>
<u>University of New York</u>. Department of Psychology.
"The relationship of ESP scores to knowledge of tar-
get location, and to birth order and family size."
(Abstract in JP 31:168-69, June 1967.)

1968. Lou Dagel. M. S. <u>Trinity University</u> (Hartford).
Department unknown. "A study utilizing reinforce-
ment in a two-choice general ESP test situation."
(On file at ASPR library.)

1971. Clifton Peterson. M. S. <u>Wisconsin State University</u>.
Department unknown. "Relationships among attitudes,
memory, and extrasensory perception." (Abstract in
JP 36:94, Mar. 1972.)

1971. Howard Eisenberg. M. S. <u>McGill University</u>. Department of Psychology. "Telepathic information
transfer in humans of emotional data."

1971. C. Plug. M. A. <u>University of South Africa</u>. Department unknown. "A study of the psychological
variables underlying the relationship between ESP and
extraversion."

OPPORTUNITIES FOR GRADUATE WORK

Having shown that parapsychology is gaining increasing recognition in the academic community and having reviewed the doctoral and master's work that has been done
on the subject in the past, this section will provide a list

of current opportunities for research experience in the field.
This list is based in part on a survey* recently prepared by
the Education Department of the ASPR giving the names of
84 institutions which offer either formal or informal courses
in parapsychology, some for credit, some not. Only institutions providing opportunities for research and/or graduate
work in the field are mentioned below.

Andhra University (Waltair, India). Dr. K. Ramakrishna
        Rao of the Department of Psychology and Parapsychol-
        ogy supervises graduate work in parapsychology.
        Both M. A. and Ph. D. degrees are offered. (For fur-
        ther qualifications, see 315.)

University of California (Davis). Dr. Charles T. Tart of
        the Department of Psychology supervises students for
        the Ph. D. in psychology. Thesis topics may be on
        parapsychology.

City College of the City University of New York. Dr. Ger-
        trude R. Schmeidler of the Department of Psychology
        supervises graduate work in parapsychology for either
        the M. A. or Ph. D. degree.

Dream Laboratory (Department of Psychiatry, Maimonides
        Medical Center, Brooklyn, N. Y.). Persons inte-
        rested in doing volunteer research work should apply
        to the Director, Dr. Stanley Krippner.

Duke University (Durham, N. C.). Faculty members in
        several departments supervise students for the M. A.
        or Ph. D. degree on thesis topics in parapsychology.
        (For information, write to Mr. W. G. Roll, Psychi-
        cal Research Foundation, Duke Station, Durham, N.
        C. 27706.)

University of Edinburgh. Dr. John Beloff of the Department
        of Psychology supervises graduate work in parapsy-
        chology for the M. S. or Ph. D. degree.

Finch College (New York City). Dr. Roslyn Hayes of the

_____
*Single copies of this survey, entitled "Courses and other
study opportunities in parapsychology, " are available from
the Education Department, ASPR, 5 West 73rd Street, New
York, N. Y. 10023, upon receipt of a stamped ($. 16), self-
addressed envelope.

Department of Psychology supervises individual research.

Foundation for Research on the Nature of Man (Durham,
N. C.). Summer training fellowships are offered for
students who are acquainted with parapsychology and
have made at least a beginning in actual research.
The Ralph Drake Perry Fellowship and a limited number of Visiting Research Fellowships are available
for persons who have started on a research career in
parapsychology.

Franklin Pierce College (Rindge, N. H.). Dr. William J.
Jack of the Department of Psychology in credit courses
in psychology provides opportunity for parapsychological experiments and supervises student research projects.

University of Freiburg (West Germany). Dr. Hans Bender
of the Institut für Grenzgebiete der Psychologie und
Psychohygiene (78 Freiburg i. Br., Eichhalde 12)
supervises students for the Ph. D. in parapsychology.

Loyola College (Montreal). The Department of Psychology
offers a course in experimental parapsychology.

University of Michigan (Ann Arbor). Undergraduate students
are allowed to make independent studies of parapsychological topics for credit.

New School for Social Research (New York City). Dr.
Robert Brier of the Department of Psychology teaches
experimental parapsychology in a course which provides for a research project.

Notre Dame College, St. John's University (Staten Island,
N. Y.). Mr. Charles Honorton teaches a course in
parapsychology (four credits) in which research projects may be carried out.

Psychical Research Foundation (Durham, N. C.). Some summer aid in the form of a research-oriented stipend is
offered to students who have already engaged in research and are familiar with the field. In 1972 the
position of visiting research assistantship was established (see 326).

Oakland University (Rochester, Minn.).   Dr. Richard Brooks
    of the Department of Philosophy offers a senior collo-
    quium program (four credits) and supervises students
    in parapsychological research or reading projects.

Society for Psychical Research (London).   Studentship Trust
    Fund.   This fund offers aid up to $1, 800 per year to
    selected graduate students who wish to do postgradu-
    ate work in parapsychology in British universities.
    (Information and application blanks may be obtained
    from Mr. John Cutten, SPR, 1 Adam & Eve Mews,
    London, W8 6UQ, England.)

South West Minnesota State College (Marshall).   Drs. Curtis
    Wagner and Charles Reinert of the Department of
    Physics supervise an interdisciplinary degree in
    physics and psychology (and biology), with concentra-
    tion in parapsychology or paraphysics.

University of Virginia (Charlottesville).   The Division of
    Parapsychology (Department of Psychiatry) offers oc-
    casional fellowships for students (undergraduate and
    graduate) and visiting scientists for research in para-
    psychology.

Wesleyan University (Middletown, Conn.).   Dr. Alan Price
    of the Department of Psychology supervises under-
    graduate or graduate research or reading tutorial for
    credit.   It is possible that an M. A. degree in para-
    psychology will be offered in the future.

West Florida University (Pensacola).   Dr. William Mikulas
    of the Department of Psychology supervises M. A.
    theses in the area of parapsychology.

West Georgia College (Carrollton).   Drs. Henry Moore and
    Horace Stewart of the Department of Psychology
    supervise students for the M. A. degree for work in
    parapsychology.

RECOGNITION BY OTHER DISCIPLINES (CHRONOLOGY)

    In addition to the acceptance of parapsychology by in-
stitutions of higher learning, another way of assessing academic attitude toward the field is to note events which indi-

cate approval by specialists in other disciplines. A partial
listing of such events, in chronological order, is now presented.

1871.   The Dialectical Society (London) reported on psi phe-
        nomena, especially those associated with mediumship.

1922.   A special commission was created under the Brain
        Institute (U.S.S.R.), headed by Academician V. M.
        Bekhterev, to study the problem of mental suggestion,
        including telepathy.

1924.   At the Eleventh Congress of Psychoneurologists (U.S.
        S.R.) reports were delivered on the experimental in-
        vestigation of mental suggestion, including suggestion
        at a distance.

1937.   The American Institute of Mathematical Statistics ap-
        proved the statistical methods used in parapsychology.

1937.   The Aristotelean Society and the Mind Association
        (Great Britain) held a symposium on parapsychology.

1938.   The American Psychological Association held a round-
        table on "Methods in ESP research." (Papers pub-
        lished in JP 2:247-72, Dec. 1938.)

1939.   The Southern Society for Philosophy and Psychology
        held a symposium on ESP methods. (Papers published
        in JP 3:85-115, June 1939.)

1949.   Fulbright Scholarship for a travel grant in parapsy-
        chology was awarded to S. G. Soal of the University
        of London to visit the Duke University Parapsychology
        Laboratory.

1950.   The Rockefeller Foundation gave a grant to Duke Uni-
        versity for research in the Parapsychology Laboratory.

1950.   The [British] Royal Society of Medicine, Psychiatry
        Section, sponsored an address on parapsychology by
        J. B. Rhine.

1950.   The [British] Society of Experimental Biologists held
        a symposium on parapsychology.

1951.   The Royal Institution of Great Britain heard an ad-

dress by R. H. Thouless entitled "Thought transfer-
ence and related phenomena." Published in the Proceedings of the Royal Institution and reprinted in JP
16:23-40 (Mar. 1952).

1952.   The [U. S.] Office of Naval Research gave a grant to
the Duke University Parapsychology Laboratory for J.
G. Pratt's investigations of anpsi.

1954.   The American Philosophical Association, Eastern Division, held a symposium on parapsychology.

1955.   The Ciba Foundation held a symposium on extrasensory
perception. (See 88.)

1959.   Sixth Madras [India] Psychological Conference held a
symposium on parapsychology.

1960.   The Canadian Physiological Society held a symposium
on parapsychology at the University of Manitoba.

1961.   The Ittleson Family Foundation made a grant to the
Menninger Foundation for research on creativity and
psi phenomena.

1961.   United States Air Force Cambridge Research Laboratories, Hanscom Field, conducted ESP experiments.
(William R. Smith et al., Testing for extrasensory
perception with a machine, Bedford, Mass.: Air
Force Cambridge Research Laboratories, Office of
Aerospace Research, United States Air Force, 1963;
31p; reviewed in JASPR 58:137-43, Apr. 1964.)

1965.   The British Association for the Advancement of
Science invited J. B. Rhine to speak on ESP at one
of the annual Granada Lectures in the series entitled
"Communication in the modern world." (Published
in JP 30:84-105, June 1966.)

1966.   International Symposium on Parapsychology held in
Moscow. Sponsored by the Central House of Medical
Workers, the Union of Soviet Societies for Friendship
and Cultural Ties with Foreign Countries, and the
House of Friendship with the Peoples of Foreign
Countries.

1967.   Lockheed Missiles and Space Company Management

Association (Sunnyvale, Calif.), in joint sponsorship
with Foothill College, held a symposium on parapsychology.

1967.   The American Psychological Association held a sym-
        posium entitled "DOP Future frontier of parapsychol-
        ogy" at its annual convention.

1967.   The New York Academy of Sciences held a seminar
        on parapsychology.

1968.   Moscow Symposium on Technical Parapsychology held
        under the direction of E. K. Naumov.

1969.   The American Association for Humanistic Psychology
        held a three-hour session on parapsychology at its
        annual convention.

1969.   The American Association for the Advancement of
        Science granted affiliation to the Parapsychological
        Association.

1970.   The Scientific-Technical Society for Radiotechnics and
        Electrocommunication, Bio-information Unit, organized
        a symposium on telepathy held in Moscow under the
        chairmanship of I. M. Kogan.

1971.   The Parapsychological Association held a one-day sym-
        posium on parapsychology at the annual convention of
        the American Association for the Advancement of
        Science.

1972.   The American Psychiatric Association held a symposi-
        um on parapsychology entitled "Science and psi:
        Transcultural trends" at its annual convention under
        the auspices of the Task Force in Transcultural Psy-
        chiatry.

1972.   The American Association for Humanistic Psychology
        presented a program on unorthodox healing at its an-
        nual convention.

1972.   The Parapsychological Association held a half-day
        symposium entitled "Understanding parapsychological
        phenomena: A survey of four possible areas of inte-
        gration" at the annual convention of the American
        Association for the Advancement of Science.

RECOGNITION BY PROFESSIONAL JOURNALS

Another sign of interest in and at least partial acceptance of parapsychology by other disciplines was shown in the
1960s by the unusual circumstance that three major scientific
journals devoted entire issues to parapsychology. These
special issues are described below.

343 "ESP Today." Corrective Psychiatry and Journal of
      Social Therapy vol. 12, no. 2 (Mar. 1966). 140p.
      Special issue.

The editor, Ralph S. Banay, points out that it "is
time that the pages of a psychiatric journal were opened to
a comprehensive and succinct presentation of topics and
authors of outstanding merit in the field of extrasensory perception to give impetus to further research and a closer and
better integrated relationship between this field and the rather
stagnant realm of scholarly mental sciences" (p. 63).

There are 11 articles in all. Paranormal dreams
are the subject of two by Montague Ullman and Richard K.
Greenbank, respectively. Psi and psychiatry and/or human
psychology is the topic of a review paper by Frederick W.
Knowles and of individual contributions by Laurence J. Bendit, Jan Ehrenwald, Gertrude R. Schmeidler, and Berthold
E. Schwarz. W. H. C. Tenhaeff reviews parapsychological
research in the Netherlands. Gardner Murphy proposes that
the personality may be enriched by extrasensory as well as
sensory means. Remi Cadoret writes on physiology and
ESP and Bernard Grad points out the implications of "laying
on of hands" for psychotherapy and the placebo effect. Although the subjects of these papers are admittedly diverse,
each provides a window through which members of the
various clinical professions can glimpse new facts and ideas
relevant to their work. Illustrated; bibliography after most
papers (190 items); bibliographic footnotes. (Reviewed in
JP 31:156-63, June 1967.)

344 "ESP Status in 1966." International Journal of Neuro-
      psychiatry vol. 2, no. 5 (Sept. -Oct. 1966). 200p.
      Special issue.

The editor, A. I. Jackman, points out that since its
inception the International Journal "has been committed to

furnishing a platform for introducing the work of scientists
committed to mensuration and its techniques.   Without mensuration there can be no real scientific appraisal....   In
view of the increasing literature and its use of valid men-
suristic evaluations in the field of parapsychology, and in
order to bring our readers up to date on the latest work
being done in parapsychology, it was decided to devote an
issue of the Journal to those articles prepared by staunch
advocates [of] parapsychology as well as articles by those
who disagree with them" (p. 354).   Section I, "Surveys of
the findings and their implications, " contains three papers,
one a general survey of parapsychology today, one on the
implications of the paranormal, and one on psi research in
Russia and Czechoslovakia.   Section II, "Psychological dimensions of ESP, " contains four papers: on attitude and
ESP scores, on precognitive dreams, on parapsychological
research in the Netherlands, and on experimentally-induced
telepathic dreams.   Section III, "Physiological and physical
relations, " has a paper on ESP responses in the form of
plethysmographic recordings, one on attempts to induce ESP
with psilocybin, and one on electrical field reinforcement of
ESP.   Section IV, "Toward an explanation," contains a paper on explanatory models of ESP and one on ESP and
memory.   Finally, Section V, "The voices of the critics, "
consists of three papers: two are surveys of criticisms,
one of which stresses the repeatability issue, and the third
presents a survey of primarily psychological counter-hypothe-
ses to psi.   Illustrated; bibliography after most papers (340
items).   (Reviewed in JP 31:163-67, June 1967.)

345   "Contributions on Parapsychology. "   The Psychoanalytic
      Review vol. 56, no. 1 (Winter 1969). 144p. Special
      issue.

      The editor, Marie Coleman Nelson, says this collec-
tion of 10 papers was put together in order to counteract
ignorance of and aversion to parapsychological phenomena
evidenced by the "Psychoanalytic Establishment. "   The papers
deal with "various aspects of psychoanalytic parapsychology
and the altered states of consciousness associated with psi
phenomena" (p. 3).   Paranormal dreams are the subject of
papers by Jule Eisenbud, Stanley Krippner, Andrea Fodor
Litkei, and Herbert S. Strean.   Berthold E. Schwarz writes
on meaningful coincidences and Allen Spraggett presents an
interview with Nandor Fodor.   Two papers by William
Blanchard and Justin Kaplan stress altered states of con-

sciousness, particularly negative ones. There is a reprint of an article by Walter Franklin Prince on the cure of two cases of paranoia by direct appeal to the purported persecutory spirits. The issue concludes with a review article by Martin Ebon of four books on parapsychology. Illustrated; bibliographic footnotes; bibliography after some papers (59 items). (Reviewed in JASPR 64:121-24, Jan. 1970, and abstracted in JP 34:243-44, Sept. 1970.)

VI. GLOSSARY OF TERMS

ABSENT SITTING   see PROXY SITTING

ALTERED STATE OF CONSCIOUSNESS.   A state of aware-
    ness which is experienced as being qualitatively diffe-
    rent from one's usual sense of oneself.   See also
    DISSOCIATION; HYPNAGOGIC STATE; LUCID DREAM;
    PSYCHEDELIC DRUG; SOMNAMBULISM; TRANCE.

ANIMAL MAGNETISM   see MESMERISM

ANPSI.   Psi in animals.   See also PSI-TRAILING.

APPARITION   see PHANTASM

APPORT (noun).   The arrival of an object in a closed room,
    indicating the apparent passage of matter through mat-
    ter.   Also, the object itself.

ASTRAL BODY.   Primarily a theosophical term for the
    "double" or replica of the self, which is said to leave
    the physical body as in out-of-the-body experiences.

ASTRAL PROJECTION   see OUT-OF-THE-BODY EXPERI-
    ENCE

AUTHENTICATION.   The verification of the facts associated
    with spontaneous psi experiences by independent state-
    ments from witnesses, newspaper or other written ac-
    counts, or other corroboratory details supporting the
    statement of the percipient concerning his experience
    and the events to which it is related.

AUTOMATIC WRITING.   Writing that is not under the con-
    scious control of the writer.   See also PLANCHETTE.

AUTOMATISM. Any sensory or motor activity carried out by a person without conscious control. See also AUTOMATIC WRITING; DOWSING; CRYSTAL-GAZING; SHELL-HEARING.

AUTOSCOPY. The act of seeing one's double, or one's body as if from a point outside the center of consciousness.

BILLET READING. A test in which the sitter writes a question on a slip of paper and seals it in an envelope; the medium then attempts to answer the concealed question and to give additional information relevant to the sitter.

BILOCATION. The experience of seeming to be in two different locations at the same time.

BOOK TEST. A test for survival used in mediumistic sittings wherein an effort is made to exclude telepathy between the medium and sitter by having the communicator transmit a message referring to items on specific pages in a book. See also NEWSPAPER TEST.

CARD-GUESSING EXPERIMENT. An ESP experiment in which cards are used as targets. (Results so obtained can be quantitatively compared with chance expectation as well as with results of other card-guessing experiments conducted under various conditions.)

CARGO CULT. A cult common in primitive societies, especially in the South Pacific, in which the members have previsions of "cargo" (white man's goods) or other desirables which will come to them if they make certain sacrifices or perform required acts.

CLAIRVOYANCE. Extrasensory awareness of physical objects or events.

CLOCK CARD TEST. A quantitative ESP test of British origin in which the position of the hands of a clock is used as the target.

COLLECTIVE HALLUCINATION. An hallucination experienced simultaneously by two or more persons who are together at the time. See also RECIPROCAL HALLUCINATION.

COMMUNICATOR. A personality purporting to be that of a

deceased person which communicates with the living, usually through a medium.

CONTROL.   In trance mediumship, the personality which habitually relays messages from the communicator to the sitter.

CROSS CORRESPONDENCE.   A communication through two or more mediums unknown to each other such that the whole message is not clear until the separate fragments are put together.

CRYPTESTHESIA.   A synonym for ESP (coined by Richet).

CRYPTOMNESIA.   An unconscious memory of an event forgotten by the conscious mind.

CRYSTAL-GAZING   see SCRYING

DEATHBED EXPERIENCE.   Apparent awareness of the presence of deceased loved ones or a state of exaltation on the part of a dying person.

DÉJÀ VU.   An illusion of memory in which a new event feels as if it had been experienced before.

DEMONIACAL POSSESSION.   Possession by a demon.   See also POSSESSION.

DIAGNOSIS, PARANORMAL.   The diagnosis of illness by means other than those recognized by medical science. See also UNORTHODOX HEALING.

DIRECT VOICE.   A phenomenon of mediumship in which an isolated voice without a visible source is heard, usually (but not always) issuing from a trumpet which floats around the room.

DISCARNATE ENTITY.   A disembodied entity.

DISSOCIATION.   A splitting of the self such that one part behaves independently of the other, each functioning as a separate unit.   See also ALTERED STATE OF CONSCIOUSNESS.

DOWSING.   The use of a divining rod (forked twig or other instrument) to locate underground water or hidden ob-

jects by means of following the direction in which the
rod persists in turning. See also AUTOMATISM;
PENDULUM.

ESP   see EXTRASENSORY PERCEPTION

ESP PROJECTION.   An out-of-the-body experience during
which the "projectionist" is seen at a distant point
and/or brings back a veridical description of what he
observed at that point. See also TRAVELING CLAIR-
VOYANCE.

ECTOPLASM.   A substance alleged to issue from the body
of a medium and out of which materializations are
sometimes formed.

EXTRASENSORY PERCEPTION (ESP).   Knowledge of or response to an external event or influence by nonsensory
means.

FAITH HEALING   see DIAGNOSIS, PARANORMAL; UNORTHO-
DOX HEALING

FIRE-IMMUNITY.   The ability to come into direct contact
with fire or red-hot coals without being burned.

FREE MATERIAL   see QUALITATIVE EXPERIMENT

GHOST   see HAUNTING; PHANTASM OF THE DEAD

GLOSSOLALIA.   Speaking in "pseudo-tongues." See also
XENOGLOSSY.

GUIDANCE, INNER.   The experience of being meaningfully
influenced by thoughts and ideas which do not conscious-
ly belong to the person having them, sometimes purporting to come from a spiritual source.

HALLUCINATION.   A visual or auditory experience similar
to a sense perception, but without sensory stimulation;
it is termed "veridical" when it corresponds to a real
event taking place elsewhere. See also COLLECTIVE
HALLUCINATION; RECIPROCAL HALLUCINATION.

HALLUCINOGENIC DRUG   see PSYCHEDELIC DRUG

HAUNTING.   The more or less regular occurrence of hallucinatory phenomena associated with a particular place and usually attributed to the activity of deceased spirits.

HIGH-SCORING SUBJECT. A person who, in psi experiments, consistently obtains results better than chance expectation

HYPNAGOGIC STATE. The drowsy state just before falling asleep; hallucinations occurring at this time are called "hypnagogic hallucinations."

IMMORTALITY. The belief that life is everlasting. See also REINCARNATION; SURVIVAL.

INTERVENTION. Act of avoiding a precognized event, or some aspects of it.

LEVITATION. The raising of objects or bodies in the air by supposedly paranormal means.

LUCID DREAM. A dream in which the dreamer is aware that he is dreaming.

LUCIDITY. A synonym for clairvoyance (coined by Richet).

LUMINOUS PHENOMENA. The appearance of luminous substances with no explicable origin, usually associated with physical mediumship or ecstatic estates.

MATERIALIZATION. A manifestation of physical mediumship in which human forms or objects become visible in apparently solid form by allegedly paranormal means.

MATTER PASSING THROUGH MATTER see APPORT

MEDIUM, MENTAL. A person who regularly receives messages purporting to come from the deceased and transmits them to the living. See also COMMUNICATOR; CONTROL; TRANCE.

MEDIUM, PHYSICAL. A person who sits regularly, usually with a group of other persons, to produce physical effects alleged to be paranormal. See also APPORT; ECTOPLASM; LEVITATION; MATERIALIZATION.

MENTAL PHENOMENA see MEDIUM, MENTAL

MESMERISM. An early term for hypnotism; named after
  Franz Mesmer, who attributed hypnotic phenomena to
  a subtle effect, "animal magnetism," which was supposed to pass to the subject from the operator.

METAPSYCHICS. Synonym for psychical research (coined by
  Richet).

MOTOR AUTOMATISM see AUTOMATISM

MULTIPLE PERSONALITY. The formation of three or more
  selves through the splitting of the personality in a dissociated state. See also SECONDARY PERSONALITY.

NEWSPAPER TEST. A test for survival used in mediumistic sittings wherein an effort is made to exclude telepathy between medium and sitter by having the communicator transmit a message referring to items on specific newspaper pages; this test can also yield evidence
  of precognition when reference is made to newspapers
  not yet published.

OBJECT-READING see PSYCHOMETRY

OCCULTISM. Collective term for various esoteric theories
  and methods for attaining hidden powers. See also
  THEOSOPHY.

OUIJA BOARD. A board marked with letters and numbers,
  plus a smaller board with a pointer. The user places
  a hand on the latter and by means of his involuntary
  movements the pointer spells out a message. See also
  PLANCHETTE.

OUT-OF-THE-BODY EXPERIENCE. The experience, which
  can be either spontaneous or induced, of seeming to
  be in a place separate from one's physical body. See
  also AUTOSCOPY; BILOCATION; ESP PROJECTION;
  TRAVELING CLAIRVOYANCE.

PK see PSYCHOKINESIS

PK PLACEMENT TEST. A method of testing psychokinesis
  (see below) in which the subject tries to influence falling objects to land in a designated area of the throwing
  surface.

PARANORMAL. A synonym for psi, psychic, or parapsy-
    chological: beyond or beside ("para") what should oc-
    cur if only the normal laws of cause and effect are
    operating.

PARAPSYCHICAL. A synonym for paranormal, i.e., attri-
    butable to psi.

PARAPSYCHOLOGY. The branch of psychology which deals
    with behavior that cannot be explained by known physi-
    cal principles; modern term for psychical research.

PENDULUM. A device, such as a weight on the end of a
    thread, which can, when moved automatically, spell
    out a message. See also AUTOMATISM; OUIJA
    BOARD; PLANCHETTE.

PERCIPIENT. A subject in an ESP test, or a person who
    has a spontaneous psi experience.

PHANTASM OF THE DEAD. An appearance suggesting the
    presence of a person (or animal) who is no longer
    living.

PHANTASM OF THE LIVING. An appearance suggesting the
    presence of a living person (or animal) who is not
    there.

PHOTOGRAPHY, PSYCHIC OR SPIRIT see PSYCHIC PHO-
    TOGRAPHY; SPIRIT PHOTOGRAPHY

PHYSICAL PHENOMENA see MEDIUM, PHYSICAL

PLACEMENT TEST see PK PLACEMENT TEST

PLANCHETTE. A board on rollers which rests on a pencil
    suspended over a writing surface, used in a form of
    automatic writing. See also OUIJA BOARD.

POLTERGEIST. Poltergeist phenomena involve the unex-
    plained movement or breakage of objects, etc., and
    often seem to center around the presence of an adoles-
    cent; they differ from hauntings in that apparitions are
    rarely seen.

POSSESSION. A state in which a person's organism appears
    to be under the control of another center of conscious-
    ness.

POST-MORTEM COMMUNICATION. A communication alleged-
    ly from a deceased to a living person, usually through
    a medium.

PRECOGNITION. Knowledge of a future event which could
    not have been predicted nor inferred by normal means.
    See also NEWSPAPER TEST; RETROCOGNITION.

PREMONITION see PRECOGNITION

PREVISION see PRECOGNITION

PROPHECY see PRECOGNITION

PROXY SITTING. A mediumistic sitting in which the person
    desiring to receive communications is represented by
    someone else, a "proxy," at the sitting.

PSI-MISSING. The use of psi so that the target the subject
    is trying to hit is missed more often than would be ex-
    pected if only chance were operating. See also
    SECONDARY EFFECT.

PSI PHENOMENA. Occurrences resulting from the opera-
    tion of ESP and/or PK.

PSI-TRAILING. A form of anpsi in which a pet finds its
    owner in a distant location where it has never been
    before.

PSYCHEDELIC DRUG. A pharmacological agent, such as
    LSD or psilocybin, which induces an altered state of
    consciousness.

PSYCHIC PHOTOGRAPHY. The paranormal projection of
    mental images on photographic plates or film. See
    also SPIRIT PHOTOGRAPHY.

PSYCHIC SURGERY. A form of unorthodox healing in which
    it is alleged that portions of diseased tissues are re-
    moved without the use of instruments.

PSYCHICAL RESEARCH. The study of phenomena which
    cannot be explained in terms of established physical
    principles; older term for parapsychology.

PSYCHOKINESIS (PK). The direct influence of mind on

matter.   See also PK PLACEMENT TEST.

PSYCHOMETRY.   Object-reading, or the ability of some
    mediums and sensitives to divine the history of or
    events connected with a material object when holding it.

QUALITATIVE EXPERIMENT.   A test for psi using target
    material which does not permit precise statistical eval-
    uation of the results obtained.

QUANTITATIVE EXPERIMENT.   A test for psi using target
    material which permits precise statistical evaluation of
    the results obtained.   See also CARD-GUESSING EX-
    PERIMENT.

REM TECHNIQUE.   Method of studying dreams by means of
    the electroencephalograph which shows when rapid eye
    movements (REMs) occur; REMs are coincident with
    periods of dreaming.

RAPS.   Percussive sounds, sometimes tapping an intelligible
    message, for which no known agency can be discovered.

RECIPROCAL HALLUCINATION.   An hallucination elements
    of which are shared by two persons out of sensory range
    of each other.   See also COLLECTIVE HALLUCINATION.

REINCARNATION.   A form of survival in which the mind, or
    some aspect of it, of a deceased individual is reborn
    in another body.   See also IMMORTALITY; SURVIVAL.

RETROCOGNITION.   Knowledge of a past event which could
    not have been obtained by normal means.   See also
    PRECOGNITION; PSYCHOMETRY.

SCRYING.   The use of a crystal or other bright reflecting
    surface upon which to project hallucinatory images; e.g.,
    crystal-gazing.   See also SHELL-HEARING.

SEALED WRITING   see BILLET READING

SEANCE   see SITTING

SECONDARY EFFECT.   In ESP experiments this term re-
    fers to an extrachance pattern attributable to psi which
    was not the primary aim of the experiment.   See also
    PSI-MISSING.

SECONDARY PERSONALITY. An alteration of character and
memory, amounting to a change of personality, which
generally happens during sleep and seems to be the
result of disease, shock, or unknown causes; it usually
alternates with the primary personality. See also
MULTIPLE PERSONALITY.

SENSITIVE. A person who is "psychic," that is, who has
frequent psi experiences and can at times induce them
at will; similar to a medium, except that communications purporting to come from deceased are usually
not involved. See also MEDIUM.

SENSORY AUTOMATISM see AUTOMATISM

SHEEP-GOAT EFFECT. The relationship between belief in
ESP and ESP scoring level, believers (sheep) tending
to score above chance and disbelievers (goats) at or
below chance.

SHELL-HEARING. A form of sensory automatism in which
hallucinatory voices and other sounds are heard in a
sea shell held to the ear. See also SCRYING.

SITTER. A person who sits with a medium or sensitive.

SITTING. An interview with a medium or sensitive for the
purpose of obtaining messages from the deceased or
other types of psi information.

SLATE WRITING. The supposedly paranormal appearance
of written messages on slates in the presence of a
medium.

SOMNAMBULISM. Sleep walking; in hypnosis, a deep stage
of trance in which the subject may exhibit capabilities
beyond his conscious control.

SPIRIT COMMUNICATION. A communication, usually obtained through a medium, purporting to come from a
deceased personality.

SPIRIT PHOTOGRAPHY. The projection of images, usually
self-portraits, on film or photographic plates allegedly
accomplished by the activity of deceased persons. See
also PSYCHIC PHOTOGRAPHY.

SPIRIT SOUNDS   see RAPS

SPIRITUALISM.   Doctrines and practices based on the belief
     that survival of death is a reality and that communica-
     tion between the living and the deceased occurs, usually
     via mediumship.

SPONTANEOUS PSI PHENOMENA.   Unanticipated experiences
     of ESP or PK occurring in the course of daily living.
     See also HALLUCINATION; HAUNTING; POLTERGEIST;
     VERIDICAL DREAM.

STAGE TELEPATHY.   The use of various methods of simu-
     lating telepathy, usually devised by magicians for the
     purposes of entertainment.

STIGMATA.   The production by suggestion of blisters or
     other cutaneous changes on the feet, hands, or else-
     where on the body of the subject.

SUBLIMINAL PERCEPTION.   Behavior indicative of aware-
     ness of stimuli that are below the threshold of normal
     perception.

SUPERNORMAL COGNITION.   A synonym for psi (coined by
     Osty).

SURVIVAL.   Continued conscious existence for at least a
     time after bodily death.   Differs from immortality in
     that eternal existence is not implied (although neither
     is it ruled out).   See also DEATHBED EXPERIENCE;
     IMMORTALITY; MEDIUM, MENTAL; POST-MORTEM
     COMMUNICATION; REINCARNATION.

SYNCHRONICITY.   Term coined by Jung to indicate that an
     acausal principle could account for psi occurrences,
     or, as he preferred to call them, "meaningful coinci-
     dences."

TABLE-TIPPING.   A form of automatism in which several
     persons place their fingertips on a table, causing it
     to move and rap out messages by means of a code.

TELEKINESIS.   The movement of objects at a distance by
     paranormal means.   See also APPORT; PSYCHOKINE-
     SIS.

TELEPATHY. Extrasensory awareness of another person's mental activities.

THEOSOPHY. In general refers to an occult system of ideas claiming to be divine wisdom; in particular it is associated with the Theosophical Society founded in 1875 by Madame Blavatsky.

TRANCE. A dissociated state characterized by lack of voluntary movement in which various forms of automatism are expressed; usually exhibited under hypnotic or mediumistic conditions. See also ALTERED STATES OF CONSCIOUSNESS.

TRANSFIGURATION. The alleged capacity, usually mediumistic, of taking on recognizable bodily characteristics of deceased persons.

TRAVELING CLAIRVOYANCE. A form of clairvoyance in which the subject (often in hypnotic trance) seems to "travel" to a distant point, and describes events actually taking place at that point. See also ESP PROJECTION.

UNCONSCIOUS CEREBRATION. Thinking that takes place unaccompanied by awareness of a mental process being involved.

UNORTHODOX HEALING. Healing effected by non-medical techniques (such as prayer, the "laying on of hands, " etc.) and inexplicable in terms of present-day medical science. See also PARANORMAL DIAGNOSIS; PSYCHIC SURGERY.

VERIDICAL DREAM. A dream presumptively paranormal in that it corresponds in some of its details with events beyond the dreamer's sensory range.

WATER WITCHING see DOWSING

XENOGLOSSY. The ability to speak in a language normally unknown to the speaker. See also GLOSSOLALIA.

VII. NAME AND SUBJECT INDEX

This is an index to Parts I through V. It should be noted that references to the subject matter covered in Part I are supplements to Annotated List of Books, not a complete index to it. The main content of each book has already been provided by means of the broad subject heading under which its title is found, supplemented by the list of additional books containing substantial amounts of material on that subject that appears in the introduction to each category. Additional entries in this index are to finer subject categories such as ouija board, PK placement tests, psychic photography; to well-known cases of hauntings, poltergeists, etc.; and to persons and organizations.

Some of the entries refer the reader to the major parts of the book, e.g., "Academic parapsychology see Part V." The Arabic numbers following the entries stand for item numbers (except when preceded by the lower-case letter p, for which see below). The capital letters which follow the item numbers for some persons and institutions indicate the following: A, author; C, contributor of one or more chapters in a book; E, editor; I, author of an important introduction or preface; SP, sponsoring organization. If the item contains one or more pictures, the number is followed by a capital P (for an index to illustrations, see Appendix 2). An underlined D indicates a doctoral dissertation (whether M.D., Ph.D., or D.Sc.) and an underlined M, a master's thesis; these entries are followed by a lower-case p (page) and number, which refers to a page in Part V of this book. Because of the complicated nature of some of the entries, it may be helpful to give several examples:

The first entry below indicates that Bernard Aaronson is the editor of and contributor to item 1 and also a contributor to items 18 and 23 (in Part I, the Annotated List of Books). The entry for Remi Cadoret shows that he received a doctorate, noted on page (224), and is also a contributor

to item 343. Benson Herbert is listed as having contributed
to item 175 and also as being the subject of item 322. Finally, the entry for Mary Craig Sinclair indicates that she
is the subject of item 61, which also contains her picture.

300, 317
Dreaming 11, 20, 23, 25,
117, 169, 170; see also
Lucid dreams
Dreams, precognitive 133,
137, 142, 153
Dreams and psi phenomena
11, 18, 23, 25, 59, 66,
78, 87, 121, 133, 137,
140, 145, 146, 152, 154,
161, 169, 170, 230, 232,
234, 236, 237, 242, 263,
300, 317; see also Dreams,
precognitive; Lucid dreams,
Rapid eye movement tech-
nique
Driesch, Hans 47-C, 157-
A, 328
Drugs, psychedelic 1, 3, 6,
7, 8, 10, 15, 24, 25, 87
Drugs and psi phenomena
see Pharmacology and psi
phenomena
Ducasse, C. J. 127-C,
131-C, 159-C, 213-A,
246-A, 247-A&P, 248-A,
249-C
Duke University Parapsychology Laboratory 53, 55-P,
57-P, 61, 174, 176, 188,
272, 318, 320
Dunne, J. W. 125, 133-A,
138, 153, 179-C, 218
Duval, Pierre (pseud.) 54-
C

ESP projection 122
Ear of Dionysius case 168,
249, 265
Eastman, Margaret M p228,
112-C
Ebin, David 10-E
Ebon, Martin 34-A, 81-A,
249-C, 271-A, 340-E,
345-C
Ecstasy 7, 14, 122, 169,

170, 179, 264
Ectoplasm 177, 256
Eddy, Horatio see Eddy
brothers
Eddy, William see Eddy
brothers
Eddy brothers 180-P
Edmonds, John W. 223-P,
224-P, 226-P
Edmunds, Simeon 158-A
Ehrenwald, Jan 89-C, 141-
A, 142-A, 143-A, 144-A,
159-C, 168-C, 343-C
Eilbert, Leo M p226
Eisenberg, Howard M p228
Eisenbud, Jule 87-C, 140-
C, 145-A, 186-A, 345-C
Elberfeld horses 27, 30, 41,
196; see also Clever Hans
Electroencephalography 4,
16
Electroencephalography and
psi phenomena 167; see
also Rapid eye movement
technique
Elguin, Gita H. D p225
Elliott, Mrs. Warren 115,
154, 269
Ellis, Albert 140-C
Ellwood, Gracia Fay 135-A
Ely, Donald P. 90-C, 175-
C
Encyclopedias and parapsy-
chology see Part II
Eva C. see Marthe Béraud
Evans-Wentz, W. Y. 249-C
Evidence for psi 47, 52,
55, 73, 74, 88, 93, 106,
151, 156, 157, 159, 161,
171, 183, 184, 185, 188,
189, 192, 217, 238, 245,
246, 254; see also Counterhypotheses to psi; Statistical methods used in para-
psychology; Testimony,
psychology of
Exorcism 34, 79

234-P, 256-C

McConnell, R. A. 60-A,
88-C, 166-A, 168-C, 249-
C
McCreery, Charles 167-A
McDougall, William 47-C,
54-P, 86-A, 179-C, 328
MacKenzie, Andrew 76-A,
233-A, 234-A
McKenzie, Hewat 105
Mackenzie, William 27-C
Maeterlinck, Maurice 28-A
Magazines, parapsychologi-
cal see Periodicals,
parapsychological
Maimonides Medical Center
see Dream Laboratory,
Maimonides Medical
Center
Mangan, Gordon L. 194-A
Mapes, J. J. 226-P
Marais, Eugene N. 29-A
Marcel, Gabriel 249-C
Marchant, James 256-E
Margenau, Henry 89-C,
90-C, 93-C
Margery see Crandon,
Mina Stinson
Maria Reyes de Z. see
Zierold, Maria Reyes
Marsh, Maurice D p225
Marshall-Hall, Edward
256-C
Masters, R. E. L. 15-A
Materialization 45, 94, 95,
96, 163, 177, 216, 242,
264; see also Ectoplasm
Matthews, G. V. T. 88-C
Maupin, Edward 4-C, 23-
C, 89-C
Medicine and psi phenome-
na see Unorthodox healing
Meditation 1, 2, 4, 16, 23,
219
Mediumistic communication,

modus operandi 98, 102,
112, 114, 243, 245, 254,
264
Mediums and sensitives see
under same in Part I. See
also Communicators; Con-
trols, mediumistic, Cross
correspondences; Develop-
ment of mediumship and/or
psi; Mediumship, fraudu-
lent; Multiple personality;
Proxy sittings; Trance
Mediumship, development of
see Development of medi-
umship and/or psi
Mediumship, fraudulent 86,
94, 96, 101, 115
Meehl, Paul 291-C
Meerloo, Joost A. M. 87-
C, 90-C
Memory 17, 21, 344; see
also Déjà-vu
Mesmerism 9, 87, 223,
228, 278; see also Hypno-
sis
Methodology in psi research
89, 154, 157, 166, 171;
see also Experimental psy-
chical research; Tests for
psi
Millar, E. C. P. 88-E
Miller, Neal E. 4-I&C
Mills, Clara U. 135-P
Mind-body problem 86, 91,
124, 126, 131, 189, 190,
246, 247
Mirabelli, Carlos 153
Miracles 171, 220, 276,
280, 281
Mitchell, T. W. 195-A
Monroe, Robert A. 119-A
Montredon, Evelyn (pseud.)
54-C
Morgan, Bryan 279-E
Morris, Joanna D. 333-E
Morris, Robert L. 56-C,
176-C, 326, 333-E

VIII. INDEX OF BOOK AND PERIODICAL TITLES
(by item number)

Appendix 1

BOOKS CONTAINING GLOSSARIES

Since there is no up-to-date, comprehensive dictionary
of psychical research terms, we felt it would be useful to
give, in addition to the glossary in Part VI, some further
guidance regarding such terms. As already noted, the encyclopedias by Fodor (201) and Spence (208) are useful for
older terms. For more modern terms the glossary appearing in each issue of the Journal of Parapsychology (329)
should be consulted. Also useful are some general psychological dictionaries such as A Comprehensive Dictionary of
Psychological and Psychoanalytical Terms, by H. and A.
English (McKay, 1958), Drever's Dictionary of Psychology
(rev. ed., Penguin 1964), and the encyclopedia edited by
Eysenck (304).

For those who do not have access to the above tools
or who wish to supplement them, the books in Part I which
contain glossaries are listed below, in order of the number
of terms contained in the glossary. To facilitate location
of a book, its number is given; for orientation as to its contents and the age of the terms defined, its title and original
date of publication are also provided.

No. of terms	Book no.	Title	Date
203	49	Occult and supernatural phe- nomena	1952
143	209	Catalogue of the John William Graham Collection	1950
123	169	Human personality and its sur- vival of bodily death	1903
112	281	Eleven Lourdes miracles	1957
99	179	Psychic source book	1951
86	164	ESP reader	1969
66	203	Catalogue of the Library of the London Spiritualist Alli- ance	1931

No. of terms	Book no.	Title	Date
58	58	Parapsychology: Frontier science of the mind	1957
52	52	Experimental parapsychology	1966
50	70	Mind to mind	1948
48	56	Parapsychology today	1968
45	54	Progress in parapsychology	1971
44	200	Biographical dictionary of parapsychology	1964
42	57	Extrasensory perception after sixty years	1940
41	46	ESP: A scientific evaluation	1966
38	167	Science, philosophy and ESP	1967
37	144	Telepathy and medical psychology	1948
33	138	Foreknowledge	1938
33	73	Ghosts and apparitions	1938
33	87	The psychic force	1970
32	262	Evidence of identity	1939
32	265	Evidence of personal survival from cross correspondences	1939
32	271	Test your ESP	1970
31	263	Evidence of purpose	1938
28	142	New dimensions of deep analysis	1954
26	231	Memories, dreams, reflections	1963
26	50	Studies in spiritism	1910
22	69	Experimental telepathy	1938
17	275	Tests for extrasensory perception	1954
14	96	The physical phenomena of spiritualism	1907

BOOKS AND ENCYCLOPEDIAS CONTAINING ILLUSTRATIONS

Though there is a demand for materials depicting parapsychological topics or persons associated with the field, such items are difficult to locate. Therefore, as a help to searchers, relevant illustrations in the books listed in Part I and the encyclopedias in Part II are indexed below. It should be noted that not all the books in Part I described as having illustrations appear in this index since in a few cases these illustrations are not relevant to parapsychology--e.g., Marais (29) and Ehrenwald (141).

The index is in two parts. The first lists persons associated with psychical research whose pictures appear in the titles in Parts I and II, while the second indicates illustrative material under a number of broad subject headings. In both instances the digit(s) following the index entry indicates the number of the book or encyclopedia. Thus, a searcher wishing to locate a picture of, say, Basil Shackleton, will find one in Modern Experiments in Telepathy (62). If he is interested in illustrations on dowsing, the entry on this topic in the subject index will lead him to four titles (36, 41, 49, 185). An asterisk after a number indicates a particulary rich source of illustrative material.

Name Index

Subject Index

Appendix 3

BOOKS WITH 100 OR MORE BIBLIOGRAPHIC REFERENCES

Although Part I is in itself a bibliography of 282 books, it is a highly selected list. Therefore, in order to supplement it not only with citations to other books but also to periodical articles, the titles in Part I having 100 or more bibliographic references are given below. Within the broad subject headings used in Part I, the books are listed (at left margin) by their entry number. To further pinpoint each book its title is given in brief, following which the number of bibliographic references is given in parentheses--to be understood as the number of individual items unless expressed as "pages."

Altered States of Consciousness

1. Psychedelics (20 pages)
2. Psychosynthesis (159)
3. LSD, marihuana, yoga and hypnosis (49 pages)
4. Biofeedback and self-control (1540)
5. Cosmic consciousness (208)
7. Chemical ecstasy (125)
9. Abnormal hypnotic phenomena (637)
13. New psychology of dreaming (257)
16. On the psychology of meditation (205)
18. Psi and altered states of consciousness (206)
20. Organization and pathology of thought (787)
21. Mental imagery (14 pages)
22. Daydreaming (11 pages)
23. Altered states of consciousness (879)
24. On being stoned (121)
25. Unfinished man (202)

Anpsi

26. Strange world of animals and pets (182)
30. Clever Hans (124)

Anthropology and Psi Phenomena

32. Trance and possession states   (277)

Automatisms

36. The divining rod   (19 pages)
37. Crystal-gazing   (12 pages)
38. Singer in the shadows   (267)
39. Automatic writing   (273)
41. Water witching U. S. A.   (112)

Criticisms

49. Occult and supernatural phenomena   (203)

Experimental Psychical Research

52. Experimental parapsychology   (1251)
57. Extrasensory perception after sixty years   (361)
58. Parapsychology: Frontier science of the mind   (229)
59. Extrasensory perception (Schmeidler)   (149)
62. Modern experiments in telepathy   (199)
64. From anecdote to experiment in psychical research (130)
67. Experiments in mental suggestion   (159)
70. Mind to mind   (61 items plus 6 pages)

Hauntings and Poltergeists

77. Can we explain the poltergeist?   (329)

Interdisciplinary Studies

87. The psychic force   (239)
88. Extrasensory perception (Ciba Foundation)   (149)
89. Psi favorable states of consciousness   (142)
90. Psi factors in creativity   (190)

Out-of-the-Body Experiences

100. Enigma of out-of-body travel   (116)

Philosophy and Psi Phenomena

130. New world of the mind   (102)

Psychiatry and Psi Phenomena

140. Psychoanalysis and the occult (204)
141. Neurosis in the family (149)
142. New dimensions of deep analysis (138)
143. Psychotherapy: Myth and method (225)
144. Telepathy and medical psychology (100)
145. Psi and psychoanalysis (332)

Psychical Research in General

158. Miracles of the mind (361)
165. Roots of coincidence (116)
167. Science, philosophy and ESP (200)
179. Psychic source book (298)
182. Personality of man (101)
185. Psychical research today (128)

Psychokinesis

186. World of Ted Serios (145)

Psychology and Psi Phenomena

196. Experimenter effects in behavioral research (21 pages)

Reference
        A number of books listed under this heading are bibliographies:

199. Literature of the doctrine of a future life
202. Price guide to the occult and related subjects
203. Catalogue of the library of the London Spiritualist Alliance
204. Bibliographies on parapsychology ... and related subjects
205. Short-title catalogue of works on psychical research
206. Supplement to short-title catalogue
209. Catalogue of the John William Graham Collection
210. Bibliography and index of psychic research
211. Bibliography of parapsychology

Religion and Psi Phenomena

212. Interpretation of cosmic and mystical experiences (369)
217. Psychic phenomena and religion (144)

Appendix 4

BOOKS BY READING LEVEL RATING

In order to guide readers and librarians in selecting books on psychical research in terms of their level of difficulty, the book numbers of the titles in Part I are listed below by their reading level ratings (see p. 20).

Reading Level 1: 10, 26, 29, 35, 38, 44, 62, 70, 76, 79, 81, 103, 104, 105, 113, 117, 119, 121, 122, 128, 132, 134, 156, 159, 161, 163, 164, 172, 174, 180, 217, 218, 223, 231, 233, 234, 235, 237, 242, 250, 252, 253, 260, 271, 277, 282.

Reading Level 2: 5, 7, 8, 9, 11, 12, 14, 15, 19, 22, 24, 25, 27, 28, 30, 31, 33, 36, 37, 41, 42, 43, 45, 46, 47, 49, 51, 54, 55, 56, 57, 60, 63, 64, 65, 66, 67, 69, 71, 72, 73, 74, 75, 78, 80, 82, 83, 84, 85, 94, 95, 96, 97, 98, 99, 100, 101, 102, 106, 107, 108, 110, 111, 112, 114, 116, 118, 120, 124, 129, 130, 133, 135, 136, 137, 138, 139, 144, 146, 150, 151, 152, 155, 157, 158, 160, 162, 165, 166, 167, 168, 170, 171, 176, 177, 178, 179, 182, 183, 184, 185, 186, 188, 189, 190, 192, 212, 213, 214, 215, 216, 219, 220, 221, 224, 225, 227, 228, 230, 232, 236, 238, 240, 241, 243, 245, 248, 249, 251, 254, 255, 256, 261, 262, 263, 264, 265, 266, 267, 268, 269, 270, 272, 274, 275, 276, 278, 279, 280, 281.

Reading Level 3: 1, 2, 3, 4, 6, 13, 16, 17, 18, 20, 21, 23, 32, 34, 39, 40, 48, 50, 52, 53, 58, 59, 61, 63, 68, 77, 86, 87, 88, 89, 90, 91, 92, 93, 109, 115, 123, 125, 126, 127, 131, 140, 141, 142, 143, 145, 147, 148, 149, 153, 154, 169, 173, 175, 181, 187, 191, 193, 194, 195, 196, 197, 198, 199, 200, 201, 202, 203, 204, 205, 206, 107, 108, 109, 210, 211, 222, 226, 229, 239, 244, 246, 247, 257, 258, 259, 273.

Appendix 5

BOOKS BY TYPE OF LIBRARY INDICATOR

In order to aid smaller libraries in selecting books on
psychical research, the titles listed in Part I which are suitable for high school, college, and small and medium-sized
public libraries are indicated below, together with the titles
recommended for all libraries. There is no listing for large
public or university libraries as most titles are recommended
for these. Also, such libraries are more likely to be in a
financial position to compile their own acquisition lists than
the smaller libraries.

The book numbers of the titles are listed by the type
of library for which they are recommended. Each type of
library should consider not only those titles specifically
recommended for it, but also those given under the heading
"A. Books Recommended for All Libraries." Titles that
are still in print are indicated by an H and/or P following
the book number. (If available as a xerocopy from University Microfilms, for our purposes a book is considered in
print.) Hardcover editions are indicated by H, paperbacks
by P.

[H] Books Recommended for High School Libraries (total: 6)

113 H, P 122 H, P 161 P   172 P   233 H, P   272

[C] Books Recommended for College Libraries (total: 165)

1 P	3 H	4 H	5 H, P	6 P	7 H
8 H, P	9 H	10 P	11 H	14 H	15 H
16 H	18 H	20 H	21 H	22 H, P	23 H, P
24 H	25 H	29 H	32 P	33 H	35 P
36 H	37 H	39 H	40	41 H	42 H
43	45 H	47 H	48	49 P	51 H
52 H	54 H	56 H	62	66 P	69

(College Libraries, continued)

70 P	71 H	72 P	73 H	76 H, P	77 H
79	82 H	85 H, P	86 H	87 H	88 P
90 H	93 H	94	96	98 H	99
100	103 H, P	104 H, P	105	108	109
110	111 H	114 H	115	116 H	117 H
118 H	119 H	121 H, P	122 H, P	124	125 H
128 H	129 P	130 P	131 H	132 H, P	136
138	140 H, P	142	143 H	144 H	145 H
146	147 P	148 H	149 H, P	150 H	153 H
154 H	157	158 H	162 H	165 H	167 H
171	173	175 H	177	179	184 H
187 P	189 P	191 P	193 H, P	194 P	196 H
197 P	198 P	200 H	204 H	208 H	209
211 H	212 H	213	214	215 H	218 P
220	221	223 H	225 H	227 H	228 H
229 H	230 H	232 H, P	235 H, P	238	240 H
243	245	246 H	248 P	250 H	251
252 P	253 H	255 H, P	256	257 P	258 P
259 H	261	263 H	264	265	266
267	268 H	272	273 P	275 P	276 H
278 H	279 P	281			

[S] Books Recommended for Small Public Libraries (total: 14)

5 H, P	72 P	88 P	112 P	113 H, P	114 H
119 H	122 H, P	161 P	172 P	233 H, P	234 H, P
246 H	282 H, P				

[M] Books Recommended for Medium-Sized Public Libraries (total: 117)

1 P	3 H	4 H	5 H, P	7 H	8 H, P
10 P	11 H	15 H	16 H	21 H	22 H, P
23 H, P	24 H	25 H	29 H	33 H	35 P
36 H	37 H	42 H	43	45 H	49 P
52 H	54 H	56 H	62	70 P	71 H
72 P	73 H	76 H, P	77 H	79	82 H
85 H, P	86 H	88 P	90 H	93 H	94
96	98 H	99	100	103 H, P	104 H, P
105	108	110	112 P	113 H, P	114 H
116 H	117 H	119 H	121 H, P	122 H, P	128 H
130 P	131 H	132 H, P	133 H, P	136	138
142	145 H	148 H	149 H, P	150 H	157

(Medium-Sized Public Libraries, continued)

158 H	161 P	165 H	167 H	172 P	173
179	184 H	189 P	208 H	214	215 H
218 P	220	221	223 H	227 H	228 H
233 H, P	234 H, P	235 H, P	238	243	245
246 H	249	250 H	251	252 P	253 H
255 H, P	256	257 P	261	263 H	264
265	266	268 H	272	275 P	277 H, P
278 H	281	282 H, P			

[A]   Books Recommended for All Libraries (total: 59)

12 H, P	13 H	26 P	28 H	30 H	38 H
44 H	46 H, P	53 P	55 H, P	57 H	58
59 P	60	61 H, P	63 H	64 H	74
78	81 H, P	106	120 H, P	134 P	135 P
137 P	152	155	156 H, P	159	160 P
163 P	164 H	166 P	168 H, P	169	170 H
174 H	180 H	182	183	185 P	186 P
188 H, P	192 H, P	201 H	216 H, P	217 P	219 H, P
224 H	231 H, P	236 P	237	239	241 H, P
242	260	271 P	274 P	280 H, P	

Appendix 6

ABBREVIATIONS

General Terms

ed.	edition	p	page or pages
ed., eds.	editor, editors	pap	paperback
enl.	enlarged	Pt.	part
n. d.	no date	rev.	revised
n. s.	new series	suppl.	supplement
no.	number	trans.	translated
OP	out of print	v.	volume (or volumes if
orig. publ.	originally pub-lished		preceded by number)

Parapsychological Organizations

A. S. P. R.	American Society for Psychical Research
F. R. N. M.	Foundation for Research on the Nature of Man
P. A.	Parapsychological Association
P. F.	Parapsychology Foundation
P. R. F.	Psychical Research Foundation
S. P. R.	Society for Psychical Research

Parapsychological Periodicals

IJP	International Journal of Parapsychology
JASPR	Journal of the American Society for Psychical Research
JP	Journal of Parapsychology
JSPR	Journal of the Society for Psychical Research
PASPR	Proceedings of the American Society for Psychical Research
PR	Parapsychology Review
PSPR	Proceedings of the Society for Psychical Research

Non-Parapsychological Periodicals

A. L. A. Booklist	American Library Association's Booklist
Abstr. FolkloreStud.	Abstracts of Folklore Studies
Am. Anthropol.	American Anthropologist
Am. Hist. Rev.	American Historical Review
Am. Imago	American Imago
Am. J. Clin. &Exp. Hypn.	American Journal of Clinical and Experimental Hypnosis
Am. J. Clin. Hypn.	American Journal of Clinical Hypnosis
Am. J. Ment. Def.	American Journal of Mental Deficiency
Am. J. Orthopsychiat.	American Journal of Orthopsychiatry
Am. J. Psychiat.	American Journal of Psychiatry
Am. J. Psychoanal.	American Journal of Psychoanalysis
Am. J. Psychol.	American Journal of Psychology
Am. J. Psychother.	American Journal of Psychotherapy
Am. J. Sociol.	American Journal of Sociology
Am. Notes & Queries	American Notes and Queries
Am. Sociol. Rev.	American Sociological Review
America	America
Ann. Am. Acad.	Annals of the American Academy of Political Science
Antiq. Bkmn	Antiquarian Bookman
Arch. Gen. Psychiat.	Archives of General Psychiatry
Arena	Arena
Athenaeum	Athenaeum
Atl. Mon.	Atlantic Monthly
Aust. J. Psychol.	Australian Journal of Psychology
Behav. Res. &Ther.	Behaviour Research and Therapy
Behav. Sci.	Behavioral Science
BestSell.	Best Sellers
BookWeek	Book Week
BookWorld	Book World
Booklist	Booklist and Subscription Books Bulletin
Bookman	Bookman
Bookman[Lond.]	Bookman [London]
Bookmark	Bookmark
Books&Bkmn	Books and Bookmen

BooksToday	Books Today
BostonEve. Trans.	Boston Evening Transcript
Br. J. Educ. Psychol.	British Journal of Educational Psychology
Br. J. Math. &Stat. Psychol.	British Journal of Mathematical and Statistical Psychology
Br. J. Med. Psychol.	British Journal of Medical Psychology
Br. J. Psychiat.	British Journal of Psychiatry
Br. J. Psychol.	British Journal of Psychology
Br. J. Stat. Psychol.	British Journal of Statistical Psychology
Brain	Brain
Bull. At. Sci.	Bulletin of the Atomic Scientists
Bull. MenningerClin.	Bulletin of the Menninger Clinic

Can. Forum	Canadian Forum
Can. J. Theol.	Canadian Journal of Theology
Can. Psychiat. Assoc. J.	Canadian Psychiatric Association Journal
Cathol. Libr. World	Catholic Library World
Cathol. Psychol. Rec.	Catholic Psychological Record
Cathol. World	Catholic World
Chic. SundayBookWeek	Chicago Sunday Book Week
Chic. SundayTimes	Chicago Sunday Times
Chic. SundayTrib.	Chicago Sunday Tribune
Child& Fam.	Child and Family
Choice	Choice
Christ. Cent.	Christian Century
Christ. Sci. Monit.	Christian Science Monitor
ChurchHist.	Church History
ChurchQ. Rev.	Church Quarterly Review
Churchman	Churchman
Commonweal	Commonweal
Compr. Psychiat.	Comprehensive Psychiatry
Concor. Theol. Mon.	Concordia Theological Monthly
Contemp. Psychoanal.	Contemporary Psychoanalysis
Contemp. Psychol.	Contemporary Psychology
Contemp. Rev.	Contemporary Review
Critic	Critic

DetroitNews	Detroit News
Dial	Dial
Dialogue	Dialogue
Discovery	Discovery

DownsideRev.	Downside Review
Economist	Economist
Eugen. Rev.	Eugenics Review
Expos. T.	Expository Times
Extrapolation	Extrapolation
Fant. &Sci. Fict.	Fantasy and Science Fiction
Forum	Forum
Frontier	Frontier
Geogr. J.	Geographic Journal
Guardian	Guardian
Heythrop. J.	Heythrop Journal
HibbertJ.	Hibbert Journal
HomileticRev.	Homiletic Review
Independent	Independent
Individ. Psychol.	Individual Psychologist
Int. J. Clin. &Exp. Hypn.	International Journal of Clinical and Experimental Hypnosis
Int. J. Ethics	International Journal of Ethics
Int. J. Psychoanal.	International Journal of Psychoanalysis
Int. Philos. Q.	International Philosophical Quarterly
Interpretation	Interpretation
J. Abnorm. Psychol.	Journal of Abnormal Psychology
J. Am. Folklore	Journal of American Folklore
J. Am. Hist.	Journal of American History
J. Am. Inst. Hypn.	Journal of the American Institute of Hypnosis
J. Am. Med. Assoc.	Journal of the American Medical Association
J. Am. Psychoanal. Assoc.	Journal of the American Psychoanalytic Association
J. Am. Soc. Psychosom. Dent.	Journal of the American Society of Psychosomatic Dentistry
J. Anal. Psychol.	Journal of Analytical Psychology

J. Bible&Relig.	Journal of Bible and Religion
J. ChildPsychol. & Psychiat.	Journal of Child Psychology and Psychiatry
J. Crim. LawCriminol.	Journal of Criminal Law, Criminology, and Police Science
J. Forens. Sci. &Soc.	Journal of Forensic Science and Society
J. Gen. Psychol.	Journal of General Psychology
J. Mark. Res.	Journal of Marketing Research
J. Ment. Sci.	Journal of Mental Science
J. Nerv. &Ment. Dis.	Journal of Nervous and Mental Disease
J. PastoralCare	Journal of Pastoral Care
J. Philos.	Journal of Philosophy
J. Philos., Psychol., &Sci. Method	Journal of Philosophy, Psychology, and Scientific Method
J. Psychosom. Res.	Journal of Psychosomatic Research
J. Relig.	Journal of Religion
J. Relig. &Health	Journal of Religion and Health
J. Sci. Stud. Relig.	Journal for the Scientific Study of Religion
J. Transpers. Psychol.	Journal of Transpersonal Psychology
KenyonRev.	Kenyon Review
Kirkus	Kirkus
Libr. J.	Library Journal
Life-Threaten. Behav.	Life-Threatening Behavior
Listener	Listener
Lit. &Psychol.	Literature and Psychology
Lit. Dig.	Literary Digest
Lit. Rev.	Literary Review
LivingAge	Living Age
MD	MD
MainCurr.	Main Currents in Modern Thought
Manch. Guard.	Manchester Guardian
Manpower&Appl. Psychol.	Manpower and Applied Psychology
Med. Opin. &Rev.	Medical Opinion and Review
Ment. Health	Mental Health, London
Ment. Hyg.	Mental Hygiene, N. Y.
Midstream	Midstream

MidwestFolklore	Midwest Folklore
Mod. Sch.	Modern Schoolman

N. Engl. Q.	New England Quarterly
N. Y. EveningPost	New York Evening Post
N. Y. Her. Trib.	New York Herald Tribune (daily)
N. Y. Her. Trib. Books	New York Herald Tribune Books
N. Y. Her. Trib. WklyBook Rev.	New York Herald Tribune Weekly Book Review
N. Y. Her. Trib. WklyRev.	New York Herald Tribune Weekly Review
N. Y. Rev. Books	New York Review of Books
N. Y. Times	New York Times (daily)
N. Y. TimesBookRev.	New York Times Book Review
N. Y. TimesSat. Rev.	New York Times Saturday Review
N. Y. Trib.	New York Tribune
N. Y. World	New York World
Nation	Nation
Natl. Obs.	National Observer
Natl. Rev.	National Review
Nature	Nature
NewRepub.	New Republic
NewStatesman	New Statesman
NewStatesman&Nation	New Statesman and Nation
NewYorker	New Yorker
Newsweek	Newsweek
NorthAm. Rev.	North American Review

Observer	Observer
Occup. Psychol.	Occupational Psychology
Omega	Omega
Outlook	Outlook

PartisanRev.	Partisan Review
PastoralPsychol.	Pastoral Psychology
Percept. &Mot. Skills	Perceptual and Motor Skills
Percept. Cogn. Dev.	Perceptual-Cognitive Development
Pers. Biol. &Med.	Perspectives in Biology and Medicine
Pers. Psychiat. Care	Perspectives in Psychiatric Care
Philos. &Phenomenol. Res.	Philosophy & Phenomenological Research

Philos. Books   Philosophical Books
Philos. Q.   Philosophical Quarterly
Philos. Rev.   Philosophical Review
Philosophy   Philosophy
PsychedelicRev.   Psychedelic Review
Psychiat. &Soc. Sci. Rev. Psychiatry and Social Science
                           Review
Psychiat. Dig.   Psychiatric Digest
Psychiatry   Psychiatry
Psychoanal. &Psychoanal. Psychoanalysis and Psychoana-
  Rev.   lytic Review
Psychoanal. Q.   Psychoanalytic Quarterly
Psychoanal. Rev.   Psychoanalytic Review
Psychol. Rec.   Psychological Record
Psychol. Rep.   Psychological Reports
Psychol. Today   Psychology Today
Psychosom. Med.   Psychosomatic Medicine
Psychosomatics   Psychosomatics
Publ. Wkly   Publishers' Weekly
Punch   Punch

Q. Rev.   Quarterly Review

Ration. Liv.   Rational Living
Relig. Stud.   Religious Studies
Repr. Bull.   Reprint Bulletin
Rev. Existent. Psychol. & Review of Existential Psychology
  Psychiat.   and Psychiatry
Rev. Hist. Relig.   Revue de l'Histoire des Religions
Rev. Metaphysics   Review of Metaphysics
Rev. Revs.   Review of Reviews [American]

St. LouisLibr. Bull.   St. Louis Library Bulletin
SanFranc. Chron.   San Francisco Chronicle
Sat. Rev.   Saturday Review
Sat. Rev.[Lond.]   Saturday Review [London]
Sch. &Soc.   School and Society
Sci. Am.   Scientific American
Sci. &Soc.   Science and Society
Sci. Books   Science Books
Science   Science
Scott. J. Theol.   Scottish Journal of Theology
Self-culture   Self-culture
SewaneeRev.   Sewanee Review

Spectator	Spectator
SpringfieldRepub.	Springfield Republican
Surv. Gr.	Survey Graphic
Survey	Survey
Tablet	Tablet
Theol. Today	Theology Today
Time	Time
TimesLit. Suppl.	Times Literary Supplement
U. S. Q. BookRev.	U. S. Quarterly Book Review
Va. Q. Rev.	Virginia Quarterly Review
VictorianStud.	Victorian Studies
WallSt. J.	Wall Street Journal
WilsonLibr. Bull.	Wilson Library Bulletin
Wis. Libr. Bull.	Wisconsin Library Bulletin
YoungReadersRev.	Young Readers Review
Zygon	Zygon

Appendix 7

ADDRESSES OF PUBLISHERS NOT READILY AVAILABLE

American Society for Psychical Research
5 West 73d Street
New York, N. Y. 10023

Parapsychology Foundation
29 West 57th Street
New York, N. Y. 10019

Psychical Research Foundation
Duke Station
Durham, N. C. 27706

R. M. Bucke Memorial Society
4453 de Maisonneuve Boulevard
Montreal 215 Canada

Society for Psychical Research
1, Adam & Eve Mews
London W8 6QU England